Strategic Advertising Mechanisms

Strategic Advertising Mechanisms

From Copy Strategy to Iconic Brands

Jorge David Fernández Gómez

Bristol, UK / Chicago, USA

First published in the UK in 2021 by
Intellect, The Mill, Parnall Road, Fishponds, Bristol, BS16 3JG, UK

First published in the USA in 2021 by
Intellect, The University of Chicago Press, 1427 E. 60th Street,
Chicago, IL 60637, USA

Originally titled: *Mecanismos estratégicos en publicidad.*
De la USP a las Lovemarks

Original work copyright © Advook Editorial S. L.

A catalogue record for this book is available from
the British Library.

Copy editor: Newgen KnowledgeWorks
Cover designer: Aleksandra Szumlas
Production manager: Naomi Curston
Typesetting: Newgen KnowledgeWorks

Print ISBN 978-1-78938-430-7
ePDF ISBN 978-1-78938-431-4
ePUB ISBN 978-1-78938-432-1

Printed and bound by Hobbs.

To find out about all our publications, please visit
www.intellectbooks.com
There you can subscribe to our e-newsletter,
browse or download our current catalogue,
and buy any titles that are in print.

This is a peer-reviewed publication.

Contents

Foreword

Like many good things, this book is a paradox. It is a book that catalogues the classic mechanisms of branding. Yet its publication coincides with a moment when classical branding models and communication theories are being challenged by the ascendancy of social media and new digital paradigms.

The question the reader must ask is whether this makes the book more or less relevant? The answer for me is emphatically the former. For two reasons.

First, we cannot challenge or question what we do not know or understand. Or, at least, we cannot do so meaningfully. To deconstruct any idea properly, we must first know how to construct it. Otherwise, we do not achieve disruption, but merely destruction.

The second reason is arguably more profound. In terms of human interaction and communication, what really changes? As Bill Bernbach famously observed,

> It took millions of years for man's instincts to develop. It will take millions more for them to even vary [...] a communicator must be concerned with unchanging man. With his obsessive drive to survive, to be admired, to succeed, to love, to take care of his own.
>
> (Bernbach in Boches 2014)

Ultimately, brands and marketing serve very basic needs – our need for certainty, fair value, simplicity, esteem, identity, accountability and quality. Like human instinct, these needs are unlikely to vary dramatically over time. This implies that the models and mechanisms on which the brands that serve them are built will endure and evolve no matter what new channels, platforms or interfaces come our way. Coca-Cola, Mercedes and Heinz were great brands before TV was invented. They remain so now in the internet age. And, with good management, will continue to flourish in the media eras to come.

As Tancredi memorably puts it in Tomasi di Lampedusa's *The Leopard* ([1958] 2002), 'everything must change so that everything can remain the same'. I suspect that the models and mechanisms explored in this book will provide lessons and learning for many years to come. I commend it to you accordingly.

Charles Vallance
Chairman and Founding Partner at VCCP

Introduction

Although this book addresses such diverse concepts as advertising, commercial communication, corporate communication, marketing and branding, it is above all about advertising strategy. There are not many books in the advertising literature that have taken a communication approach to this strategic area per se. By our reckoning, creativity, design, new technologies and the industry's trends have tended to be the focus of current works and, therefore, the main objects of study for researchers, scholars and advertising communication professionals. Certainly, most of the literature published, for example, in Europe and the United States generally addresses topics of this type. To confirm this, suffice it to glance through the most recent publications on the subject on the online sales portal of any distribution company in the publishing industry or in the most recent catalogue of a more or less specialized publishing house.

In addition, the few books on advertising strategy that have been published lately either put the focus on strategy from the perspective of advertising structure and activity – addressing the history of strategic planning and recuperating the figure of some planner or other – or have a clearly functionalist objective and, therefore, a know-how-based approach. In both cases, any exercise of a conceptual or reflective nature from an academic viewpoint tends to be systematically ignored. As to the former, there are works such as the meritorious *98% Pure Potato* (2016) by John Griffiths and Tracey Follows, who track the origins of the discipline, highlighting the founding fathers and their immediate adherents. It is precisely some of these pioneers in strategic planning, like Stephen King and Stanley Pollitt, who have received literary tributes, usually in the shape of compilations of their most relevant works. This is the case with the essential *A Master Class in Brand Planning: The Timeless Works of Stephen King* (2008), a book edited by Judie Lannon and Merry Baskin, who compile some of the writings of the father of planning, accompanied by the reflections of some of the most eminent experts on the subject. Briefer but just as indispensable is *Pollitt on Planning* (2000), edited by Paul Feldwick and published by APG and BMP DDB, which includes three now-classic articles written by the other father of planning, a prologue by Baskin

1

and an introduction by Feldwick himself. Also noteworthy is *How to Plan Advertising* (1997), a collective book coordinated by Alan Cooper with contributions from the most eminent experts in international planning.

As regards the latter, Margo Berman's *The Blueprint for Strategic Advertising* (2017) deserves a mention for its extreme pragmatism. Some professionals have also bequeathed their strategic approaches, for pedagogical purposes, in book form with more or less success. Those standing out in this group include the interesting *Disruption: Overturning Conventions and Shaking Up the Marketplace* (1996) by Jean-Marie Dru, chairman of the BDDP Group in Paris, which does not only offer lessons but where there is also room for reflection. Just as notable is *A Handbook of Advertising Techniques* (1989), by Tony Harrison, creative director of Saatchi & Saatchi in Frankfurt (a misleading title because it is a study of positioning). All in all, in this category there are plenty of works that lack rigour, originality or relevance, and which are largely characterized by being a cross between self-congratulatory and self-help books.

Likewise, after a careful reading of some books whose covers are emblazoned with the words 'advertising strategy', it is clear that, albeit placing the spotlight on the topic from a conceptual angle, they do not strictly deliver on the promise of their titles. Many books on advertising that broach subjects relating to technology, business or creativity and which contain the word 'strategy' in their titles do not usually dwell on the concept and only address the core topic – technology, business or creativity – using the term 'strategy' mistakenly (when not directly out of ignorance), to cover them with an intellectual sheen or simply as a claim to sell more copies. The concept is also abused when referring to advertising activity, including the afterthought 'strategy' in a creative proposal or in the development of a digital campaign or a media plan, although strictly speaking they have nothing to do with strategy and, in many cases, are merely tactical decisions. Under this all-encompassing prism, any decision that is made is strategic – a plan, a stage, an action, a medium and the like – everything is strategic. We have called this imprecise, vague and diffuse use of the term 'strategic advertising monism'.[1]

It is necessary to go back a few years to find some studies that, even though they do not coincide exactly with the contents and aims of this book, at least have something in common with the philosophy underlying their conception. These include classics like *Strategy in Advertising* (1967) by Leo Bogart; *Stratégie Publicitaire et Marketing* (1971) by Raymond Audy; *Advertising Strategy: A Communication Theory Approach* (1980) by Larry Percy and John Rossiter; *Essentials of Advertising Strategy* (1981) by Don E. Schultz; *Advertising Management* (1982) by David Aaker and John Myers; *Truth, Lies & Advertising: The Art of Account Planning* (1998) by account planner Jon Steel; *Estrategias de comunicación* (2001) by Rafael Alberto Pérez; and the seminal *Planning Advertisements* (2013) by Gilbert Russell, a work first published in 1935. More recent and equally commendable contributions include *Advertising Account Planning* (2015) by Larry Kelley and Donald Jugenheimer, and Paul Feldwick's informative and interesting *The Anatomy of Humbug: How to Think Differently About Advertising* (2015). Albeit all with their strengths and weaknesses, they have led to the evolution of strategic advertising thought in academia, and in some of them it is even possible to glimpse a conceptual approach similar to the one that we intend to follow here. Nevertheless, none of these previous works is exactly in keeping with our proposal.

Strategic Advertising Mechanisms: From Copy Strategy to Iconic Brands describes the most important strategic mechanisms in the history of modern advertising. Specifically, it offers an analysis of mechanisms ranging from the so-called 'classics' like copy strategy (devised by the hygiene giant Procter & Gamble, hereinafter P&G) to the most recent proposals such as iconic brands. It should, however, be stressed that by calling these advertising strategies 'mechanisms' we are coining a new term in advertising jargon, a personal decision on which we would like to elaborate. Our decision is based on the fact that there is no consensus among researchers in this regard. Proof of this is that other authors have chosen to call them 'philosophies', 'methods', 'techniques', 'models', 'thoughts', 'procedures' and even in a hyperbolic fashion 'ages'. The reason why we have decided to call them 'mechanisms' is that we believe that this term offers a better description of this strategic concept.

We say this because, in our view, advertising mechanisms have to do with current trends in brand management or with the specific strategic decisions of an organization when selecting the most suitable branding paradigm for managing its brand. In other words, a strategic advertising mechanism like copy strategy only makes sense from a product-orientated branding perspective that, through communication, disseminates a unique rational attribute and the reason why the product in question is purchased. Of course, if we approach a brand from an emotional and motivation psychology angle – which implies assuming a personality branding perspective – mechanisms like copy strategy or 'reason-why' cease to be valid because they merely highlight tangible benefits, for which reason it is necessary to implement mechanisms like brand image and the star strategy that operate under motivational and symbolic strategic premises. Having made this clear, we will now attempt to explain the hierarchization involved in establishing different levels between the diverse constituent elements of brand management through communication.

The evolutionary conception of brand management should be structured according to three levels of categorization which, in descending order, are as follows: (1) paradigms, (2) theories and (3) strategic advertising mechanisms. They are hierarchized concepts defined from the broadest to the most specific. Thus, the most general concept would be that of 'paradigm', which addresses the most long-term vision of brand management (we have established three major paradigms: product branding, personality branding and consumer branding). We can then talk about different 'theories' that, as secondary conceptual contributions, flesh out those paradigms (e.g. the first paradigm would include behaviourism as a psychological basis, economic liberalism, the 'economic man' as a theoretical consumer model and the concept of marketing mix). And, lastly, there are 'strategic advertising mechanisms' resulting in applied strategic advertising methodologies, which form the basis of this book. It should be cautioned that these paradigms, theories and strategic advertising mechanisms can coexist. As a matter of fact, the unique selling proposition (USP), which saw the light of day over 60 years ago, is still valid, sharing the limelight with much more modern mechanisms like Lovemarks and Passionbrands.

Having explained why we have coined the term 'mechanism' to define our object of study, the time has now come to clarify the reasons why we have selected the mechanisms covered here from all those populating the advertising universe. First and foremost, we intend to analyse only those strategic mechanisms that have been theoretically relevant in the field of advertising, namely, those that have not been the exclusive preserve of advertising agencies, advertisers or consultants. Second, there are so many of these proposals that it would be impossible to list them all here. This is the case of the numerous mechanisms (some of which do not strictly fit in with what we understand by strategic advertising mechanism) which, throughout the history of modern advertising, have been devised by the major multinational advertising groups and have been included in their in-house work manuals or what could be understood as working methodologies. We are referring to J. Walter Thompson's 'T-Plan' (the agency that subsequently conceived other mechanisms like the 'Thompson way' and 'total branding'), McCann Erickson's the McCann selling strategy, Ogilvy & Mather's 'creative strategy', DDB's 'relevance, originality and impact' (ROI), Lintas' 'Lintas' link', BBDO's 'strategy review board', the Grey Group's 'brand character', DMB&B's 'belief dynamics' and the Young & Rubicam creative work plan. Likewise, there are several proposals that have been put forward by important advertisers with the aim of providing the agencies with which they work with something more than a briefing, like the Unilever Principles for Great Advertising (UPGA) or Nestlé's 'five stages of advertising development'. To our mind, both the contributions made by advertising agencies and those by advertisers are very interesting and, in some cases, relevant to professional practice. However, they have not been a priority when preparing this book, because our chief objective is to analyse only those mechanisms that have had repercussions outside the companies that developed them, making a place for themselves in the professional world and academia, that is, in universities, business schools, professional associations and the like.

On the other hand, some works have already analysed, for better or for worse, the strategic mechanisms to which we are referring. This is the case of Don E. Schultz's aforementioned book, *Essentials of Advertising Strategy*, one of the first to examine advertising strategy from an applied perspective. In the chapter entitled, 'How to develop an advertising strategy', the author offers a brief overview of different mechanisms like the USP, brand image and positioning, placing the focus on their most practical and functional development (their ultimate objective). Similarly, in the chapter entitled, 'What do the experts say?', the author discusses diverse methods mostly devised by advertising agencies, dwelling above all on the different models developed by the major multinational groups. In their *Advertising Management*, David Aaker and John Myers also briefly address these mechanisms in the chapter entitled, 'Creating and producing copy'. In fact, most contemporary advertising manuals usually review some of these strategic mechanisms under different labels as some point or another.

By the same token, the majority of the mechanisms have a common basis, for the most part coinciding with that of the most popular mechanism of the moment, which, going beyond the frontiers of the professional world, is disseminated in books, academic papers or any other type of medium (press interviews, blogs, social networking sites, TV programmes and so on and so forth), thus becoming part of advertising knowledge. In this respect, Soler remarks, '[a]fter reviewing these manuals [those of agencies and advertisers describing their work philosophy], it can be observed that they have several things in common, as if they had all originated from the same school' (1997: 127). In effect, the very functionalist nature of contributions of this type justifies this course of action, because they are work manuals whose purpose is to facilitate processes, methodologies and decision-making; in essence, know-how. Neither do they aim to reflect on or theorize about strategic advertising thought, nor lay its foundations. As Soler rightly observes, '[i]t is necessary to bear in mind that the purpose of these manuals is to unify criteria and provide all those people intervening in communication strategy with guidelines' (1997: 127). A good example of this is copy strategy that is no more than a guide for others to conceive their own strategic mechanisms: to the point that some authors dedicate a chapter to P&G's original copy strategy, before going on to address the different mechanisms indebted to this original conception largely devised by multinational advertising groups. The fact that chapters are devoted to explaining these mechanisms – close relatives of the original copy strategy – evinces this. A more recent example is the fad among many advertising agencies of creating brand-centric emotional mechanisms since the publication of *Lovemarks: The Future Beyond Brands* (2004), a book written by Kevin Roberts, the former worldwide CEO (as can be read on the cover of the book itself) of Saatchi & Saatchi. In light of its success, it is nowadays an authentic mission statement of personality branding philosophy.

As will be seen throughout the pages of this book, it goes without saying that these strategic advertising mechanisms have a clearly promotional objective. In other words, they are aimed more at popularizing some or other aspect (methodology, teams, philosophy, etc.) of the communication agencies devising them than at pondering on advertising strategy. For this reason, the most robust strategic advertising mechanisms from a conceptual point of view endure, while the rest (those in which greater priority is given to form than to content and whose popularity is due more to that appealing or striking façade) perish in the attempt and, therefore, have little to no chance of appearing in academic works addressing advertising in a more or less serious fashion, and much less in this book (which, as we have already stressed, intends to be scrupulous in this respect). Certainly, we are not interested – for they are not in keeping with our objectives – in the many working methodologies popularized by agencies (mainly multinational groups), which, at best, have only been applied in an in-house context. Moreover, as we have already stressed, without the intention of offending anyone and with the experience gained from having worked at different types of communication agencies, we have to admit that, behind some of those more or less fortunate Anglicisms, acronyms or terms, there is often a disproportionate desire to sell the agency in question. That groundbreaking methodology, that unparalleled creative philosophy or that mechanism on which some or other new technological or psychological tool is based, is no more than a name devoid of meaning. And, this alleged vacuity is not only attributable to the new times. Quite the contrary, it is a long-standing feature of an industry like ours in which precedence is given above all to novelty, and which has the imperative need for differentiation through new philosophies, professional roles, working methodologies and so on in order to justify the intangible and complex proposal of assessing and valuing the advertising 'product' from an economic angle. In other words, the quest for differentiation as a commercial tool is a constant in the communication industry. And these formulas to which we are referring 'sell'.

Albeit an exaggeration, the most evident proof of this is the United States in the 1960s, a moment when, on the strength of dubious experiments of a purportedly motivational nature, it was claimed that it was possible to alter the desires of consumers to the whim of the marketing industry, an idea with a more commercial than critical purpose, as will be seen. We are referring to the age of myth according to which a number of mysterious 'hidden persuaders', like a sort of Orwellian Big Brother, could guide people's behaviour. A context that Vance Packard exploited in his bestselling *The Hidden Persuaders* (1957), in which he decries the way in which people like Dichter and Vicary hypothetically manipulated consumers. This context was also ideal for carrying out an experiment employing a technique known as 'subliminal advertising', with which it was supposedly possible to modify the judgement of individuals – namely, below their threshold of conscience – which, as the researcher Vicary himself confessed, ultimately proved to be a fraud.[2] We now know that he devised his hypothetical strategic mechanism with an eye to reviving his failing marketing company, as did many others. One thing that is for sure, though, is that Packard sold many books – as Reeves[3] himself denounced in due course – and that the long shadow of the myth of the 'hidden persuaders' still haunts us today. Despite the time that has passed, some strategic advertising mechanisms operate in a way similar to that of Vicary's bogus experiment, with little theoretical substance (which, as has been seen, is the least of it), but with large doses of impact and appeal aimed at attaining the desired brand notoriety.

At any rate, and in spite of their unquestionable relevance, these mechanisms are of no interest here because they do not correspond to our most immediate objectives. Running the risk of being repetitive, we insist that our interest lies in those mechanisms that have transcended the borders of the corporate world and which have unequivocally permeated the advertising discipline with a capital A. For, in our view, only in this way can advertising thought be discussed and modified and evolve. So as to provide future advertising professionals with a solid education, new theories, methodologies, philosophies and strategies devised by different actors in the advertising industry have to pierce their hermetic doors and enter new knowledge forums. This has been the case with the major milestones and the most outstanding figures in advertising, all of which are currently covered in the curriculum of any communication or business studies course.

The time has now come to address the structure of this book. The order in which we have organized the different strategic advertising mechanisms described here is not exclusively chronological, but basically has to do with their conceptual nature. As already explained above, we contend that there are three major brand management paradigms – product branding, personality branding and consumer branding – in which each one of the mechanisms analysed here is framed. For this reason, we have organized them in terms of their conceptual orientation. Having said that, those mechanisms belonging to the same brand management paradigm are ordered chronologically. Thus, we start by addressing copy strategy, 'reason-why' copy, the USP and the dominant idea – all rational mechanisms – because they are in keeping with the philosophy of product branding. We are of the mind that this is a pioneering paradigm with respect to marketing studies. Certainly – at least in our view – the product branding approach spawned advertising, marketing and, of course, brand management. These rational theories are then followed by brand image, the psychological axis, the star strategy, Lovemarks and Passionbrands – all mechanisms relating to personality branding – for, even though some of them are years apart (nearly 45 years in the case of Ogilvy's brand image, conceived in the 1970s, and Kevin Roberts's Lovemarks, devised in the 2000s), they all share a conceptual approach that led to the boom of emotional communication theories. The last two chapters of this book are devoted to consumer branding, which places the emphasis on user orientation and cognitive psychology. The first of these addresses positioning, one of the most popular strategic advertising mechanisms in the history of marketing, while the second examines a mechanism that we believe is a hybrid between the cognitivist rules governing positioning and emerging anthropological approaches – albeit indebted to semiotics and motivation research – embodied by iconic brands. This is actually the paradigm that has produced the fewest mechanisms in the history of modern advertising, perhaps because it is the one that is – consciously – the furthest removed from classical advertising communication and because it employs other types of communication tools. We are referring to a communication associated with the web environment, social media and content management, which combines media and formats, merging classical theories, such as repetition, with other more current ones like the famous co-creation. This new and more complex strategic conception involves the formulation of other mechanisms not strictly related to advertising, which fall outside the scope of this book and, moreover, have already been studied in a previous contribution of ours, *Principios de Estrategia Publicitaria y Gestión de Marcas: Nuevas Tendencias de Brand Management* (2013). We will now offer a brief description of each one of the book's eight chapters.

Chapter 1 analyses one of the pioneering strategic mechanisms in the history of advertising and, to be sure, the first to be developed by an advertiser. Specifically, 'Procter & Gamble's copy strategy: When the advertiser made products and advertising' deals with one of the most popular and longest-standing rational strategic advertising mechanisms. The hygiene giant's copy strategy was not only one of the first serious and rigorous working methodologies in advertising, with all that it involved from a professional point of view – having a definitive influence on subsequent strategic mechanisms and, of course, on the different actors in the communication industry (chiefly advertising agencies and advertisers) – but also one of the first contributions to advertising strategy and theory and marketing in general. However, this first chapter also follows the trail of the closest precedents of copy strategy, including the first rational strategic theories and the popular reason-why copy conceived by Hopkins, one of the fathers of advertising copywriting.

Chapter 2, 'Rosser Reeves's USP: The reality in advertising is the product', continues to delve deeper into rational, product-orientated strategic mechanisms, but this time focusing on an advertising agency, rather than on an advertiser, specifically the Bates Group. Greatly influenced by Hopkins, Rosser Reeves, the creator of the USP, would be one of the first admen in history to immortalize his strategic concept in a book titled *Reality in Advertising* (1961) (Hopkins had already done so in his famous *Scientific Advertising* [1923], but from a perspective highly focused on ad copywriting) and, above all, to popularize one of the most notable strategic mechanisms in the history of modern advertising. Indeed, the USP is perhaps the most memorable strategic mechanism in this book, due both to its prestige in the conceptual realm since it was disseminated in book format, and to the fact that it has been the most used in the communication industry. Be that as it may, it seems that this famous mechanism had precedents which, in a way, dim Reeves's fame, specifically a strategic mechanism conceived by an adman called Finn in an American agency in the second decade of the twentieth century, called the 'dominant idea'; an issue that is also addressed in this chapter.

Chapter 3, 'David Ogilvy's brand image: The rise of emotion in advertising communication', covers the first contribution to emotional strategic advertising mechanisms framed in the context of personality branding. As will be seen throughout these pages, they are the most numerous mechanisms of all and, by extension, those that have been reviewed and updated most throughout the history of advertising strategy. In fact, this book analyses strategic mechanisms of this type conceived in the 1960s and others that, notwithstanding the years separating them, emerged in the first decade of the new millennium. In this chapter, an analysis is performed on the theoretical bases of David Ogilvy's brand image, which was the first mechanism of its kind to be employed in the advertising industry. It also examines those of other similar mechanisms, from the so-called 'emotional advertising' to the influential motivation research, through the most outstanding figures of this new current of advertising thought, as is the case with Martineau. Likewise, an attempt is made to explain the reasons behind the rise of this type of strategic mechanism, while of course tracing the precedents of what Ogilvy called 'brand image'. As will be seen, these precedents are striking to say the least.

Chapter 4, 'Henri Joannis's psychological axis: The advent of motivational research in European advertising', deals with the book's first strictly European contribution (Ogilvy was an Englishman who had emigrated to the United States, where he fine-tuned his advertising skills and pursued a successful professional career), specifically of a French provenance. Also belonging to strategic advertising mechanisms of an emotional type, Joannis proposed a working methodology entirely based on motivational psychology. Specifically, this chapter focuses on his popular – both in academic and professional circles – 'psychological axis'. Equally influenced by Dichter (as regards his faith in motivation research) and Reeves (with respect to a suspect product-orientated approach), it is fair to claim that Joannis developed one of the most rigorous and balanced strategic mechanisms in the history of advertising, a claim that this chapter sets out to demonstrate.

Also of a French origin and with an identical conceptual basis, Chapter 5 examines one of the most acclaimed emotional strategic advertising mechanisms in modern advertising. In 'Jacques Séguéla's "star strategy": To sell the Hollywood star system to sell brands', the intention is to analyse one of the most controversial admen (particularly for his literary legacy) and one of the most notorious and unusual strategic approaches in advertising history, since Séguéla compares the creation of the Hollywood star system with brand conception and management. As regards both its name – a legacy of copy strategy studied in Chapter 1 – and its conceptual proposal – resorting to the solidest bases of emotional advertising and personality branding – this strategic advertising mechanism opened up important new strategic communication channels, as is the case with Chevron's theories, which are also examined in this book.

'Kevin Roberts's Lovemarks: The return of emotional mechanisms in the new century', the title of Chapter 6, is the last emotional strategic advertising mechanism relating to personality branding that we have chosen. Certainly, with his Lovemarks Roberts recuperates the most classical postulates of the emotional mechanisms studied in the previous chapters. Besides reviewing the new developments that the mechanism meant for the academic literature on advertising strategy – which can be covered mainly thanks to the publication of the eponymous book *Lovemarks: The Future Beyond Brands* – in this chapter a comprehensive analysis is performed on the reasons behind such developments that, as will be seen, go beyond those exclusively associated with academia or the dissemination of advertising knowledge. In point of fact, in addition to Lovemarks, other contemporary mechanisms, such as Passionbrands, with a similar or identical purpose are also discussed.

Chapter 7, 'Jack Trout and Al Ries's positioning: The appearance of cognitive psychology in advertising', addresses one of the few important strategic advertising mechanisms with a cognitive basis and, therefore, one of the scant contributions made by the consumer branding paradigm to advertising strategy. Even though it is true that on the subject of branding (particularly from a markedly academic perspective) there are some very interesting proposals, examined in a previous book (Fernández Gómez 2013), the fact remains that from a strictly advertising perspective strategic contributions of this type – combining a consumer approach with cognitive psychology and strategic advertising mechanisms of co-creation – are very few and far between. Accordingly, this chapter is devoted to one of the mechanisms that gave rise to this type of strategic philosophy and, more importantly, perhaps the most popular advertising concept in the history of advertising and marketing. Indeed, 'positioning' is the most widely employed term in the communication sector, and unquestionably the most written about in both the academic and general interest literature. Accordingly, this chapter is devoted to inquiring into the term's roots, characteristics, implications and distinctive traits, and even into several theories that distance the concept from its putative fathers Trout and Ries, while placing it in the orbit of Reeves, one of the great advertising strategy gurus.

This book ends with 'Douglas Holt's iconic brands: When cognitive psychology and motivation research converge'. Based on the emerging cultural branding approach, the presuppositions and the theoretical framework of iconic brands as an advertising mechanism are much more comprehensive and complex than those of previous proposals. Thus, cultural branding theories are the most developed in the consumer branding paradigm, which we believe is theoretically and professionally more advanced than product branding and personality branding. Although with an eminently cognitive psychological perspective – strategic advertising mechanisms like positioning and brand management models such as those pertaining to the identity approach are proof of this – and product-centric – as regards its tangible attributes, namely, its characteristics, advantages, uses, etc. and so on – consumer branding has evolved and developed in a miscellaneous manner. Hence, it is associated with motivation research – a school that has very little to do with cognitive theories – and different disciplines including anthropology, sociology and the humanities. So, the iconic brand mechanism draws from these very solid and eclectic theoretical bases, for which reason it should come as no surprise that the concept emerged in the academic world. Effectively, Douglas Holt, the mechanism's father, is a university professor and branding researcher, which means that it is the only one covered in this book whose development is not linked to professional advertising. Nonetheless, its advent outside the industry has not prevented it from becoming a staple in the advertising industry.

Strategic Advertising Mechanisms: From Copy Strategy to Iconic Brands compiles the most important strategic mechanisms that have emerged in the relatively brief history of modern advertising. It is an ostensibly exhaustive and clearly analytical work whose intention is to delve into both the characteristics of each one of the strategic approaches described in this introduction – defining them, analysing their distinctive traits and implications, tracing their precedents and so on – and aspects linked to their conception and formulation – their context, creators, dissemination and the like. However, as will be seen throughout these pages, it is a work that includes reflection and debate not without criticism, in which assumed truths are discussed, illustrious admen unmasked and, above all, myths are dispelled. This last aspect is, in our opinion, its best calling card.

1

Procter & Gamble's Copy Strategy: When the Advertiser Made Products and Advertising

As already noted, the company Procter & Gamble (P&G) has been one of the driving forces behind the so-called 'product branding', almost an understatement when bearing in mind that it was precisely this multinational that pioneered the creation of a management model for its brands, paving the way for what has come to be known as brand management. As will be seen, the brand approach developed by the American company laid the foundations of what is understood now as product branding. In other words, it would not be unreasonable to claim that P&G was the pioneer of these embryonic brand management standards. But, moreover, the company, in line with the brand management models that it continues to develop, conceived what can be considered to be one of the first strategic advertising mechanisms of a rationalist nature in the history of advertising, the so-called 'copy strategy', also generally known as copy platform or creative strategy, a mechanism that competed with Rosser Reeves's unique selling proposition (USP) and certainly influenced the American advertising man when he was devising it.[1] Before performing a more in-depth analysis on the copy strategy, what follows is a brief overview of the achievements of P&G in the field of branding, on the one hand, and the context in which these rationalist techniques emerged, on the other.

1.1. P&G or the prehistory of brand management

Before continuing, it is necessary to answer a basic question: what is meant by product branding? Very briefly, because it is question that is evidently beyond the scope of this work, product branding can be summed up in the idea that commercial and communication management should be subordinated to the product. This approach to the product affects all of the spheres in which a company operates,

12

from aspects of strategic business management to the techniques employed to advertise its products. In order to consolidate this approach, it is essential to take into consideration the economic current prevailing at the time, based on the free market, that contained the germ of so-called 'modern capitalism'. This aspect is associated with the concept of the 'invisible hand', a term coined by the Scottish philosopher Adam Smith in his *The Theory of Moral Sentiments* (1759) and popularized in his greatest work, *The Wealth of Nations* (1776). The 'invisible hand' is a metaphor that in economics expresses the self-regulatory capacity of the free market, based on profit maximization and resource optimization. This economic–anthropological perspective led to another school of thought that can be summarized in the concept of *homo economicus*.

According to the 'economic man' – an abstraction very much in fashion in economic science at the time – individuals consume rationally on the basis of maximization criteria. Namely, everyone optimizes their usefulness in an attempt to obtain the greatest benefits possible with the least amount of effort. This idea, grounded in a theoretical model that also dates back to the time of Adam Smith,[2] was taken up again in the theories of 'rational choice' – some of which were developed later on by sinister thinkers inspired by Nazi ideology. By the same token, this paradigm is directly linked to 'self-management' business models pertaining to branding. In plain English, a brand that is adequately managed by a company through the implementation of optimal marketing policies will triumph, which associates it with behaviourism. Indeed, product branding is indebted to the behavioural psychology – all the rage at the time – of theories such as Pavlov's 'conditioned reflex'.[3] As a result, advertising resorted to the pre-scientific psychology of the nineteenth century and theoretical models, such as the AIDA and DAGMAR approaches,[4] and to one of the disciplines that, in the main, is most related to the behavioural school – at least with respect to its operational aspects – namely, marketing. Lastly, the paradigm derived from this still nascent discipline.

In 1960, McCarthy published *Basic Marketing: A Managerial Approach*, the forerunner of the 'four Ps'. In his book, he coined the famous terms 'product', 'price', 'place' and 'promotion', which were destined to become some of the most important concepts in marketing. However, the first scholar to consider the marketing mix, as it is understood nowadays, was not McCarthy, but Borden.[5] In point of fact, McCarthy's 'four Ps' are a simplification of Borden's original concept (Grönroos 1994: 349). Effectively, Borden describes what he believes marketing should be like in a concise text, explicitly entitled 'The concept of the marketing mix',[6] and as with McCarthy's work, it is now regarded as a marketing classic:

> The marketing mix of a firm in large part is the product of the evolution that comes
> from day-today marketing. At any time the mix represents the program that a

management has evolved to meet the problems with which it is constantly faced in an ever changing, ever challenging market. There are continuous tactical man-euvers: a new product, aggressive promotion, or price change initiated by a com-petitor must be considered and met [...] All such problems call for a management's maintaining effective channels of information relative to its own operations and to the day-to-day behavior of consumers, competitors, and the trade.

(Borden 1965: 394)

All the aforementioned factors are, to a great extent, behind the concept of the paradigm at hand. In fact, such an important asset nowadays as the brand, under the approach of product branding, was no more than an addendum to a company's product policy. To our mind, this vision can be considered as the prehistory of brand management; to wit, they were the first attempts made by some com-panies to manage their brands (understanding the 'brand' concept in a germinal manner). Undeniably, the development of marketing and advertising, and above all branding, still had a long way to go, for which reason it could be contended that they were rudimentary strategies. It was the major western business groups that were the first to practise these marketing techniques. Heding et al. (2009: 30) are of this mind: 'Procter & Gamble gave birth to the first management practices of brand management with its product management approach'. Certainly, P&G was behind the promotion of a new management concept and, for many, pioneered modern brand management. This is how Dyer et al. (2004: 60) see it:

> A new generation of managers rising to senior status during this period – people such as Deupree, Ralph Rogan, and Stockton Buzby – laid the groundwork for brand man-agement as they decentralized responsibility for brand promotions. Launching Crisco was a formative experience in this regard. The most influential figure in defining brand management, however, was Neil McElroy, and the pivotal brand was Camay.

And they have a point. In 1930, Neil McElroy, the person in charge of the adver-tising for the soap Camay, a P&G portfolio brand, produced a memo in which he outlined a new brand management system, which would have a huge impact on the business management world. In was precisely in that report that he planted the seeds of product branding, thus revolutionizing both the brand concept as it was viewed at the time and the way in which those assets should be managed. McElroy's proposal revolved around the development of an annual plan for each brand in which the marketing policies to be implemented were enumerated; the plan was based on the study and analysis of the product, the distributors and the suppliers. Thenceforth, the brand manager began to take strategic control, namely, establishing independently the annual plans and choosing the most appropriate marketing tools in each situation. As Clark (1989: 34) notes, 'P&G started the practice of what is known as "brand management" whereby managers take overall responsibility for individual brands just as though they are companies in their own rights.' McElroy's brand manager (or chief) system became a classic organizational model for many advertising companies and has served ever since as an organizational principle for the marketing departments of many companies. Dyer et al. (2004: 60–61) also reach the same conclusion in their study of the American giant:

> [T]he experience of fighting for resources against P&G's entrenched, big-budget brands convinced McElroy, then a young advertising manager, that the company needed to formalize assignments of its marketers in brand-specific teams and to give these teams a large degree of autonomy in running specific marketing campaigns. From this background and with this impetus, brand management was already coalescing as a de facto policy by the mid-1920s. McElroy took a major step toward formalizing it as an organizational structure in a May 1931 memo, outlining what he referred to as 'the duties and responsibilities of the brand men'.
>
> Specifically, McElroy's memo charged brand managers with studying shipments of their brands by units and territories, analyzing where sales were heavy and where they were light, and extracting from that data conclusions about which tactics were working.

As can be seen, P&G introduced a radical change in business management in general, and in marketing management in particular.[7] And what is more important, in a visionary way and at a moment when management was primitive and unsophisticated, the company introduced a series of working methods that have survived the passing of time. Dyer et al. (2004: 41) discuss how in around 1890 P&G began to plan its business on an unprecedented scale and to interiorize a series of principles that are still clearly fundamental. In their opinion, neither was this transformation planned nor was it a timely occurrence: 'It was more like a chain reaction, as one round of change set off another somewhere else within the enterprise. Strategic crisis drove new product development, creating new marketing experiments (consumer packaging, branding, mass advertising).' However, as held by other authors, the authentic revolution sparked by P&G was doubtless the concept of product branding:

> From an external point of view, though, the most dramatic impact came in the marketing of the product. Harley Procter and Ivory's other 'brand managers' (to apply a term Procter & Gamble itself would not invent for another fifty years) were venturing into unexplored territory [...] Only after a period of experimentation and analysis did the first, elemental understandings emerge about how brands were going to work.

Chief among these early lessons was the basic idea that to sell brands, Procter & Gamble had to connect with consumers. [...] The consumer may not yet have become 'boss' by 1890, but Procter & Gamble was beginning to learn how to listen to her and certainly coming to understand that if it listened better than its competitors did, its brands would win in the marketplace.

(Dyer et al. 2005: 66)

P&G was also the company that developed what is regarded as one of the first strategic advertising mechanisms of a rational nature, called 'copy strategy'. As a matter of fact, as will be analysed below, P&G would play a crucial role both in establishing the highly product-centric marketing policies, and in devising and applying markedly rational advertising strategies like the aforementioned copy strategy and the USP, which will be examined in the following chapter.

1.2. The birth of rationalist advertising

The roots of rationalist advertising should be sought in Chicago in 1898, when the talent of John E. Kennedy and Claude C. Hopkins, regarded nowadays as the fathers of advertising copywriting, caught the attention of Albert B. Lasker,[8] a partner of the agency Lord and Thomas. Similarly, Clark (1989: 64) sees in Lasker the '"father" of modern advertising', because hitherto the concept had been very rudimentary and mainly based on product information that was repeated in the press. However, it was in fact his encounter with Kennedy that changed the course of advertising, because the latter understood it in following terms: 'Advertising is salesmanship in print' (Clark 1989: 39). This was truly a novelty, relevant enough for Rosser Reeves (1961: 120), a person never inclined to offer gracious compliments, to have called him a 'remarkable man'. For Kennedy

believed that an ad should be salesmanship in print, not just news or publicity. Advertisers had to do more than merely inform people about their products, he said. They had to persuade the public to purchase. Lasker, impressed by this thinking, hired Kennedy for a staggering $50,000 a year.

(Meyers 1984: 25)

In this vein, John O'Toole, the head of the agency Lasker, believes thus:

It seems so simple and obvious today. But what this definition did in 1904 was to change the course of advertising completely and make possible the enormous role it now plays in our economy. For, by equating the function of an advertisement with the function of a salesman who calls on a prospect personally, it revealed the true nature of advertising. For the first time, the concept of persuasion, which is the prime role of a salesman, was applied to the creation of advertising.

(Clark 1989: 39)

Although Lasker should be merited with the discovery of such outstanding figures as Kennedy and Hopkins, it was these two men who actually revolutionized advertising thinking. The former because he included persuasion in the marketing mix, as noted above, and the latter thanks to his reason-why copy concept, namely the issue at hand. In fact, Hopkins can be regarded as the creator of argumentative copy or, what is the same, the reason why people purchase a product: 'His carefully crafted ads stressed the unique qualities of a product and listed specific reasons why it should be bought. People in the industry called this "scientific selling"' (Meyers 1984: 26). And to professionalize the industry he resorted to market research, a then incipient and unrefined technique. In the words of Mayer (1958: 203–04), 'Hopkins was a great believer in getting what he called "data", and hired people to do product research for him (What's in this product? How is it made?) whenever he had a new and particularly difficult job.' But it would be Hopkins (1966: 13) himself who best defined his posture in the first paragraph of his seminal *Scientific Advertising*:

> The time has come when advertising has in some hands reached the status of a science. It is based on fixed principles and is reasonably exact. The causes and effects have been analysed until they are well understood. The correct methods of procedure have been proved and established. We know what is most effective, and we act on basic laws.

Hopkins employed the primitive technique of coupons as the embryo of modern market research – refining it to measure the effectiveness of his sales pitches and even to choose the typographies of his advertisements. These techniques were very popular because they provided relevant information in terms of profitability and, to a great extent, eliminated risks:

> In every aspect of his advertising the mail-order man enjoys an efficient control of his expenditure and an observable relationship between advertising and sales. This control is what Claude Hopkins meant by Scientific Advertising, and practitioners in this limited area are still using Hopkins's measurement and arguments today.

(Mayer 1958: 46)

As already noted, the method would have a huge impact on the advertisements and advertising creatives of the period. It should be recalled that, after the signing of the Armistice, capitalism entered its monopolistic phase and that environment in which companies had the need to sell mass products in a highly competitive market was conducive to the development of a more specialized and professional sort of advertising. This is how Eguizábal (2007: 74) portrays the moment:

> Versus a much more pacific and passive market like the traditional economy, capitalism was edified on a more dynamic, ever-changing and aggressive type of competition, in which, sooner or later, competitors discovered advertising as a civilized (with respect to the aggressions to which competition had led in the first capitalism) and modern (and, therefore, more sophisticated) tool for forging ahead.

In this sense, advertising techniques tended to be improved so as to adapt them to the new market reality. There was no room for old advertising based on exaggeration – when not on barefaced lies – or repetition in a much more mature and complex market. It was during this continuous quest for improving communication that rationalist advertising, also called 'informative-persuasive' advertising, emerged. During its early years, in light of the social sciences' incapacity to furnish advertising with coherent research methodologies, the creation of the message had to take second place to the copywriter's ingenuity and intuition:

> The success of Madison Avenue during its first hundred years – from J. Walter Thompson to Rosser Reeves to Mary Wells – was largely due to the quirky creative vision of several eccentric entrepreneurs. Until recently, advertising was inward-looking, as much a form of personal expression as a tool of persuasion. Ads traditionally reflected the attitudes, tastes, and feelings of such individualistic copywriters as C. C. Hopkins and Bill Bernbach.
>
> (Meyers 1984: 41)

Although Meyers's accusations are evidently overdue – leading him to decry innocent people like Hopkins and Reeves who, strictly speaking, represented the first foray into market research – it was an indisputable fact, albeit 30 years before. Sure enough, to combat the arbitrariness of copy at the time, advertising creatives turned to more refined techniques such as the psychological model summarized in the famous acronym AIDA, briefly described above. So, on the basis of the consideration of the consumer as a reasonable and conscious being and employing psychological techniques such as AIDA, people like Kennedy and Hopkins began to develop what would later be known as 'scientific advertising'.[9] It is from that moment on that we can speak of rationalist advertising. And, as Sánchez Guzmán

(1989: 152) has rightly pointed out, 'a version of this type of advertising, going by the name of USP, was adopted by the American agency Ted Bates & Company in 1940'. The time has now come to analyse these new strategic advertising mechanisms deriving from Hopkins's concept.

1.3. Reason-why copywriting and Hopkins as the pillars of rationalist advertising

Hopkins undoubtedly did more than encourage P&G to develop its copy strategy[10] and Reeves to formulate his USP and, by and large, help to understand the development of modern advertising. In the specialized literature, it is often claimed that with Hopkins everything changed and that he revolutionized the way of doing and understanding advertising. In this respect, David Ogilvy, one of the most successful advertising men in history, alleged that Hopkins 'is to advertising what Escoffier is to cooking' (in Roman 2009: 60). As a matter of fact, he wrote the introduction to the new edition of Hopkins's famous book *Scientific Advertising* in 1966, which starts with the following weighty words:

> Nobody, at any level, should be allowed to have anything to do with advertising until he has read this book seven times. Claude Hopkins wrote it in 1923. Rosser Reeves, bless him, gave it to me in 1938. Since then, I have given 379 copies to clients and colleagues. Every time I see a bad advertisement, I say to myself, 'The man who wrote this copy has never read Claude Hopkins.' If *you* read this book of his, you will never write another bad advertisement – and never approve one either.
>
> (Oglivy 1966: 7, original emphasis)

In *Reality in Advertising*, Reeves (1961: 55) himself would acknowledge that Hopkins's 'genius for writing copy made him one of the advertising immortals'. What was it about Hopkins that made two such irreconcilable characters as Ogilvy and Reeves concur for once in their lives? Mayer, who has conducted an in-depth analysis on all three of them – referring to the closing words written by Politz for the 1952 reedition of *Scientific Advertising* – hits the nail on the head: '[W]ithin the area he covered, his measurements were absolutely valid. To determine the value of advertising, he took as his standard of measurement, *sales* – the only accurate measuring rod' (1958: 45, original emphasis).

In the same vein, Roman (2009: 60) claims that Hopkins's deep-seated advertising concept as a sales mechanism united Ogilvy and Reeves. Indeed, Hopkins (1966: 97) departed from an eminently commercial perspective of advertising: 'Advertising is salesmanship', he declares. 'Its principles are the principles of salesmanship. Successes and failures in both lines are due to like causes. Thus every advertising question should be answered by the salesman's standards.' And this approach, which was so closely linked to the purely commercial transactions of peddlers with their hyperbole and half-truths, created a very powerful bond between 'professionalized' advertising creatives like those being analysed here. Years later, Ogilvy himself would recognize that Reeves reinforced his natural predilection for sales, introducing this aspect in Hopkins's theory, specifically sending him the manuscript of *Scientific Advertising* before it was published (Roman 2009: 60). In a speech in tribute to Reeves, Ogilvy said the following: 'In 1938 you gave me a typed copy of the Hopkins book. It changed my life. I know it by heart. Every year I give away twenty copies, to wordsmiths. They never comprehend' (in Roman 2009: 118). This starting point has been crucial to the longevity of the idea that Hopkins appreciated and popularized most. For only such a functional and practical consideration of things can justify the fact that offer service (Hopkins 1966: 23) became an essential communication vehicle at the time and in the years to come, as Eguizábal (1998: 339) notes:

> 'Scientific advertising' and direct response advertising gave way to new ideas and new messages. The death of Lasker (1952) also brought the curtain down once and for all on a way of understanding advertising. There were those (including Jim Young of Walter Thompson) who believed that nothing had been invented in advertising in the past 25 years and, admittedly, Hopkins continued to cast a long shadow: top professionals like Reeves and Ogilvy never forgot the masterfulness of the author of *Scientific Advertising*.

In effect, the influence of Hopkins with his sales approach and confidence in rational benefits was the most acknowledged among advertising creatives on Madison Avenue at the time. His theories had a powerful impact on his professional colleagues and, above all, on Reeves. As Herreros Arconada (2000: 200) notes, 'Rosser Reeves is the most widely known copywriter among the new generations of advertising men because he honed the reason-why copywriting technique.'

1.4. The copy strategy

In the enlarged reedition of the classic *Advertising Management*, Batra et al. (1996: 462–76) dedicate a chapter to what they call 'Advertising copy testing and diagnosis'. Here, when broaching the subject of copy-testing strategy, they underscore aspects like recognition and recall to measure the effectiveness of advertisements. Namely, they put the accent on how agencies like P&G understand advertising and, generally speaking, employ the same jargon as the hygiene giant. In reality, it should come as no surprise that P&G baptized its advertising creation with a name so closely linked to research techniques – the copy strategy – given its predilection for these. Indeed, P&G was an unswerving advocate of research, an activity to which it dedicated a great deal of time, effort and money. According to Mayer (1958: 264),

> Several big client companies have thought up their own advertising testing procedures. Procter & Gamble has a particularly elaborate set of tests, performed mostly by Burke Research of Cincinnati and guarded by the company and its agencies with security precautions that would do credit to the Atomic Energy Commission.

Thirty years later, Clark (1989: 37) would also refer to P&G's famous secretiveness, while similarly alluding, albeit less effusively, to the influence of Burke and his research methods on the company:

> The most widely used copy test method in the US, however, even though it is frequently scorned by men in agencies, is a recall one. Burke's Day-After Recall was developed by Burke Marketing Research for Procter and Gamble and it has been described as 'an industry standard for evaluating TV commercial effectiveness'.
>
> (Clark 1989: 107)

Clark himself revealed the steely mechanics applied by the company when designing its advertisements – he literally calls it the agency's 'indoctrination': 'All agencies who work for Procter and Gamble know they will have to work within close confines and under constant scrutiny' – 'Procter and Gamble style advertising with its reliance on safety and research testing [...] may help sell products but it is hardly admired' (Clark 1989: 36), which made other copywriters treat the agencies working for P&G rather scornfully. Sure enough, P&G's blind faith in research earned it a fair amount of criticism. Meyers (1984: 146) claims that 'Burke is P&G's Bible', which in his opinion undermined advertising quality: 'Copywriters at the company's agencies are aware of this strict criterion, and as a result, they've been forced to devise commercials that repeat an item's name five or six times in 30 seconds' (Meyers 1984: 146). And, more categorically, he adds, 'Burke's "scientific" process sucks the creative life out of a campaign and leads to annoying advertising that inner-directed viewers tend to tune out' (Meyers 1984: 146).

These objections, which were mainly voiced by the so-called 'creative agencies', were also extensible to many other advertising workers. But the fact is that P&G's success converted it into an attractive client and, beyond its way of understanding the advertising business, it was, and perhaps still is, the most sought-after advertiser. In a laudatory chapter – entitled, 'Competing with Procter & Gamble', and with the suggestive subtitle, 'Who's afraid of the big bad wolf?' – that he dedicates to P&G in *Ogilvy on Advertising*, Ogilvy (1983: 155), one the 'rebels' who sermonized on creativity and ingenuity, remarks that the success of P&G was because it used 'market research to identify consumer needs'. To which he adds, '[t]hey use research to determinate the most effective strategy, and never change a successful strategy' (Ogilvy 1983: 156). Curious words for a denier of research such as Ogilvy, as will be seen in the following chapters. Perhaps the prospects of winning the P&G account encouraged more than one advertising man to rethink his philosophy. All considered, and although most of the criticisms aimed at P&G were well-founded, others were totally inconsistent. For instance, Meyers (1984: 146) goes so far as to claim that P&G's TV spots 'are so busy drumming brand identity into our heads that they neglect to show how the products can help us'; when, as is common knowledge, P&G was a fierce defender of argumentative copy and its copy strategy was a replica of the former, as we will now try to explain.

That being said and despite the criticism, P&G had good reason to resort to research, for it was one of the main advertisers in the world. In his classic *Advertising and Sales Promotion Strategy*, Tellis (1998: 8) holds that 'Procter & Gamble is the largest advertiser in the United States today; spending as much as $2.7 billion on advertising in 1994'. And this was nothing new. In his book, Mayer (1958: 35) includes the list of the 'top advertisers' previously published in *Advertising Age* (1956), which ranks P&G second only to General Motors, with a global spending of US$93,000,000. Some years later, Meyers (1984: 145) went on to qualify its prominent position, asserting that '[for] Procter & Gamble, the nation's largest packaged-goods advertiser […] sales increased thirty-fold between 1945 and 1975'. For his part, Ogilvy (1983: 155) diverges from the product category and provides only figures: 'They spend $700,000,000 a year on advertising, more than any other company, and their sales are $12,000,000,000 a year.' In short, according to Clark (1989: 31–32), P&G was the world's largest advertiser, insofar as it accounted for some 18,000 to 20,000 30-second commercial spots on American TV alone.

It was mostly thanks to its commitment to advertising that P&G became the business empire that it was and still is to a certain extent: 'Procter and Gamble recognised the importance of advertising almost from the beginning and in 1913 the company was the US's top advertiser' (Clark 1989: 32). Clark (1989) describes how Harley Procter, the son of one of the founders, was already reasoning back in 1876, before the launching of what would become known as P&G Ivory soap,[11] that what the company's new product needed was a distinctive name and good advertising. This visionary ability to understand advertising strategy in branding was decisive for the company. It can be contended that its pioneering confidence in advertising and the large sums that it invested to this end justified its desire for control. For these reasons it was logical for the company to study conscientiously where and how to spend its advertising budget. Hence, there is nothing odd in the fact that it opted for advertising techniques that placed the accent on the product, its attributes and the reasons why it was purchased, summarizing this in its copy strategy. Be that as it may, the company also resorted to rationalist advertising strategies like the USP.

There is no general consensus among communication experts on whether the copy strategy influenced the USP or vice versa. Quite to the contrary, there are many opinions in this respect, some of which are contradictory. To our mind, it is a much more complex issue than first meets the eye. The fact that both concepts were developed progressively (there was no eureka moment in either case); that they emerged in the privacy afforded by the workplace (advertiser and agency, respectively); and that their postulates were not made public until some or other text was published or some or other internal document was leaked makes it very hard to make any serious value judgement. To this should be added, moreover, a very specific, rich and dynamic context in which there was no lack of novel advertising (the success of Hopkins's reason-why copy, for example) or psychological (the AIDA-type models), economic (the new free trade winds that had begun to blow with the advent of modern capitalism) and, of course, sociological (the famous 'economic man' concept, for instance) ideas. All this inevitably affected both and, therefore, opting for one or the other is no mean feat. In this connection, we will now analyse the copy strategy, before doing the same with the USP in the following chapter.

As already observed, the copy strategy was devised by P&G, one the most important multinational groups in the world, which, as explained above, also revolutionized the marketing world with its new brand management methods. Well, the mass product giant has also made a very valuable contribution to the advertising world.[12] 'Your chances of competing successfully against this juggernaut will be improved if you understand the reasons for its overwhelming success', Ogilvy (1983: 155–57) remarks in the space that he dedicates to P&G in *Ogilvy On Advertising*, before offering a description of its techniques. For the master document as a brief that P&G created has become a modern advertising classic, to the point that 'most of the major agencies have adopted the term "copy strategy"; albeit with variations and their own methodology, in part because of the convenience of developing something "exclusive and refined"' (Moliné 1996a: 101). Hence, the copy strategy currently appears in many forms and is still useful in many mass consumption product categories, inasmuch as 'it has evolved over time and from being an advertiser's document has become the basis of the majority of strategies implemented by agencies' (González Martín 1996: 365–66). As a matter of fact, when Moliné explains the concept in his book *La comunicación activa*, he dedicates a chapter to P&G's copy strategy (i.e. that of the advertiser) and another to the agency kind. Such was the influence of this advertising technique on the advertising industry that there was not one agency that did not develop its own version. In this sense, for González Martín (1996: 366) the creative work plan[13] (CWP) developed by the agency Young & Rubicam was a newer and more widespread version of the copy strategy. Moliné (1996a: 108–18), for his part, goes a step further, contending that Ogilvy & Mather's creative strategy, Leo Burnett's 'diagnostic model', J. Walter Thompson's T-Plan, NCK's 'creative work document', Dorland & Grey's 'creative work plan' and so on and so forth are also indebted to the original copy strategy.

At this point, there is question that should obviously be broached: what is a copy strategy exactly? Suffice it to look to P&G itself, which answers it in following terms:

> The copy strategy is a document that identifies the basis on which we expect that the consumer prefers to buy our products, instead of those of our competitors. It is that part of marketing strategy that refers to advertising. The basic content of the copy strategy derives directly from the product and the basic need of the consumer for whose satisfaction the product is intended. A copy strategy should clearly express the fundamental benefit promised by the brand, which is the primary basis of the purchase.
>
> (in Moliné 2000: 189)

So, the copy strategy is based on the advertiser's marketing strategy and brief, yet it should not be confused with these. It is a concise strategic document that, on the basis of the product per se, 'identifies the benefits to be presented to consumers, but it doesn't cover execution. How the benefits will be presented is the creative team's job' (Arens et al. 2009: 211). In other words, the creative aspects are a matter for the agency, but the strategic ones are the reserve of P&G (Clark 1989: 36). Arens et al. (2009: 211) flesh out the tool's mechanics as follows:

1. An objective statement. A specific, concise description of what the advertising is supposed to accomplish or what problem it is supposed to solve. The objective statement also includes the name of the brand and a brief, specific description of the target consumer.

2. A support statement. A brief description of the evidence that backs up the product promise; the reason for the benefit.
3. A tone or brand character statement. A brief statement of either the advertising's tone or the long-term character of the brand.

As can be observed, the mechanism restricts the attributes or benefits of the product, which occasionally limits the strategic possibilities (sometimes it is necessary to preserve a corporative slogan that defines the company's policy). In the interview that he gave Clark (1989: 35) in *The Want Makers*, Robert V. Goldstein, the vice president in charge of the company's advertising at the end of the 1980s, could not have been more categorical in this respect: 'If you make a better product for meeting consumer needs you ought to tell them about it,' and according to him, the ideal medium is mass advertising. In his view, 'the role of advertising is to sell the product. There is a great variety of ways, but basically only one objective' (Clark 1989: 35). This thinking is a direct legacy of Hopkins, despite the 70 years separating them. It is little wonder that, in his opinion, strategic advertising techniques have barely changed at all in 100 years: 'I don't think the advertising creation process is dramatically different from when the first Ivory Soap ad was made in eighteen-something or other' (Clark 1989: 35). It was precisely this straitjacketed character that gave it a bad name among agencies and the industry in general, as will be seen later on. Clark (1989: 36) says that this type of advertising was basically at the root of the public's loathing of the advertising industry. P&G was well aware of this, and it was Goldstein himself who attempted to save the day:

> 'We don't have a single style of advertising', he protested. 'We have advertising that's musical and advertising that's not. We have real people and glamorous celebrities. Advertising that is basically heavily demonstration and advertising that is very cosmetic and selling dreams'.
>
> (Clark 1989: 36)

As well as the heterogeneous list of advertising resources – there is room for aspects such as the tone and components of the advertisement per se – Goldstein is absolutely right if what is understood by dreams are dishes that sparkle or hair that is smooth and glossy after being washed.

After clarifying the concept of copy strategy, we will now specify its characteristics by associating them with those of the USP, the other rationalist technique that will be covered in this book. As noted above, both techniques are closely connected and our aim is to identify those connections. Moliné (1996a: 106) has no doubts whatsoever:

On the other hand, it [the copy strategy] is not too far removed from the USP. Not by a long chalk. The crux of the problem that we are trying to resolve, how to define campaign strategy, leads us to the same solution.

The first common denominator between the copy strategy and the USP that should be underscored is their communicative nature. Although both are strategic advertising mechanisms and should be understood as such, it is true that both collaborate in building the brand, but from the unequivocal perspective of communication. That both are product centric is the second aspect that they share. When alluding to the copy strategy, González Martín (1996: 365) says that 'it is a condensed document that determines the product's essential argument, specifying communication content, but without saying more (besides insinuating the tone) about the final form that the messages should adopt'. This perspective of product branding is a totally logical aspect of the copy strategy when bearing in mind that P&G developed branding models focusing exclusively on the product.

With respect to the USP, however, product orientation was an option freely chosen by the agency and by Reeves himself. Lastly, as to the third connecting element, the driving force behind the purchase is a specific benefit. To wit, resorting to the product's tangible or rational benefits as the campaign's focus. As Ed Harness, former P&G chairman, declares, '[i]f the consumer does not perceive any real benefits in the brand, then no amount of ingenious advertising and selling can save the brand' (in Roman and Maas 2003: 16). Indeed, 'the copy strategy or creative platform, as others prefer to call it', notes González Martín (1996: 365), 'acts principally on the cognitive component, steering the creative one towards the quest for convincing arguments of an eminently functional nature'. As will be seen in the following chapter dealing with the USP, this characteristic is not lost but, quite to the contrary, enhanced. The reason for this is blindingly obvious: both mechanisms have a remarkably rationalist common core that, as already noted, can be traced in the reason-why copywriting technique. As Reeves (1961: 55) himself confessed, he learnt a lot from Hopkins – for him, he was a genius. He admired his intelligent advertising copy and his farsightedness to use in advertising a characteristic of the product that, without being either novel or exclusive, nobody had singled out before. And in both trust is placed in the sound judgement of the consumer to choose the best purchase option, that is, we are referring to the so-called 'rational consumer'.

After analysing the similarities between both mechanisms, we will now examine what is held to be the first rationalist strategic advertising mechanism developed by an advertising agency: the USP.

2

Rosser Reeves's USP: The Reality in Advertising Is the Product

To talk about Reeves's unique selling proposition (USP) is to talk about the rationalist strategic mechanisms of advertising. Obviously, it is not the only technique based on these psychological assumptions, as seen in the first chapter. Furthermore, it has been claimed that it is excessively in debt to the theories of the masterly Hopkins, as also already noted. As a matter of fact, we do not even know as yet if it was its forerunner (it appears that P&G was working on its copy strategy at about the same time as Reeves was doing so on his USP). And there are still doubts about whether or not Reeves was actually the father of the concept in question. So, why exactly has the USP been chosen as the first strictly advertising contribution (the proposal of an advertising agency) to the strategic advertising mechanisms of this book?

Well, first and foremost, due to the recognition that this commercial concept has achieved not only among the advertising community – in *The Mirror Makers*, Stephen Fox contends that 'for the 1950s, Reeves was the most influential theoretician of how advertising worked' (1997: 187) – but also in the academic world. This is an indisputable fact judging by the words of most of the communication experts analysed here. Robert Jones (2017: 35), a strategist at Wolff Olins and a professor at the University of East Anglia, includes the acronym in what he calls the 'masters of branding' and compares Reeves with outstanding figures like Ogilvy and Bernbach. Similarly, for Feldwick (2015: 63) the worldwide brand planning director at DDB, the USP 'is supported in textbooks and advertising courses'. He has a point when taking into account its continued presence, since its inception, in the most relevant textbooks on the subject. This is also the case with the seminal *Advertising Management*, where it is claimed, '[t]he Reeves approach was undoubtedly successful' (Batra et al. 1996: 449); in *Strategic Advertising Campaigns* by Schultz (1991: 309), who credits it with a 'strong persuasive advantage; may force competitors to imitate or choose more aggressive strategy'; and in the fundamental *Essentials of Contemporary Advertising*, a manual in which Arens et al. (2009: 15) refer ironically to its persistent and, in a way, exaggerated use. Perhaps its overuse justifies a certain weariness on the part of the advertising industry: 'it would be hard to overestimate the influence that Reeves's idea of the Unique Selling Proposition has had on both agencies and clients to date; even, paradoxically, among creative departments who would regard Reeves's own work with deep contempt' (Feldwick 2015: 62). All in all, as Moliné (2000: 193), one of the founders of the legendary agency MMLB (the genesis of modern advertising in Spain), concludes, the USP concept 'ended up forming part of a package of basic advertising skills'. Indeed, it also occupies a very important place in the non-English literature. For instance, the historian Eguizábal (2007: 48) declares that it is 'one of the most influential discoveries in the past decades'. This is an opinion shared by Sánchez Guzmán (1989: 153) who reckons that it is 'one of the most important contributions to the advertising world'. And, lastly, González Martín (1996: 367) who describes it as one of the most well-known creative philosophies. In effect, the USP is doubtless one of the most popular concepts in advertising (see Moliné 1996a: 96).

Second, it is one of the most influential advertising techniques. It is not for us to challenge the application of the USP, since its advent up until the present day, by advertising agencies of all kinds (from multinational to local ones, through national and specialized agencies). This is how Ramon Ollé (2005: 120), the former head of planning at Grey Group Spain, sees it when suggesting that the 'USP has become one of the most used theories by advertising men'.[1] Burtenshaw et al. (2006: 88) refer to its 'efficiency', defending the formula versus the complexity of differentiating products at present. In the now classic *Advertising and Sales Promotion Strategy*, even Tellis (1998: 91) holds that the USP concept is still in use. A good example of this is the statistics provided in the 7 October 1996 issue of the specialized journal *Advertising Age*: when asked about basic strategic mechanisms, 69 per cent of North American advertising agencies mentioned the USP. Namely, 35 years after the publication of Reeves's book, the survey ranked it in prominent position way ahead of other strategic mechanisms employed by advertising agencies.

Lastly, and what is perhaps of most interest here, it was the first relevant and rationalist strategic mechanism devised by an advertising agency. In this connection, irrespective of the reasons, this mechanism will now be carefully considered in this chapter.

2.1. The USP as a strategic advertising mechanism

In his now classic *Reality in Advertising*, when discussing the fierce competition in the advertising world, Reeves (1961: 52) notes, '[t]he U.S.P. almost lifts out of the ruck and wings its way to some corner of the mind'. And in another passage of the book, he cautions in an even more mercantilist tone, '[t]o a company that is not achieving this extra edge [USP], the difference is not so much money lost as it is sales lost' (Reeves 1961: 24). The interesting thing is that, although it may seem otherwise, this sort of statement so typical of Reeves; it is not only commercial hot air. Quite to the contrary, as Reeves (1961: 46) himself declared, the USP theory allowed Ted Bates & Company to increase its sales from US$4 million to 1500 million during the 1940s. But not only Reeves praised its achievements – which would be rather suspect. In *Madison Avenue U.S.A.*, Martin Mayer (1958: 53), one of the top experts in the North American advertising world of the period,[2] claims, 'he was from the beginning (to quote a former employer) "a wild one", an experimenter in the arcane reaches of client contact, a brilliant creator of sales arguments and a theoretician of the business'. This should come as no surprise judging by the arguments deployed by Reeves himself to convince the journalist:

> 'What this agency has done which is different from any other agency', says Rosser Reeves, chairman of the board of Ted Bates & Company, 'is to apply reason to advertising. We've grown from $2,900,000 in billings in 1940 to about $100,000,000 in 1957. Nearly $60,000,000 of what we do today comes from increases in client appropriations since they came to us – and in seventeen years we've never lost an account'.
> (Mayer 1958: 53)

Some years later, William Meyers, another journalist specializing in advertising, explained in *The Image Makers*, a book that also addresses the golden era of the American advertising industry, 'Ted Bates & Company, the agency he [Rosser Reeves] helped launch in the early 1940s on a shoestring budget, is today a $3 billion conglomerate with offices in more than fifty countries all over the world' (1985: 23). Nor does he go unnoticed in the overview of the advertising industry in the 1980s offered by Eric Clark (1989: 15) in *The Want Makers*, which refers to him as 'the great American advertising man'. And when dealing with the years during which Madison Avenue steered the course of global advertising in a recently published biography on David Ogilvy, Roman (2009: 118) has the following to say about him: 'Reeves joined Bates as a copywriter and rose to chairman, building the agency into the fourth largest in the world.'

It is more than likely that the majority of the clients of Ted Bates's agency at the time obtained very positive results with the USP – for example, the figures provided by Reeves himself in the interview that he gave in *The Art of Writing Advertising* (Higgins 1987: 94–124), in which he boasts about the results obtained by Bates in campaigns for Anacin, M&M and Viceroy. In other words, in view of the figures, it seems that highlighting only one rational attribute of products in the advertisements produced in the mid-twentieth century guaranteed, to certain extent, the marketing success of brands. It was due in part to its proven effectiveness that the USP made a place for itself in the brief history of modern advertising.

However, it is indisputable that Reeves himself had something to do with the success of his advertising formula: 'But Reeves's salesmanship is probably the deciding factor' (Mayer 1958: 58). Indeed, this controversial advertising man was both the catalyst and exponent of this novel strategic mechanism, defending and promoting it in such an aggressive manner that he sometimes overstepped the limits. Meyers (1984: 22) tells how Reeves was known as the 'the blacksmith' on Madison Avenue because he believed that advertising should be used to 'bludgeon' people into buying. His 'go-for-the-jugular' style revolutionized Madison Avenue to such an extent that he can be regarded as one of the people responsible for reinventing the advertising industry: 'he helped build a cottage industry into a global communication power' (Meyers 1984: 23). So, differences aside, the USP theory tells us a lot about Reeves's personality and modus operandi. As Moliné (1996a: 99–100) claims,

> That style is evinced in his own book. As his was the only reality in advertising, he was brutally honest when expressing his doubts about the tendencies and methods being developed at the time. For Reeves, the USP was a comprehensive technique that encompassed the process of putting together a campaign, from its strategic approaches to creativity, and by and large he refused to admit that other contributions were capable of widening its scope or enhancing it.

Eguizábal (2007: 49) is of the same mind:

> In 1961, Reeves published his book emphatically entitled *Reality in Advertising* in which he presented the basic principles of the USP and, in passing, inveighed against the Freudian approaches in American advertising and 'image theory', which he contrasted with what he called the 'theory of reality'.

Whatever the reason, the USP will go down in history because 'Rosser Reeves, the legendary co-founder and president of Ted Bates, has managed to understand what "makes a person buy"' (Bendelac 1997: 7).

2.2. What is the USP?

In order to answer this question, it is first convenient to recall what Stanley Bendelac, the chief operating officer at Bates Europe and the president of Delvico Bates until 2005, wrote in his prologue to the Spanish edition of *Reality in Advertising*, which the communication group re-edited in 1997:

> USP is a precise term with an unequivocal meaning. First and foremost, it is a peculiarity inherent to the brand. It should promise a 'benefit' that no one else offers in its product category. Secondly, a USP should be directly related to the needs and desires of consumers and incite action. Thirdly, each USP should offer consumers or users a clear proposition as regards the benefit offered by the service or product.
>
> (Bendelac 1997: 9)

Now, this is how Reeves himself answers the question:

> Actually, U.S.P. is a precise term, and it deserves a precise definition [...]:
> 1. Each advertisement must make a proposition to the consumer. Not just words, not just product puffery, not just show-window advertising.[3] Each advertisement must say to each reader: 'Buy this product, and you will get this specific benefit [...]'
> 2. The proposition must be one that the competition either cannot, or does not, offer. It must be unique – either a uniqueness of the brand or a claim not otherwise made in that particular field of advertising [...]
> 3. The proposition must be so strong that it can move the mass millions, i.e., pull over new customers to your product.
>
> These three points are summed up in the phrase: 'Unique Selling Proposition'. This is a U.S.P.
>
> (1961: 47–48)

As can be observed after carefully reading both definitions, the term USP is relatively simple: to look for an attribute, benefit or quality possessed by a product that differentiates it from its competitors and to get that message across, for in Reeves's (1961: 34) opinion, '[t]he consumer tends to remember just one thing from an advertisement – one strong claim, or one strong concept'. This is how Ollé (2005: 120) understands it when claiming that

> the idea is very simple: we investigate what that product can do, what are its differential attributes and we focus our communication efforts on that sole idea that we consider to be differential (what Reeves calls a unique selling proposition).

We cannot be far off the mark when making this assertion since most of the literature reviewed underscores the same characteristic when referring to the USP. From classic works such as *Strategy in Advertising*, whose author Leo Bogart (1967: 63) has the following to say in this respect: 'The foundation for a successful campaign, Reeves wrote, was the "Unique Selling Proposition", the embodiment of those qualities (real or putative) which distinguish a brand from its competition and offer the consumer a unique benefit', to more recent and specific works, including *Branding: A Very Short Introduction*, whose author Robert Jones (2017: 35–36) declares,

> The proposition expressed the benefits the product offered consumers. Its apogee was the idea of the 'unique selling proposition', or USP [...] the concept that your advertising should communicate a benefit for the customer that was (as far as possible) unique to your product.

Even in those publications that do not regard Reeves as the father of the USP work method, this strategic advertising mechanism is referred to in the same way: 'Superiority claim based on unique physical feature or benefit. Most useful when point of difference cannot be matched readily by competitors' (Schultz 1991: 309).

In contrast, although Moliné (1996b: 37) does not endorse this characteristic of simplicity, arguing that the USP concept is not always adequately interpreted, he recognizes the universally accepted principle of focusing, as has been seen above: 'With the USP (unique selling proposition), Rosser Reeves determined once and for all the need to establish clearly the objectives of communication strategies and concentrate efforts on one sole concept: a unique selling proposition.' He understands that the USP's mechanisms are not as simple as first meets the eye and explains the term's most complex and profound meaning by resorting to a dictionary and translating the different meanings that, to his mind, contain the English term 'unique'.

> On the one hand, in English it is 'single', 'sole', to wit, unique and sole in the sense that there is nothing else. On the other, in the dictionary 'unique' is defined as 'being without a like or equal', namely, not only should there be one proposition, but this should not have been used by another competing brand in its advertising.
>
> (Moliné 1996a: 97)

And further on, he adds, '[b]ut "unique" also has a third meaning: matchless, and Reeves had the ability to play with that third meaning, that of unparalleled, matchless' (Moliné 1996a: 98).

In the same vein as Moliné – in this case, with a clear commercial aim – Reeves (1961: 46–47) himself also questioned this principle of candour explained above, when alleging thus:

> Today, U.S.P. is perhaps the most misused series of letters in advertising. It has been picked up by hundreds of agencies and has spread from country to country. It is now applied, loosely and without understanding, to slogans, slick phrases, strange pictures, mere headlines – in fact, to almost anything which some writers consider slightly different from what they find in competing advertisements.

To our mind, and without wanting to detract from the theories of Moliné, one of the most outstanding communication experts in Spain, or from Reeves's – even though with these words his only intention was to promote his agency, as already noted – we are of the opinion that a careful reading of the American advertising man's book alone demonstrates the simplicity of the concept in question. It is also true that with time and basically as a result of the success and popularity of the USP, its original precepts were perhaps overstated and obscured. Indeed, we still contend that the USP is a very simple and candid formula. And a look as its history only reinforces this opinion.

As a matter of fact, its conception cannot be excessively convoluted when bearing in mind that the USP was originally based on a quote attributed to Samuel Johnson[4] (1709–84), a person who had absolutely nothing to do with the advertising world: 'Promise, large promise, is the soul of an advertisement' (Woodruff 1979).[5] Reeves grounded his theories and arguments in this remark made by Dr Johnson, a doyen of English literature. Namely, he translated an eminently poetic idea into the jargon of advertising. The merit of the advertising man of the Bates Group supposedly lies in this exercise of adaptation, for his consideration of marketing derived from a cognitive advertising benchmark destined to be the germ of the modern kind.

However, there is a work predating that of Reeves – written in the 1910s,[6] according to the experts – featuring a strategic advertising mechanism identical to the USP. The book in question is *Master Merchandising and the Dominant Idea*, authored by McJunkin and Finn and published in Chicago by the McJunkin Advertising Company (we understand that this company was owned by the first of the authors, another coincidence with Reeves's case). As can be deduced from its title, the book addresses the 'Dominant Idea' which is, as will be seen below, a model faithful to the USP. Better said, the USP is a calque of the dominant idea. Sabaté et al. explain this rather mockingly as follows:

An example clearly illustrates this advertising constant that we could call a recurrent invention: the same thing is invented and reinvented as many times as required. For decades, we have seen this with the USP, subsequently morphing into the emotional selling proposition – we assume for those who have never read Reeves – and then later on into the multiple selling proposition – which looks very much like the invention of a dissatisfied advertiser. But, long before that, there was already talk of the dominant idea that should be present in every campaign and establish the connection between the advertiser and the consumer. As explained by Joseph H. Finn, an advertising man from another time, '[...] the campaign which is not based upon a distinct, interesting central idea, falls short of its possibilities'. And it is even as if Reeves suffered from advertising amnesia, because back in the 1910s the advertising men McJunkin and Finn formulated that same principle: the agency McJunkin Advertising Company, with offices in Chicago, New York and Cleveland, published a magnificent book entitled *Master Merchandising and the Dominant Idea* in the 1910s. A careful reading will confirm that the USP that Reeves recreated several decades later was already about.

(Sabaté et al. 2010: n.pag.)

In fact, the similarities between the theories of Reeves and those of McJunkin and Finn, who wrote the chapter dealing with the dominant idea in the aforementioned book, are quite remarkable. Thus, what follows is a comparative analysis between the characteristics of the USP and those of the dominant idea.

2.3. *Characteristics of the USP or revamping the dominant idea*

The three aforementioned principles of the USP described by Reeves in his book are reflected in the dominant idea. To summarize them as a reminder, the 'rules' of the former will be listed before comparing them with the premises of the latter. First, a well-defined proposition is required: buy this product and you will obtain this specific benefit. Second, it should be a unique proposition, something that the competition cannot or does not offer. And, third, the proposition should sell.

The first 'rule' of the USP is faithfully reflected in McJunkin and Finn's work; one could say that it is the basic premise of both books. As already observed, McJunkin and Finn (191?: 28) established their work as a whole on the assumption that a campaign that is not grounded in a distinctive, central and interesting idea will not be a success. For his part, nor did Reeves (1961: 46–47) tire of repeating this idea, as noted when discussing the definition of the USP concept.

The second 'rule', that the selling proposition be unique, is one of the topics on which Reeves (1961: 54) elaborates most in his book:

[I]t is astonishing how many radical differences come swimming to the top – differences either in the product, or in the use of the product, which had not been suspected before. When this happens, the U.S.P. is often startling in its selling power.

And he even stops to analyse what he understands as the 'three broad roads that lead to Rome, and finding a U.S.P. in the product (very much like finding a pearl lying in an oyster) is only one' (Reeves 1961: 54). The second would involve inducing the client to improve or modify the product. 'A U.S.P. is thus specially tailored and built in – not only to the benefit of the manufacturer, but to the benefit of the public as well' (Reeves 1961: 55). And, lastly, his third 'broad road' consists in making the public see something in the product that they have not noticed before. 'This is not a uniqueness of the product, but it assumes uniqueness, and cloaks itself in uniqueness, as a claim' (Reeves 1961: 55). The uniqueness of the product is also reflected in *Master Merchandising and the Dominant Idea*, albeit perhaps in a subtler fashion than in the previous rule, doubtless because hyperbolic and misleading advertising was rife when the dominant idea was conceived. Nevertheless, McJunkin and Finn (191?: 31–32) understood that selling propositions had to be unique and had his doubts about the effectiveness of any benefit that was not original: 'The business which was originated solely to imitate some other business [...] cannot use Dominant Idea plans with profit. A business without individuality gets nowhere nowadays.'

Lastly, the rule referring to the sales power of a USP and the dominant idea is practically a constant in both books. Reeves and McJunkin and Finn, alike, recognized that their arguments were directly related to sales. As already noted, Reeves created the USP concept for a clear commercial purpose. As a matter of fact, there was not one agency at the time that did not develop a communication mechanism, theory, study or strategy to help companies increase their sales. In this sense, his book is replete with his own conclusions reached on the strength of the good results obtained with the use of USPs. For instance, '[s]tudies of great numbers of brand histories show that the first big advertiser can pre-empt the U.S.P. He is the pioneer, and, protected by his penetration bulwark, his is the reward' (Reeves 1961: 57). Nor did McJunkin and Finn mince their words, despite that the fact that the agency for which he presumably worked developed its activities 30 years before Reeves's and, therefore, there were not many scientific–commercial works on which the former could fall back on. At any rate, McJunkin and Finn (191?: 40) did indeed acknowledge that 'the McJunkin Dominant Idea advertising and selling plans are simple salesmanship, first and last. They are economic factors not only in minimizing sales expense, but also in facilitating distribution, eliminating resistance, and adding power to every sales effort'.

All considered, the similarities between both persuasive mechanisms do not end here. Quite to the contrary, they also coincide in a number of minor aspects. For example, Reeves was a staunch advocate of eliminating any superfluous or secondary information from advertising. As observed above, almost throughout *Reality in Advertising* he deploys all sorts of arguments to justify that advertisements should be based only on one important idea and do away with what he considers to be unnecessary:

> The advertisement may have said five, ten, or fifteen things, but the consumer will tend to pick out just one, or else, in a fumbling, confused way, he tries to fuse them together into a concept of his own.
>
> Reality campaigns, those that climb the ladder of penetration with the most speed, do not put the consumer in this predicament. Instead, they gather their energies together into a tight coil. They present him with one moving claim or concept which he can easily remember. Like a burning glass, which focuses the rays of the sun into one hot, bright circle, they bring together all the component parts into a single incandescence of their own.
>
> (Reeves 1961: 34–35)

Curiously enough, McJunkin and Finn (191?: 23) had come to the same conclusion several decades before: 'The Dominant Idea in advertising and merchandising, therefore, is the one distinctive major selling feature [*sic*] of a business, as free as possible of confusing minors.' In this connection, if the selling proposition – the 'sales truth', as McJunkin and Finn literally called it – is sufficiently relevant and is presented in a clear way without the distraction of other less important ones, according to the author, sales are guaranteed (McJunkin and Finn 191?: 29). That is, as with Reeves, they believed that in advertising one central idea should carry all the weight:

> The advertisement which does not contain a sane and substantial reason for purchase is a waste of space, money and effort. I believe the campaign which is not based upon a distinct, interesting central idea, falls short of its possibilities. I believe that every sales effort, every bit of constructive energy, should be built consistently around this one Dominant Idea – this one selling feature that overtops all the rest.
>
> (McJunkin and Finn 191?: 28)

Furthermore, both concepts are plainly product-centric. In Reeves's case, it was a highly conventional strategic decision, undoubtedly a product of his time. In contrast, McJunkin and Finn's theories were visionary insofar as they developed them when marketing was still in its infancy.[7] Making allowances for this, all we can say about them is that they reveal a combination of intuition, ingenuity, proactivity and foresight (and, more than likely, long hours poring over the pages of the journal *Printers' Ink*[8]). It should be recalled that when McJunkin and Finn were describing their dominant idea, products were marketed under brands as identification marks and, at best, as measures of control; it was a period in which such an important discipline for commerce as marketing had yet to be developed; and that the advertising of the so-called 'peddlers' was still very rudimentary, based on devices such as exaggeration, repetition and, more often than not, falsehoods.[9] So, unsurprisingly McJunkin and Finn (191?: 30) even go so far as to declare that

> advertising will never take the place of uniformly good merchandise; advertising may make the first sale, but never the second. The product must do that. And Dominant Idea advertising and merchandising do pay – because there is no division of effort – no scattering of shot.

To conclude this comparison, mention should go to a very interesting detail: as with Reeves, the creators of the dominant idea had no qualms about resorting to research as a necessary instrument both for identifying a dominant idea and for verifying its effectiveness. In fact, Reeves, always abreast of the psychological and economic theories of the moment,[10] made a point of the fact that what he was saying was the result of research and experience – for which reason this argument was very useful for discrediting the proponents of 'brand image' and motivational studies. As Mayer (1958: 56) explains, '[e]laborate research projects, involving laboratory experiments and detailed clinical testing, lie behind many of Bates's most commonplace product claims'. To the point that in response to the remark, '[w]hich is a technical job', made by the interviewer Denis Higgins (1987: 109) in *The Art of Writing Advertising*, without hesitation Reeves replies, '[o]f course, it's a technical job'. Throughout *Reality in Advertising*, he never tires of describing the experiments and research conducted. In this vein, he once said that 'a careful study of the U.S.P. approach, the philosophy of claim, leads us to the conclusion that the U.S.P. works in a far higher percentage of the cases' (Reeves 1961: 84). Likewise, he justified the validity of the USP concept on the basis of his experience. To his mind,

> There is a certain type of campaign that delivers more leverage in usage pull. These campaigns happen to make a claim about the product, the claim happens to have the quality of uniqueness, and it happens to be a claim of an order that is of interest to the reader.
>
> (Reeves 1961: 48–49)

McJunkin and Finn (191?: 33) were not far behind when declaring thus:

> Dominant Advertising is simplicity itself. Its obvious truthfulness is one of the biggest assurances possible to the interest of the consumer. Do not confuse the Dominant Idea with another kind of Dominance – a dominance of bulk alone. Its cost is terrific compared to results won. It is not comparable in permanent value to the adequate, determined and consistent presentation of the Dominant Idea. Dominant Idea campaigns are essentially founded on a basis of sane investment.

To end, Reeves did not only draw inspiration from the dominant idea to formulate his theories of advertising reality. However, there is indeed a feature inherent to the USP concept: that is, the principle of perseverance, which will now be described below.

If there is an aspect that makes the USP unique in its conception, then that is perseverance – a characteristic that brings it very close to Ries and Trout's famous positioning strategy.[11] In the words of Bogart (1967: 68), 'Reeves insists that the frequent change of the advertising campaign message results in a loss of penetration'. Indeed, unlike other rationalist theoreticians in the advertising world such as Hopkins and McJunkin and Finn themselves, Reeves (1961: 29) claimed that 'too-frequent change of your advertising campaign destroys penetration'. And it is he himself who, throughout *Reality in Advertising*, insists on how important it is not to change concepts in advertisements and to stick to that differential advantage offered by a USP as much as possible.

> It is one of the oldest principles in advertising, yet none is more generally ignored; for there are few brands on the market today that have not changed campaigns 5, 10, 15 or 20 times in the past 20 years. 'This story is worn out', a manufacturer will say. 'The public in getting bored with it', another will tell you. 'A new story puts new pep into my brand profile', a third will confide. If 90% do not remember it, the story is certainly not worn out. If 90% are not even aware of it, they can hardly be bored. And as for the new-pep philosopher, if only he had the figures, he would discover that by changing his story he is simply getting his brand profile into as few heads as possible.
>
> (Reeves 1961: 29–30)

Reeves was actually firmly convinced of the need to persevere in communication, which was nothing new since his boss Ted Bates was a firm advocate of insistence as an essential tool in advertising strategy:

'If an idea is a good one, and applies to the product', says Ted Bates himself, 'it will be good for an indefinite length of time. You might quibble with this, but I'd say it *never* wears out; you might put a new dress on it, that's all'.

(Mayer 1958: 57, original emphasis)

According to Mayer, Bates was not the only person to believe in the value of repetition, at least since the times of N.W. Ayer. In fact, until recently it was a basic advertising procedure (Mayer 1958). With this legacy, such was Reeves's conviction in this respect that Mayer offers the following anecdote offered by the advertising man himself:

'I had a client down in the Caribbean with me on a boat', Reeves says, 'and he said to me, more or less joking, you understand, "You have seven hundred people in that office of yours, and you've been running the same ad for me for the last eleven years. What I want to know is, what are those seven hundred people supposed to be *doing*?"' 'I told him, "They're keeping your advertising department from changing your ad."'

(Mayer 1958: 58, original emphasis)

Apparently, the Bates Group had been very successful in preventing clients from altering ad copy in a capricious manner (Mayer 1958). In point of fact, Reeves (1961: 32) himself includes some principles to this effect in his famous book:

1. Changing a story has the same effect as stopping the money, as far as penetration is concerned.
2. Thus, if you run a brilliant campaign every year, but change it every year, your competitor can pass you with a campaign that is less than brilliant – providing he does not change his copy.
3. Unless a product becomes outmoded, a great campaign will not wear itself out.

In retrospect, this idea may seem rather jaded or irrelevant, but nothing could be further from the truth, for perseverance is, in our view, one of the major achievements of the USP theory developed by Reeves and, without a shadow of doubt, one of the strengths of any current approach to brand management. Rom and Sabaté (2007: 144) are of the same opinion when noting,

This point of view has also been the target of much criticism, because it considers that consumers grow tired of always being told the same thing. We believe that a USP can be used for a long time, but the way of communicating it has to change.

Actually, one of the wisest choices, and above all the one that has been implemented most successfully in disciplines such as advertising, marketing and branding, is precisely the ability to maintain an idea for a brand.

2.4. Critiques of the USP

Despite the incontestable achievements of the USP described above, it should be acknowledged that, nowadays, approaches of this sort are moot, to say the very least. As could not be otherwise, since its inception it has been criticized by all kinds of professionals: colleagues, researchers, scholars, journalists and the like. In its early years, to all appearances very closely related to Reeves's character and ways, it was decried by many of his professional colleagues who harboured serious doubts about its hypothetical effectiveness. Naturally, there was an additional reason behind this criticism, which was none other than commercial. Reeves's competitors could not possibly commend and even less assume his precepts under the threat of losing business. In this connection, as with copy strategy, the USP concept swiftly underwent slight formal modifications – albeit more important as regards content – and, under different names,[12] was employed as a work methodology by several communication companies. As observed by Mayer (1958: 59), Reeves's main rival at the time was David Ogilvy of Hewitt, Ogilvy, Benson & Mather (afterwards, simply Ogilvy & Mather), with whom he not only vied for clients, sales and market shares – a very illustrative example of their rivalry, although of no interest here – but whose disputes over advertising, which will be addressed below, caused rivers of ink to flow: 'Few disagreements in any business have been so thoroughly thrashed out as the conflict in viewpoint between Ogilvy and Reeves' (Mayer 1958).

In fact, it was Ogilvy himself who declared, on more than one occasion, that his relationship with Reeves was very complicated, which is only to be expected when taking into consideration certain aspects. First, there were family issues, because Ogilvy had been Reeves's brother-in-law for several years until he divorced Melinda Graeme Street, Reeves's sister-in-law. Second, it was Reeves who introduced Ogilvy into the American advertising business. Indeed, he took the young Ogilvy under his wing during his first years in the United States; Roman (2009: 59) says that Ogilvy was always looking for father figures and was an acknowledged idolizer who found in Reeves not only a professional mentor but also a friend. And last but not least, as already mentioned, they were fierce rivals in the advertising world. All in all, in his biography of the English advertising man – leveraging the success of HBO's TV series *Mad Men* – entitled *The King of Madison Avenue*, Roman (2009: 118) describes that tempestuous relationship as follows:

They were at various times student and mentor, competitors, friends, and, if not enemies, at least estranged when Ogilvy divorced Reeves's sister-in-law. Some theorized that Ogilvy wrote *Confessions* to compete with *Reality in Advertising*. Their rivalry was on public display at an awards dinner. Telling people he was going to upstage Ogilvy, Reeves went to the Half Moon resort in Jamaica for a week and returned with a deep bronze tan, which he set off with a white dinner jacket. Asked the next morning how the dinner went, 'You know what that Scottish son of a bitch did', Reeves spit out. 'He wore a kilt.'

Ogilvy himself described his complex relationship with Reeves, when, in 1993, the latter was included in the Advertising Hall of Fame, a select group of the most outstanding American advertising creatives, in the following terms:

> When I came to work in the United States 58 years ago, I was a typical British advertising man of my generation – a pretentious highbrow. A few days after leaving Ellis Island, I met Rosser Reeves. We acquired the habit of lunching together once a week. During those lunches, Rosser talked without stopping and I listened. What Rosser said changed my life. He taught me that the purpose of advertising is to sell the product. And he taught me how to sell. Some people will tell you that Rosser and I were rivals – even enemies. I was his disciple. Bless you, dear Rosser. You taught me my trade.
>
> (in Roman 2009: 59)

Mayer (1958: 59) understood that both men represented a microcosm that was very difficult to analyse from the outside:

> When they talk about each other, however, it must be understood that they are playing a private game, the rules of which are known to them alone. Competitive with each other both personally and professionally, they conduct their competition within the framework of a mutual admiration society.

Setting aside personal disagreements between professionals, the accent will be placed here exclusively on objections arising from conceptual issues, discrepancies or errors, leaving those resulting from jealousies or quarrels inherent to the industry for another occasion.[13] Thus, as regards Reeves's fiercest competitor, only such conflicts will be dealt with here. Ogilvy, the promoter of a current of contemporary advertising thinking in opposition to the USP called 'brand image' – which will be studied in greater depth in the following chapter – questioned the precepts that Reeves defended with such vehemence. This is how Mayer (1958: 59) sees it when noting that 'these arguments [in reference to Reeves and his USP] seem suicidally shortsighted to David Ogilvy, of Ogilvy, Benson & Mather, apostle of the "brand image" '. However, unlike the American advertising man, with a penchant for harsh criticism and outrageous controversies, Ogilvy – Meyers (1985: 35) describes him as a 'warm' person, always wearing a 'broad smile' – preferred restraint when tilting at Reeves's theories:[14]

> He is a charmer and very appealing personality, one of the few men in advertising who has a good word to say for almost everybody else in the business (even Reeves): 'He taught me more about advertising than anybody I've ever known; the pity of it is that I couldn't teach him anything.' Scenting battle, Reeves replies, 'If we ever get out of packaged goods and into luxury items, I'll be glad to go sit at David's feet and listen.'
>
> (Mayer 1958: 60)

On the whole, the Englishman's criticism was aimed at one of the aspects of which the creator of the USP boasted about most: research. For Ogilvy (1987: 100), Reeves's methods lacked ingenuity, intuition and creativity.[15] In his opinion, all this was sacrificed for an excessive reliance on research and hard figures: 'I notice increasing reluctance on the part of marketing executives to use judgment; they are coming to rely too much on research, and they use it as a drunkard uses a lamp post, for support rather than for illumination.' In this vein, he discredits Reeves's 'advertising reality' based on complicated experiments, tests and research, because, far from being useful for brand image theory, it was a liability. 'How do you decide what kind of image to build?' Ogilvy (1987: 100) wonders. 'There is no short answer. Research cannot help you much here.[16] You have actually got to use judgment.' He goes on to declare, '[b]uild sharply defined personalities for their brands and stick to those personalities, year after year. It is the total personality of a brand rather than any trivial product difference which decides its ultimate position in the market' (Ogilvy 1987: 103). It is revealing that the aim of one of the few references to Reeves in *Ogilvy on Advertising*, with *I Hate Rules* as the suggestive claim-like subtitle – which can be regarded as the Ogilvy bible – is to contest the idea of 'originality'; Ogilvy (1983: 24) was a fervent advocate of creativity and originality was his mantra. In contrast, Reeves branded it as damaging and dangerous. This last objection voiced by the English advertising man is very useful for addressing one of the most common criticisms of the USP concept, namely, the markedly product-centric approach adopted by Reeves.

Specifically, the main criticism of the USP and, by extension, of all strategic advertising mechanisms of a rationalist nature is that – unquestionably influenced by product branding – they systematically lack any affective component in their design. The USP relies blindly on the rational consumer, on stimulus-response, on operational marketing policies and on the ability of self-managed businesses to implement it adequately, while taking absolutely no account of the consumer. As has been seen, this highly rigid and narrow perspective is now water under the bridge. In this respect, Eguizábal (2007: 50) declares,

> Even recognizing the merits of his proposal, it should be noted that the rational benefits only partially explain the mechanisms of consumption (or voting); and in the review of the USP technique performed by Bates Worldwide in 1995, 'emotional benefits were also included'.

It is certainly essential to make allowances for the affective component in communication, as Sánchez Guzmán (1993: 399) remarked some years ago when explaining that 'the use of emotional resources in the message is more effective than the deployment of rational arguments'. For his part, Moliné (2000: 193), when criticizing Reeves postulates that

> the chances of discovering a benefit are not limited to the functional and rational aspects of a product or its use, for there is a vast emotional field that, in many cases, tends to be a warmer and more effective and powerful alternative for strengthening a brand and its advertising.

And further on, making a play on words between Reeves's nickname 'the blacksmith' and his highly restrictive, rigid – and steely – perspective of strategic advertising mechanisms, he concludes, '[t]he profession would show [Reeves] that the human being has a heart and sensitivity. And that precisely thanks to those emotional qualities, the brain and logic react to the objectives established by adverts' (Moliné 2000: 193). It was that short-sightedness that would undermine the USP in favour of other communication approaches. Ortega (1997: 222) is of the opinion that the 'philosophy' of 'brand image' relegates the USP concept: 'This creative approach began to replace its USP counterpart at around the beginning of the 1970s [...] With this approach, the product was displaced by the brand that, as a distinctive symbol, requires a meaning, a personality, an image.'

Rom and Sabaté (2007: 143–44) take a very different view on the foregoing and, just as we have done, first address the shortcomings of Reeves's strategic concept:

> The USP is an advertising philosophy that has been the subject of some controversy. Its rigidness has been criticized and some have deemed it to be obsolete. Mention should also go to the controversy arising in the United States and Spain as from

1997 with the formulation of an ESP opposing the USP in the context of the debate on emotional and rational advertising.

However, contrary to the widely held view in academia, they hold that Reeves took 'emotion' into account when formulating his famous USP theory. As evidence, they resort to a remark made by Reeves (1961: 81) himself: 'The totality of the advertisement must project a Unique Selling Proposition, as well as a feeling.' Rom and Sabaté (2007: 144) thus conclude, '[n]amely, that the creator of the USP was already taking into consideration the emotional side of advertising, contrary to what is widely believed'. In our view, this reflection, albeit very subtle, is not entirely in line with reality. We will now attempt to plead our case.

In his book, Reeves uses the word 'feeling'[17] only on two occasions, while frequently inveighing against 'brand image', motivational theories, Freud and everything relating to 'emotion', 'affection' or 'feeling'. If the phrase is contextualized, it is possible to understand that what Reeves was trying to do was to make slight concessions – in his book, he makes several – to a technique that was dangerously (for him and the Bates Group) taking root in the market and which could not be totally ignored for obvious commercial reasons (a more radical stance than that taken, which, as already observed, was already radical per se, might lead to the loss of a client):

> The really valuable part of the brand-image theory is its emphasis on the visual symbol. In this, the brand imagists are quite correct, for no one denies that visual symbols can stir deeply buried tides [...] So it is better to drape a product, on the nonverbal level, with as many activating and pleasant associations as possible. We simply say: 'The totality of the advertisement must project a Unique Selling Proposition, as well as a feeling.' Embellish it then, if you will, with gold or sprinkle it with stardust. Drape behind it the richest tapestries of the nonverbal school.
>
> (Reeves 1961: 81)

Nevertheless, what is really interesting here is that Reeves apparently did not fully understand the emotional mechanisms of image theory. As can be seen in the aforementioned passage, he understood 'brand image' as if it were the background of a picture, without analysing its strategic or creative possibilities. In his eyes, it was merely a formal element. 'No, we cannot do without words, which are the content, and we would be foolish not to try for the image, which is the form' (Reeves 1961: 82). Eguizábal (2007: 49), who shares this view, offers the following clarification:

More than opposing Ogilvy, Reeves turned his attention to Pierre Martineau and his *Motivation in Advertising*,[18] published in 1954, although in his criticism he tended to identify advertising, whose arguments are developed through the image (to wit, the photograph or the illustration), with brand image (which constructs an image that is more mental than physical).

In other words, Reeves could not include 'feeling' in his USP concept, as he himself admitted, because he never really understood – nor wanted to – the inner workings of image theory. Thus, as already noted, his view was much closer to scathing criticism than to recognizing 'emotion' as a strategic mechanism, as can be clearly seen in the following remark: 'For the brand imagists move in the ectoplasmic area of mood and feeling; and it is indeed dangerous ground' (Reeves 1961: 85). So much so that, in the company's re-edition of *Reality in Advertising* the ex-president of Delvico Bates Stanley Bendelac makes amends for this absence of 'emotion' in the USP concept in the following way: 'In 1995, at Bates Worldwide we decided to revamp the USP concept [...] by incorporating emotional benefits, as well' (Bendelac 1997: 9). In any case, and to conclude, there is a more empirical indicator, for of all the many campaigns involving USPs that Meyers (1984: 29–33) describes in *The Image Makers*, none of them make any allowances whatsoever for emotional arguments.

For sure, the USP leaves no one minimally acquainted with communication indifferent. In this regard, some are staunch proponents of its relevance, despite the fact that the concept is anything but new: 'In reality, the best campaigns nowadays are based on a good USP' (Soler 1997: 119). While others completely discredit this strategic mechanism:

> [I]t seems that it was the American advertising man Rosser Reeves, of the Ted Bates agency, who invented this pseudo-scientific nonsense. The USP was the characteristic that gave a product its exclusive appearance, which made it uniquely attractive. This invention gave brand advertising a false halo of expert knowledge and legitimacy. Curiously enough, the acronym USP continues to be a respectable concept for the most credulous and innocent members of the marketing world.
>
> (Olins 2003: 65)

And there are also other more benevolent critiques that call for a review of the concept:

> We could review hundreds of campaigns from that decade and, in most cases, we would find that idea of using a sole dimension of the product as the principal message. Practically always associated with its performance, its benefits, its attributes

that make the promise plausible. We are of the mind that this magical triumvirate that, over time, had been incorporated in the vast majority of agency briefings (the USP, the benefit and the reason why) now needs to be reviewed in order to enable us to adapt to a new market setting.

(Ollé 2005: 121)

Be that as it may, with all its virtues and drawbacks, the USP has become a benchmark for strategic advertising mechanisms and, more specifically, a prototype of those of a cognitive nature. And the aim of this chapter has been to demonstrate just that.

3

David Ogilvy's Brand Image: The Rise of Emotion in Advertising Communication

Nowadays, most communication experts concur that there is a need to reformulate the traditional conception of brand management based on the economic
man, the marketing mix and rational advertising techniques, and to opt for new
branding formulas. Indeed, a brand is understood as a strategic asset and not as a
mere identifying or regulatory element, for which reason its management, together
with the strategic advertising mechanisms employed, should not be limited to
the strictly behavioural parameters relating to product branding described in the
previous chapters. From a personality branding perspective, there is no room for
mechanisms such as the 'reason-why', the 'copy strategy' and the unique selling
proposition (USP), since this new paradigm calls for emotion, the management
of intangibles and symbolic consumption. There is therefore a need for new more
complex strategic advertising mechanisms. Unlike the classical conception, in
which the image is a secondary element whose purpose is to catch the attention
of the public, namely, merely a more or less faithful reproduction of a sensation
or perception – or, in other words, an eminently sensorial passive phenomenon
which has nothing to do with intelligence – in the new conception described here
image is everything.

> The iconicity of advertising images (the ability of an image to represent reality by
> partial similarity or by analogy) means that they can be 'soaked with meaning' by
> their association with a rich variety of emotions to which we are already attuned
> through our interactions with our social and natural environments.
>
> (Messaris in Rosenbaum-Elliot et al. 2011: 29)

This preponderance of the iconic stems from a clearly Freudian idea – in point
of fact, Freud is essential for the approach described here – that 'motives' can be

conscious or unconscious. And, at the same time, it is obviously another of the basic differences between both psychological models, namely, the subordination of cognitive factors to emotional ones. This is doubtless one of the notions that had the greatest influence on the creation of emotional strategic advertising mechanisms and, by extension, the new personality branding paradigm.

This theoretically new conception has now been assumed to a certain extent. In effect, taking approaches of this sort to emotional brand management is practically a truism. And, as a consequence, many branding experts vindicate the power of the image versus that of copy. They stress the need to manage brands employing techniques like branding, marketing and emotional advertising, or coin – and even plagiarize – euphonic terms like Lovemarks, 'Passionbrands', 'aesthetic brands' and the like. Ultimately, as will be seen in this chapter and in all those framed in the context of this brand management paradigm, they have a similar basis and a suspiciously similar objective – to define what are supposed to be the brand management models of the future. On quite a few occasions, furthermore, they are used as a commercial strategy to sell a methodology, tool or technique developed by an important communication group or as a mere excuse to sell books. In this connection, Kapferer complains,

> It is paradoxical that the more brands are endangered and losing their market share [...] the more books are being published emphasizing affect, love, passion and emotions as the central construct of brands ('Love brands', 'emotional branding', 'passion brands', etc.). Some authors even urge brands to become 'legendary brands', or 'iconic brands', if they want to survive.
>
> (Kapferer 2012: 12)

Be that as it may, we are examining a reality that emerged nearly 60 years ago through a twenty-first-century prism. Let us now try to explain this. As has been observed, nowadays no one doubts these 'new' methods. Nevertheless, their conception and, in the main, their application are both age-old. It is not unreasonable to contend that the first emotional branding campaigns were developed in parallel to many others that continued to place the accent on the rational advertising of the guru Rosser Reeves, that is, in the mid-twentieth century. And, as will be seen, one of its main architects – at least from a media and, obviously, commercial point of view – was an outstanding disciple of Reeves himself. We are referring to David Ogilvy, who both capitalized on and popularized the so-called 'brand image' in the 1960s. So, in theory, the foundations of emotional strategic advertising mechanisms began to be laid during that decade – although the 1950s had been decisive for their future consolidation – on the famous Madison Avenue. We say in theory because, as has occurred on many other occasions with major advertising milestones, these mechanisms are very far removed from advertising theory and science[1] and, of course, from the offices of Madison Avenue. Indeed, they are indebted, as with everything else pertaining to personality branding, to the school of psychoanalysis led by Freud and of a distinctly European origin,[2] or to the advances that were being made in semiotic research mainly in countries such as France and Italy. In other words, this approach is deeply rooted in a tradition of thought both conceptually and geographically very far removed from the United States. However, as already noted, it would be Ogilvy, an Englishman residing in that country, who disseminated what can be considered to be the first emotional mechanism in the history of advertising.

3.1. The influence of motivation research on emotional strategic advertising mechanisms

'The ad industry began enlisting fairly basic research in the very early days of modern advertising', Clark contends in *The Want Makers* (1989: 65). And there are data to support his claim: in 1879, the N. W. Ayer agency conducted the first surveys; in 1908, Harry Dwight Smith called for 'formal research'; and in 1919, Archibald Crossley was already 'conducting formal surveys'. 'Thus psychology enjoyed its greatest vogue among ad people since the heyday of John B. Watson's behaviorism in the 1920s' (Fox 1997: 183). 'It was not until the mid-1930s however, that the industry as a whole caught up with the need for such systematized information' (Mayer 1958: 206). The reason had little to do with the advances in advertising science or technique – in fact, in a discipline as functionalist as advertising, research could eliminate the risks. In 1931, A. C. Nielsen broadened his line of work to include hygiene products, which was not only an unprecedented success for a consultancy firm that was on the verge of bankruptcy as a result of the Great Depression, but was also the starting point for the famous panels and, with them, the birth of market research with a capital M.

'A major shift developed in the 1950s. Advertising generally was firmly product-orientated until well after World War II, but in the 1950s it began to be directed increasingly towards people's desires, needs and wants' (Clark 1989: 67). This shift towards intangible brand assets and personality branding was based on a new school of psychology: motivation research. Supported by psychoanalysis and, above all, by the figure of Freud – although motivation research also encompasses Adlerian and even cultural anthropology theories, since it is a melting pot of premises and techniques – the emphasis was placed on the depth psychology of consumers and their 'unconscious' desires. According to Cheskin (1957: 86), one of its advocates, motivation research is the type of research that seeks to learn what motivates individuals in making choices. It employs techniques designed to reach the unconscious or subconscious mind because preference generally is determined by factors of which the individual is not conscious.

From an academic perspective, G. H. Smith, in his seminal *Motivation Research in Advertising and Marketing*, explains that it seeks to answer the question 'why?': 'Why do people behave as they do in relation to a particular advertising, marketing, or communications problem?' (1954: 3). And Samuel, more than 50 years later, in the essential *Freud on Madison Avenue*, similarly stated thus: 'Motivation research was devoted almost entirely to the "whys" of consumer behavior, its practitioners digging deep for root causes rather than being satisfied with whatever had risen to the surface' (2010: 13).

Motivation research developed in parallel with the advertising industry, as 'the fad of the industry and the darling of its most "advanced" practitioners' (Mayer 1958: 243). So, communication companies and motivational psychology institutes joined forces to make headway in the business world and, in the process, to revolutionize the concept of advertising. In fact, the industry itself subsidized such research, even when reputable psychologists – Gallup, for example (Samuel 2010: 155–56) – or prestigious advertising creatives – with Reeves at the fore (1961: 70–74) – harshly criticized the motivational approach. This can be explained by the fact that, regardless of whether or not the application of these theories of depth psychology to communication actually works, its pull was certainly undeniable from a commercial point of view. In addition to Ogilvy, Benson & Mather's well-known commitment to the new motivational approach with their popular brand image, other agencies also jumped on the motivation research bandwagon. For instance, Norman, Craig & Kummel spread the Freudian concept of 'empathy', taking it to the extreme; as well as McCann-Erickson, along with Herta Herzog – the wife of the illustrious Lazarsfeld who embraced this trend despite not publicly subscribing to any psychological school – who 'has done far more work than any other agency in Adlerian analysis, with its heavy emphasis on power drives' (Mayer 1958: 72). Herzog, together with Harper and Armstrong, worked on verifying 'brand personalities' by means of clinical tests, such as the Rorschach test. Similarly, numerous independent research institutes have since emerged, including the pioneering Institute for Motivational Research, the Color Research Institute and the Social Research Inc., not to mention the plethora of independent consultants, including the controversial James Vicary.

In this context, professionals such as Dichter, Martineau, Cheskin, Gardner and Maslow – even though Maslow did not regard himself as a member of the group – with Freud's psychoanalytic theories as a precedent, developed a new school of thought that would have a decisive influence on advertising and, by extension, on its strategic mechanisms. A school that, in addition to developing a new marketing concept, was also an authentic billing machine. The eminently commercial nature of motivational studies is clearly echoed in the words of its main proponents. This is the case of Ernest Dichter, who can be regarded as the father of motivational psychology. In his *Handbook of Consumer Motivations: The Psychology of the World of Objects*, he maintains,

> The Institute for Motivational Research is an organization for the purpose of finding answers to the 'why' of human actions in order to develop appropriate strategy to bring about desired results and goals. The institute, under the guidance of the author, has conducted over 2,500 studies in the United States, Canada, Europe, Latin America, Africa, and Australia.
>
> (Dichter 1964: vii)

The sales spirit imbuing the books that he wrote was not exclusive to Dichter. Pierre Martineau, another eminent motivation research expert, stated in his *Motivation in Advertising: Motives That Make People Buy*, '[m]otivation research is rapidly taking shape as a new tool available to modern advertising in the search for understandings of people' (1957: 8). Louis Cheskin, in a line closer to Dichter's – both of whom represented research institutes that had to advertise – kept this promotional spirit alive in Chapter 6 of *How to Predict What People Will Buy*, in which Robert Stone, the vice president of the National Research Bureau, interviews him; all in all, it is a mission statement of motivation research's sales principles (1957: 83–109).

The synergies between the advertising industry and motivation research were such that even agencies wrote books in which parallels were drawn between them, such as Harry Henry's (then a McCann-Erickson heavyweight) significant *Motivation Research*, in which he goes so far as to state euphorically that brand image 'is probably the most important concept that has emerged in the whole history of advertising' (1958: 89). By the same token, professional associations were soon referring to motivation research. From *The Techniques of Marketing Research* (1937), the book that the American Marketing Association (AMA) would commission – in which Lazarsfeld himself was going to participate – which intended to include depth psychology, to what Samuel understands as 'the definitive indication that motivation research had reached the big time' (2010: 38), with the publication of *An Introductory Bibliography of Motivation Research* (1953), which compiles almost 500 books and articles relating to the subject matter.

Unsurprisingly, one year before, in November 1952, the Advertising Research Foundation (ARF) appointed the Committee on Motivation Research

(Newman 1957: 49–50). This committee then persuaded the ARF to publish a second work including a comprehensive glossary of motivational terms. *The Language of Dynamic Psychology: As Related to Motivation Research* (1954) is a dictionary of psychoanalytic terms coordinated by the Tufts College professors of psychology Joseph Wulfeck and Edward Bennett. It covered all sorts of concepts of motivation psychology in order to train advertisers in these then trendy research approaches: from 'libidinal-object' to 'Adlerian psychiatry', through 'symbolisms' or 'self'. In the first line of the preface, the Committee on Motivation Research even dares to claim that '[t]he key to success in every sales message is the motivating appeal' (Wulfeck and Bennett 1954: 5).

In the same vein, as indicated by Newman (1957: 50), in 1954 the ARF also published the *Directory of Organizations Which Conduct Motivation Research* and the *Directory of Social Scientists Interested in Motivation Research*. It then went on to sponsor Smith's *Motivation Research*. In the interesting *Motivation Research and Marketing Management*, Newman describes how, at the time, it seemed that all professional publications and symposia revolved around motivation research (1957: 50). However, the ultimate accolade – and, in a sense, the prologue to its decline, at least publicly – also came in the shape of a book, this time sponsored by the all-powerful AMA. *Motivation and Market Behavior* (1958) is a collective work coordinated by the professors Robert Ferber and Hugh Wales, compiling the contributions of leaders in motivation research such as Dichter, Martineau and Vicary, plus those of other critics, such as Politz and Scriven. The second part of the book contains numerous contributions almost always linked to academia and largely drawn from academic journals, addressing a large number of qualitative research techniques. In short, this evinces how the advertising industry and motivation research fed off each other.

Notwithstanding this – partly commercial – vocation, the achievements of motivation research are undeniable: on the one hand, in relation to the new conception of consumers; and, on the other, with regard to the epistemological, conceptual and methodological approaches of the new theory versus previous techniques.

3.2. Pierre Martineau: The ambassador of emotional advertising

It has already been noted in Chapter 2 that when Reeves openly criticized brand image in his famous *Reality in Advertising*, he was not actually attacking Ogilvy, its purported creator, but Martineau. To recap, Martineau was one of the principal exponents of motivation research in the United States in the 1950s and 1960s, and an author who championed symbolic consumption and emotional advertising in his publications. And, in retrospect, the father of the USP had plenty of reasons to be angry with the promoter of grand image, judging by the arguments, as subtle as they are devastating, deployed by Martineau in his main work *Motivation in Advertising*, when analysing rational advertising techniques – of which Reeves was the high priest. Unlike Ogilvy's diplomatic and moderate words, Martineau trenchantly sets forth the main principles and values of brand image and lambasts the classical advertising conception represented by Reeves. He sternly challenges all of the advertising clichés to date, from the predominance of copy over image to the sovereignty of the product over brand image, through the type of rational, instead of emotional or 'psychological' – as he himself calls them – arguments deployed. Indeed, the theoretical advertising creative refutes the very basis of the USP:

> Modern advertising is not just a posting of claims, a bare-bones statement of facts. It is far, far from being just a reliance on words and logic. It is rather a fusion of many modes of human communication, including language.
>
> (Martineau 1957: 13)

And on the basis of surmounting Reeves's persuasive mechanism, he advocates for the power of emotions:

> Advertising grew up as a statement of product virtues and superlatives – all copy and logic. But modern advertising is something entirely different. Now it uses a wide range of esthetic effects, emotive appeals, nonrational meanings. It reaches into the motive structure of the individual by many avenues of communication.
>
> (Martineau 1957: 18)

As can be observed, the alleged logic of consumption is another of Martineau's targets: 'We are not going to accomplish anything merely by stating a logical case. We are not going to persuade anybody by winning an argument with the consumer via our logic and our words' (Martineau 1957: 6). And more emphatically, he decries,

> A tremendous amount of misunderstanding about the very nature of advertising probably emanates from the classic definition that advertising is just salesmanship in print. This implies that there is an identity of method between face-to-face salesmanship and the process of persuasion through advertising, that both involve a battering down of the consumer's defenses by logical argument involving economic yardsticks and technical superlatives. This misconception, of course, completely overlooks the key element in persuasion, which is feeling.
>
> (Martineau 1957: 122)

In this respect, he believed that strategic advertising mechanisms had to be renewed, asserting that

> this is why the focus on all advertising has to be changed so that, instead of looking outward from the product to the consumer, we see the product from the consumer's eyes and thus can fit it into his life.
>
> (Martineau 1957: 8)

For the motivation researcher, the objective of advertising was very different from that pursued by rational advertising creatives. He defended the creation of a rich and positive product image or institutional image with plenty of appeal. Martineau endorsed the idea that products should possess many other attributes, in addition to their purely utilitarian aspects, if they really wanted to differentiate themselves from their market competitors. He forged one of the emotional advertising maxims when contending that '[o]ther manufacturers can match ingredients or engineering features or bargains. But they can never match the nonrational psychological overtones in the product image, the collar of subjective attitudes' (Martineau 1957: 199).

These arguments, which had infuriated the masterly Reeves so much, paved the way for the new advertising and emerging brand management approaches. Thus, as already noted, in any self-respecting branding manual it is possible to read reflections that are identical to Martineau's presuppositions: 'The greatest brands have a meaning that transcends practical benefits. That transcendence allows them to embrace change unafraid, allowing for more consistent customer satisfaction and a longer-lasting brand than competitors who focus only on immediate benefits' (Healey 2008: 21).

In short, Martineau was initially known as the head of market research at the daily *Chicago Tribune*, before going down in history as one of the pioneers of the concept of brand image. And, as has been seen, he more than debunked Reeves's theory and, in a way, broke with traditional advertising theory as a whole. In effect, by our reckoning, unlike Ogilvy, who in his oeuvre only mentions the concept of brand image a couple of times and in passing and, above all, who commercially leverages that approach, Martineau's work is a complete handbook that resolutely combines motivation research with advertising and highlights brand image, one of the concepts that has had the greatest impact on advertising. Irrespective of whether we agree or not with his arguments, methods and examples, what is unquestionable is that he took the concept of brand image to a theoretical level that was dizzying at the time[3] to such an extent in fact that it has barely been exceeded in the subsequent literature.

3.3. *David Ogilvy's brand image*

The Englishman David Ogilvy was the first adman to recommend forcefully the use of an emotional advertising mechanism framed in the context of the so-called 'personality branding models'. Indeed, in a talk entitled 'The image and the brand', which he gave during a lunch organized by the American Association of Advertising (AAA) on 14 October 1955, he pronounced a phrase that has become etched in the annals of advertising science: 'We hold that every advertisement should be thought of as a contribution to the complex symbol which is the brand image' (Ogilvy 1987: 100). He also included this same phrase in one of his key works, *Confessions of an Advertising Man*, first published in 1963. Ogilvy used such a commercially conducive forum as the AAA to make a compelling appeal in favour of the power of the image, semiotics – although he spoke of symbols and meanings – motivation research and long-term advertising objectives. All these aspects were truly revolutionary in an advertising landscape dominated by rational theories and the USP of his professional colleague and mentor Reeves, as has been seen in the previous chapter. However, Ogilvy at first mistrusted the precepts of personality branding. He rather repudiated them, as he himself acknowledged during his talk at the AAA lunch:

> I must confess that I have changed my mind on this subject. When I first arrived in this country eighteen years ago, I bought the wicked old Chicago philosophy, as practiced by Claude Hopkins. I used to deride advertising men who talked about long-term effect. I used to accuse them of hiding behind long-term effect. I used to say that they used long-term effect as an alibi – to conceal their inability to make any single advertisement profitable. In those intolerant days, I believed that every advertisement must stand on its own two feet and sell goods at a profit on the cost of the pace.
>
> Today, I have come to believe, with Garner and Levy, that every advertisement must be considered as a contribution to the complex symbol, which is the brand image. And I find that if you take that long-term approach, a great many of the day-to-day creative questions answer themselves.
>
> (Ogilvy 2006: 21–22)

In the previous chapter, it has already been seen that the English advertising man, strongly influenced by both his past as a door-to-door salesman and the respect that he professed for the fathers of rational advertising Hopkins and Reeves, was initially a staunch advocate of a more commercial advertising. However that may be, he changed his mind radically. And, in our opinion, there were two reasons behind that change. The first was of a conceptual nature. In April 1955, Ogilvy received the last number of the popular business journal *Harvard Business Review*. It contained a paper by Burleigh B. Gardner and Sidney J. Levy, two experts in motivation research – a work, which will be analysed below, in which they advocated for a more symbolic communication model – which had a lasting influence on the advertising man. Contrary to what may be assumed at first sight, for the British adman had a powerful ego, he acknowledged the original source of the idea that he was presenting: 'I didn't make that [brand image] up. I borrowed it, from an article by Burleigh Gardner and Sidney Levy in the March issue of the *Harvard Business Review*' (Ogilvy 2006: 21). He also recognized that 'The product and the brand' had changed his way of understanding communication in this regard, and all this coming from a man who had previously prided himself on creating campaigns that communicated, directly and explicitly, the virtues of a product – or even a list of these. At the time, he disavowed it, endorsing the maxim that 'every advertisement must be considered as a contribution to the complex symbol, which is the brand image – as part of the long-term investment in the reputation of the brand' (Ogilvy 2006: 21). As a matter of fact, Ogilvy set himself up as one of the main advocates of this novel advertising current, in stark and open contrast to the postulates of his colleague and mentor Reeves.

To our mind, the second reason why Ogilvy started to believe in the 'brand image' advertising current was less profound and philosophical. As has been seen in the previous chapter, he was a talented businessman and a tenacious and persevering battler, as well as a consolidated leader in the advertising industry. Namely, a person capable of embracing change and committing himself to an a priori risky path at a moment of uncertainty in the industry. And that is precisely what he did when he decided to introduce the brand image working methodology in his communication group, thus managing to associate his advertising agency with the motivation research fad which was the talk of the town at the time – and which we have briefly reviewed in this chapter. All in all, it may be surmised that it was more of a business ploy, whose aim was to broaden his new business strategy to include those clients who were calling for a less rational and explicit communication, than a profound and meditated reflection on image theory, semiotics or motivation research per se.[4] Suffice it to read the advertising man's different works on the topic to understand that they do not precisely stand out for their conceptual development of or philosophical reflections on brand image. Quite to the contrary, the few passages in his oeuvre in which he broaches the subject of brand image recall his typical advertising 'recipe books', with the only difference that he now underscores brand image he had once referred to 'direct sales'. Rom and Sabaté express this in similar terms:

David Ogilvy is usually credited with having given the brand a value equal to or greater than that of the product in advertising communication, but in his oeuvre he does not fully develop this advertising philosophy. Taking into account that brand image is an advertising trend that really began to circulate among advertising agencies at the end of the 1960s and at the beginning of the 1970s, it is odd that he did not make the most of his writings to establish and theorize it. Even so, Ogilvy & Mather was one of the advertising agencies that stood out when applying it.

(Rom and Sabaté 2007: 147)

However, Ogilvy's role in disseminating the precepts of brand image and, by extension, motivation research, semiotics and image studies in general in both academia and the business world is undeniable. To the point that, in the profession, the English advertising man is still considered to be the high priest of this advertising current. It can be claimed that he was to brand image what Reeves was to the USP.

All considered, notwithstanding its theoretical inconsistency, brand image has gone down in history as an advertising mechanism directly associated with motivation research – and largely in Europe – semiotics. In our view, it was the first communication model to be combined with the personality branding that we have been reviewing here. Whatever the reason, it is necessary to perform a conceptual analysis on this persuasive mechanism, something that we will do in the following section.

3.4. *Theoretical bases of brand image*

Despite the scant attention that Ogilvy paid to the concept of brand image in his oeuvre, there is a general consensus among advertising theoreticians that he should be given the credit of creating it. Cheverton, although anticipating the date, understands it in this way when claiming,

> By the late 1950s, admen like David Ogilvy were looking to go beyond simple promises; they wanted to build 'brand image'. If a brand could build a better image than its competitors', then it would enjoy a degree of protection.
>
> (Cheverton 2006: 4)

In effect, in the most recent marketing literature, Ogilvy is portrayed as a revolutionary as regards persuasive philosophy and as the champion of the most suggestive and implicit advertising; it should be recalled, as has been seen in the previous chapter, that in the literature of the period he was associated with a very different advertising theory of a very commercial nature based on insistent repetition. In fact, he has been attributed some of the most important communication achievements in advertising history. This is the case with the commitment to advertising 'coherence' in keeping with a previously defined brand image, trust in emotional strategic advertising mechanisms and the need to define long-term objectives (in contrast to rational product advertising in which a different advantage or attribute is shown in each ad in order to meet immediate sales goals). For example, this is how Eguizábal sees it when pointing out that

> versus the economic line and the vision of an advertising subordinated to sales as an immediate result, Ogilvy defended long-term work and insisted on the need to create a brand image that resisted the passage of time. More than extracting a USP from the object, what emotional advertising does is to attribute it personal features, a 'character'. The attribution of those emotional features to the product should be, on the other hand, a task as rigorous, measured and adjusted (to the material characteristics of the object, its history, its market, its consumer) as that of discovering its rational benefits.
>
> (Eguizábal 2007: 50)

Effectively, Cheverton contends that in those years it was thanks to Ogilvy that the brand began to be conceived differently. In his own words,

> A brand was something that you knew about, that you might be able to state facts about – and facts that you believed to be true – and that engendered feelings and emotions that went well beyond the product or even its USP. Of the three ingredients, the emotional projections were most important.
>
> (Cheverton 2006: 15)

Even though, as will be seen below, Ogilvy borrowed most of these ideas; one should give him the credit – as well as recognize his courage – for directly alluding to them in his oeuvre. Accordingly, he convincingly vindicated long-term objectives when indicating that 'every advertisement, every radio program, every TV commercial is not a one-time shot, but a long-term investment in the total personality of their brands. They have presented a consistent image to the world, and grown rich in the process' (Ogilvy 1987: 101). By the same token, as motivation researchers and semiologists had already done before him, he stressed the supremacy of pictures over words: 'Words and pictures must march together, reinforcing each other. The only function of the words is to explain what the pictures are showing' (Ogilvy 1987: 130). In point of fact, at the time Ogilvy was already referring to a technique that, allowing for the differences, was very close to what is nowadays known as storytelling, which he called – borrowing the term coined by Harold Rudolph – 'story appeal'. Sure enough, as with Rudolph, Ogilvy considered pictures that told a story as the most appealing aspect of advertising, because they awakened the public's curiosity and encouraged them to read the ad copy to see what else it was saying, thus continuing the story. According to Ogilvy, 'Harold Rudolph called this magic element "story appeal", and demonstrated that the more of it you inject into your photographs, the more people will look at your advertisements' (Ogilvy 1987: 116). Likewise, very much in the same vein as his mentor Reeves, he defended 'persistence', observing that 'if you are lucky enough to write a good advertisement, repeat it until it stops pulling' (Ogilvy 1987: 98).[5]

He also made a number of contributions to branding, as was the case with the principle of 'coherence', which he timidly outlined in his writings. Closely linked to the brand notion (and, therefore, disregarding the hitherto predominant product-centric perspective, in which the advantages fluctuated in terms of the market, competition, technology or research), Ogilvy, albeit in a very simple way – if we confine ourselves to what is currently understood as brand image – was already outlining the principles of personality branding. For instance, when he alluded to the need to maintain the same brand image aimed at a specific target audience who sees it as their own, he was thinking about the brand. As can be seen, most of the theoretical reflections on personality branding rest on this idea: from the management of intangibles to satisfying cultural needs, through self-concept. In this connection, he sarcastically and commercially decried that

> [m]ost manufacturers are reluctant to accept any limitation on the image of their brand. They want it to be all things to all people. They want their brand to be a male brand *and* a female brand. An uppercrust brand *and* a plebeian brand. They generally end up with a brand which has no personality of any kind [...] Ninety-five per cent of all the campaigns now in circulation are being created without any reference to such long-term considerations. They are being created ad hoc. Hence the lack of any consistent image from one year to another. What a miracle it is when a manufacturer manages to sustain a coherent style in his advertising over a period of years!
>
> (Ogilvy 1987: 100, original emphasis)

Despite the time that has passed, this reflection is still more valid than ever, because the brand management panorama has not changed that much. This fervent dissemination of new approaches to brand management was perhaps the British adman's greatest achievement. As already observed, Ogilvy did not invent or revolutionize anything, insofar as most of his contributions were borrowed from others. Nonetheless, his collaboration – given his prestige and position – in popularizing what would later be called 'brand personality' – an embryonic designation for the more complex paradigm of personality branding – is beyond question. Eguizábal explains this as follows:

> Fundamentally, Ogilvy started with something that already existed, the brand, but which had not been sufficiently exploited. The creation of brands marked the beginning of advertising and established as its objective not to sell but to make more money. A prestigious brand sells at a higher price and leads to higher profits than an unknown brand of the same type of product or a product without a brand, as occurred originally. In the 1950s, branded products were habitual. The brand, with its physical attributes, served to 'baptize' products, to create 'individualities' where before there had only been undifferentiated goods. What Ogilvy did was to create a personality for them. The USP insisted on the physical properties of a product, while the 'brand image' provided it with psychological traits.
>
> (Eguizábal 2007: 50–51)

To conclude with Ogilvy's brand image, it is necessary to make a few conceptual clarifications so as to avoid confusion with what is currently understood by brand or corporate image – in contrast to brand or corporate identity. As already observed, the brand image touted by the English advertising man is a much more basic concept than what nowadays could be considered to be its closest equivalent on a conceptual level, to wit, brand personality. In this regard, we concur with Rom and Sabaté:

> It was at the end of the 1960s when people began to speak seriously about brand image advertising campaigns, but not yet in the sense that we now give to this expression, but in a much simpler one [...] Brand image is an advertising philosophy whose principle is the study of the positive and negative values that this conjures up in the minds of consumers. The overly-simplistic vision of brands still implies a primitive point of view. Brand image is based on compensating through advertising the image that consumers have of brands. Thus:
> a) If the brand image is positive, advertising will reinforce this value.
> b) If the brand image is negative, advertising will change that value.
>
> (Rom and Sabaté 2007: 147)

Owing to its simplicity and pragmatism, Ogilvy's concept of brand image has serious strategic limitations. Its scope is very limited since it merely intends to highlight an advertising philosophy that should be preserved over time. In this vein, it should be specified that it is a very rudimentary persuasive mechanism of personality branding – even more so in view of the much more complex advertising approaches that have subsequently been included in this management model.

Indeed, Ogilvy's brand image completely dispenses with the conceptual depth that would be given to other emotional strategic advertising mechanisms with the introduction of values, associations and meanings or extensions of the architecture.

On the other hand, and directly associated with the foregoing, it is necessary to underscore that this term does not strictly correspond to the concept of brand image – corporate image in public relations jargon. Ogilvy's brand image is a concept of emission corresponding to business objectives that the organization manages itself and does not intend to enter into the realm of social psychology or reception. On the contrary, the current brand image that assumes branding approaches, like the identity approach (Fernández Gómez 2013), differs greatly from Ogilvy's more primitive or rudimentary conception.

3.5. Gardner and Levy's 'The product and the brand': The acknowledged forerunner of brand image

As already noted, in 1955 Gardner and Levy published a paper in issue 33 of the journal *Harvard Business Review*, entitled 'The product and the brand', which would revolutionize the communication and marketing world. As has been seen, even the famous adman Ogilvy who popularized the brand image formula admitted that he was indebted to it, for having borrowed its central idea. In their paper, the authors formulate the basic principles of the new branding paradigm. As Caro has asserted,

> 'The Product and the Brand' is considered to be the seminal text in which the principles of what would thenceforth be understood as brand image were set out for the first time, not as a simple name designating a product, but as a 'complex symbol'.
>
> (Caro 2009: 113)

In other words, it established a type of brand management in which the functional attributes of a product were exclusively taken into consideration and in which its meanings were reinforced. Certainly, 'The product and the brand' led to a still lively debate, as seen in the previous chapter, on the suitability of brand management focusing either on the product or on the accumulated brand image. At any rate, Gardner and Levy laid the foundations of what we have called 'personality branding' and, by extension, emotional strategic advertising mechanisms: from the need to understand consumers on the basis of motivation research, to the relevance of semiotics for generating meanings for brands, through the recommendation to rely on qualitative techniques to conduct communication research.

The authors base their ideas on the demystification of the psychological scientism – clearly orientated towards statistics – prevailing at the time, as already seen when analysing the influence of motivation research on communication. Accordingly, they note,

> Many current ideas about human psychology are overly simple and nonoperational in definition. Gross assumptions are made about what people want and what motivates their wanting. Quick generalizations are made and arbitrarily transferred from one situation to another, often inappropriately.
>
> (Gardner and Levy 1955: 34)

Hypotheses that, in the authors' opinion, are frequently too wide-reaching. Notwithstanding this, Gardner and Levy based most of their theories on motivation research. In this respect, they recognized that 'they are especially useful for arriving at an understanding of the attitudes and feelings which make up the image of a product and a brand' (Gardner and Levy 1955: 35). It is not for nothing that the former was the director and the latter the proxy of the company Motivation Research Social Research, Inc., which Gardner founded in 1946.

As has been explained before, Ogilvy borrowed several ideas from this paper, which he then put into his own words in *Confessions of an Advertising Man*. Specifically, he latched on to relatively minor ideas, such as the importance of 'segmentation' which Gardner and Levy highlight in their work: 'It is rarely possible for a product or brand to be all things to all people. It may be most desirable to sell to the most people, but hardly anyone can sell to everyone' (Gardner and Levy 1955: 37). Likewise, he also drew from now classical advertising principles like that of 'coherence'. In effect, back in 1955 Gardner and Levy were already referring to the need to obtain a coherent brand image, which would subsequently be called 'brand identity' or 'how the product and brand are organized in consumers' minds' (1955: 36), thus anticipating the notion of positioning that Trout and Ries would popularize years later and which will be examined in Chapter 7 of this book.

However, the main achievement of 'The product and the brand' – which corresponds to the very basis of the philosophy proposed by Ogilvy – is to recognize the importance of the brand in relation to the product: 'one of the first things a manufacturer and his advertising people need to explore is the particular constellation of goals and attitudes most pertinent to their product and brand situation' (Gardner and Levy 1955: 34). Gardner and Levy then stress that

> [s]uch explorations must take into account the character of the product (the human needs it serves and the particular way it does so), the dimensions employed in

evaluating brands of such a product, and where the particular brand stands on these dimensions.

(Gardner and Levy 1955: 34)

These words evince, on the one hand, the motivational basis of the theories put forward by these two authors and, on the other, outline ideas that would, with time and the necessary maturity, become classics in advertising thought in the case of the commitment to intangibles and the classification of human needs. Nonetheless, the most outstanding passage in the paper – which is what captivated Ogilvy and prompted him to copy it shamelessly – is the conception of the brand as a 'complex symbol'. Indeed, for Gardner and Levy,

> a brand name is more than the label employed to differentiate among the manufacturers of a product. It is a complex symbol that represents a variety of ideas and attributes. It tells the consumers many things, not only by the way it sounds (and its literal meaning if it has one) but, more important, via the body of associations it has built up and acquired as a public object over a period of time.
>
> (Gardner and Levy 1955: 35)

These psychologists even catalogued the possibilities of brand personality: 'The image of a product associated with the brand may be clear-cut or relatively vague; it may be varied or simple; it may be intense or innocuous' (Gardner and Levy 1955: 35). Because, to their mind, 'these sets of ideas, feelings, and attitudes that consumers have about brands are crucial to them in picking and sticking to ones that seem most appropriate' (Gardner and Levy 1955: 35). To this well-known motivational basis, Gardner and Levy added another novelty with respect to the classical conception of communication, which is the commitment to the management of meanings – a not too distant relative of the field of semiotics, which Levy would cultivate in many of his subsequent essays. In this respect, they caution thus:

> Something must make a greater difference; the conceptions of the different brands must be compounded of subtle variations in feelings about them, not necessarily in product qualities. A big problem in this area, then, is *what kind of symbol a given brand is to consumers.*
>
> (Gardner and Levy 1955: 35, emphasis added)

Similarly, the authors – as with Martineau – openly criticized rational advertising techniques: 'The net result is a public image, a character or personality that may be more important for the over-all status (and sales) of the brand than many technical facts about the product' (Gardner and Levy 1955: 35). With a commitment to a more implicit and suggestive advertising – as Ogilvy also assumed – '[i]t is the business of advertising to assist in the creation of brand images, to give them structure and content, to develop a pattern of consumer attitudes likely to lead to brand purchase' (Gardner and Levy 1955: 38). They even went so far as to offer a series of recommendations for creating ads:

> - Copy should be thought about in terms of its symbolic and indirect meanings as well as its literal communication.
> - Color and illustration are not merely esthetic problems since they also have social and psychological implications.
> - Media selection should be related to a brand image plan and not merely geared to circulation figures.
> - Research should seek out ideas and meanings as well as audience statistics.
>
> (Gardner and Levy 1955: 39)

These recommendations are so outstanding that we could say that Gardner and Levy, as visionaries, revealed a reality that has yet to be firmly established. We are referring to considering brand management as a management role and not as a specific function of marketing or communication departments. The authors subtly observe that 'a reputable brand persists as a stable image through time [...] Such reputations are built through time, frequently in ways that management is not aware of' (Gardner and Levy 1955: 37). Before qualifying this:

> For management to be able to handle this problem effectively it should evaluate its brand's current public image, the differences seen by different important consumer groups, and the images of competitive brands. Otherwise it does not know just what it is working against, what limitations in image must be overcome, and what strengths it has to build on.
>
> (Gardner and Levy 1955: 38)

In conclusion, it is a work that did not only serve Ogilvy as a vehicle for popularizing brand image, but also continues to have a specific relevance for marketing theory and the advertising profession.

4

Henri Joannis's Psychological Axis: The Advent of Motivational Research in European Advertising

Henri Joannis has gone down in the history of advertising not for being one of the pioneers in employing motivational psychology as a working methodology for the advertising companies at which he pursued his professional career[1] – something that quite a few people had done before him – but for being the first theoretician coming from a specific field of communication – not from that of psychology, sociology or marketing – to address the links between motivational research and advertising in a rigorous and systematic fashion. He published his theory in several books that he wrote during the second half of the twentieth century and which have since converted him into one of the most influential and, consequently, most cited advertising theoreticians in the literature on this field of knowledge. Indeed, works such as *De l'étude de motivation à la création publicitaire et à la promotion des ventes* (1969), *Le processus de création publicitaire: Stratégie, conception et réalisation des messages* (1978) and *De la stratégie marketing à la création publicitaire: La création publicitaire dans les magazines et les affiches, à la télévision, à la radio* (1995)[2] contain a very well-founded advertising theory that has since been adopted by many European theoretical advertising creatives.

This is the case in Spain, where historians of advertising grant Joannis the honour of being one of the fathers of modern advertising thought. Among many other merits, the French theoretician coined the popular concept of 'strategic axis', also called 'axis of communication' or, as it is more widely known, 'psychological axis': this last designation resulting from his avowed motivational leanings – a concept that, furthermore, forms part of the basic jargon of advertising agencies in Spain. Indeed, as Sánchez Guzmán notes, perhaps the best summary of the application of motivational research to the creation of advertising messages is H. Joannis' with his 'psychological axis' theory that, based on his own advertising experience, had a huge impact on advertising in the 1960s [*sic*].

(Sánchez Guzmán 1989: 158)

In the same vein, Rom and Sabaté (2007: 145) contend,

> At the end of the 1960s, the French advertising man Henri Joannis, influenced by these psychologistic currents, stated his view on how advertising affected consumers, which he called 'psychological axis' and which is based on a positive interpretation of the opposition of the psychological forces of the motivations and restraints arising in individuals.

In this respect, Soler points out thus:

> In *De l'Étude de Motivation à la Création Publicitaire et à la Promotion des Ventes* (1965), H. Joannis establishes that perception is partially or totally determined by what people want to perceive, what they have normally perceived or the physical and social reward that they hope to obtain from their perception. If this were so, it would mean that people can disconnect at will, perceiving only that which interests them.

(Soler 1991: 63)

In this sense, directly linked to the parameters of motivational psychology, the conception of the so-called 'psychological axis' is perhaps Joannis' chief contribution. As Checa has rightly remarked, it was he who 'developed the psychological axis theory' (2007: 160), a strategic advertising mechanism that we shall now discuss in further detail.

4.1. The psychological axis theory

Joannis certainly conceived a currently essential element in advertising theory and practice that, as already observed above, he merely called 'axis':

> The axis or driving element is the element of purchase mechanisms, which subject to advertising pressure will tip the balance in favour of our product to the greatest degree. The axis always focuses on the stimulus of a motivation or the lessening of a restraint.

(Joannis 1969: 147)

66

Unlike most of his colleagues who put the accent on creative talent, Joannis introduced a strategic phase prior to creative conception. It is in this phase that the 'axis' is defined, a component that goes beyond ingenuity or intuition, because, as he himself held, it is grounded in reflection and research. On the basis of the 'psychological axis', the central idea around which the campaign revolves is obtained. This involves the 'what to say?' The Frenchman was of the mind that 'the axis notion rests on that of conflict' (Joannis 1990: 21). In other words, with the purchase of a product the idea is to satisfy specific needs and to suppress others. 'Therefore, to choose the driving element is to choose satisfaction, whose evocation exerts greater pressure in our favour on the act of purchasing' (Joannis 1969: 148). In sum, the axis should determine what needs and restraints to implement:

> When choosing the psychological driving element of a campaign, we need to determine that whose modification has a greater effect on the mechanism as a whole: the strongest motivation or that which no product on the market satisfies, the most vulnerable restraint or that which our product lessens more than any product of our competitors, etc. At any rate, our choice will always be a motivation or a restraint.
>
> (Joannis 1969: 148)

For his part, Checa (2007: 160) explains that this strategic psychological-advertising mechanism involves the following:

> Two opposing tendencies coexist in individuals, he [Joannis] says, which determine the purchase or rejection of a product. The positive ones are motivations; the negative ones, restraints. The advertising man should be very familiar not only with the motivations that favour a purchase, but also with those that can restrain it, so by acting on it the misgivings disappear. Advertising should facilitate the necessary information to avoid rejections and to develop the motivations as much as possible.

Therefore, more than creation it is a stage of reflection. As already observed, it is a strategic decision; there is no creative formula involved. Although when choosing the axis different options are considered and thought is given to which of them is the most interesting (it is thus a quasi-creative process), it is not until the 'creative concept'[3] has been determined that it enters fully into the process of creation per se. This logic of conception is what the French advertising man called 'the process of advertising creation'. And we believe that it is one of the strategic advertising mechanisms with the longest history among those analysed in this book.

Indeed, as can be observed, Joannis developed a strategic mechanism based on what he understood as 'psycho-sociology' – a hybrid that he invented to define the importance of researching within psychological and sociological parameters. That mechanism, albeit developed more clearly in *Le Processus de création publicitaire* – his second book, in which he popularized his famous 'creative Z' – was the result of his experience, as he himself acknowledged: 'The proposed method is based on more than ten years of specific experience in applying motivation studies' (Joannis 1969: 7). He defines this perfectly in his first book:

> It [this work] puts forward a 'method' for applying psychological studies that makes it possible to shift from the abstract towards the concrete, from the psychological towards the commercial [...] Based on the knowledge that modern psycho-sociology has of the phenomena of motivation, communication, perception and attention, we shall perform a general analysis on a number of principles for creating advertisements.
>
> (Joannis 1969: 8)

As already noted, with this more or less systematic working methodology, the French advertising man claimed that to do advertising it was first necessary to plot a strategy. This is how Checa understands it when, referring to Joannis, he makes the following comment: 'All advertising creation implicitly involves a strategy, sometimes devised intuitively. To determine this it is necessary to detect a gap in the market, a product with possibilities for development, some or other unsatisfied motivation and a target audience' (Checa 2007: 161).

Likewise, Joannis was already talking about the concept of 'brand personality' some years before it caught on in marketing jargon. And, in addition, he provided a definition for the term that, albeit not corresponding exactly to what has since become established in branding studies, already displayed a similar and very explicit essence at the time:

> The affective or moral value that each one of the brands existing in the market has for the public [...] indicates the personality of each brand. The features that as a whole shape this personality constitute the brand image [...] Of course, it is beyond doubt that each brand has its own personality in the public's mind.
>
> (Joannis 1969: 53)

Attributing the notion of 'brand image' to his mentor Dichter, Joannis recognized that 'it is not enough for a brand to be known. It is also necessary that this recognition should prompt a purchase, that is, that the image presented in that way should contain motivations' (1969: 54). In this context, his perspective revolved around a maxim that went beyond the functionality of the product: advertising creatives should discover the real reasons for buying in relation to the consumers' psychological needs. 'We shall see that the idea of the driving element focuses not on the product, but on the satisfaction that the consumer feels, namely, on something that occurs within. It is abstract like any psychological idea' (Joannis 1969: 149). Sure enough, as with motivation psychologists, Joannis started by ignoring the product approach and by searching for the 'profound' motives, in Dichterian terms, that really drive human beings:

> In the life of the consumer, a product does not exist as such; it is inserted into well-defined activities, incorporated into a series of concerns, plays a role in a category of actions that humans perform to feel happy or less tired, to amuse themselves, to impose themselves on the rest, etc. If the intention is to understand what the purchase and use of a product signifies, it is first necessary to know the nature of the human concerns in which it is framed. Many industrialists and certain salesmen tend to believe that the sole context of the product is their own (the economic context) and that the only thing that counts are their prices in relation to those of their competitors. This is a mistake.
>
> (Joannis 1969: 36–37)

And he concludes more emphatically, cautioning that 'it should be understood once and for all that consumer products do not move in an economic context, but in a moral, family and human one in which money is only one of many elements' (Joannis 1969: 37). The advertising man pondered on what he called the 'psychological context', which at the time was the main source of consumer data. In Joannis's opinion, the study of the psychological context should be performed following three basic criteria: unity, nature and assessment. In his view, 'nature' is divided into the personal and family universes (both associated with functional products), on the one hand, and the social universe (closely linked to the concept of 'self-concept'), on the other. In this regard, he held that

> some products do not only represent a personal acquisition. They are united to the social universe and serve, in this universe, to claim something with respect to their users, to demonstrate what they are, what they would like to be.
>
> (Joannis 1969: 40)

However, its most evident motivational orientation can be observed in the importance that Joannis gave motivations and restraints in his strategic advertising mechanism, which was grounded in the assumption that

> the acquisition of any product is orientated towards certain human needs. But, nevertheless, this acquisition goes against other needs (even though this is only the desire not to spend money). Motivations and restraints are two impulses that create

these two categories of needs; the former are positive impulses that encourage the purchase of products; the latter are negative impulses or impediments to purchase.

(Joannis 1969: 43)

And, as already observed, he explained this reality with what he called the 'notion of conflict'. Specifically,

motivations are positive psychological forces, that is, they tend to encourage the purchase of products. It corresponds to the needs that the purchase satisfies [...] They are fixed and permanent in an individual, but only exist with respect to a given context or product.

(Joannis 1969: 43)

He understood that there were, on the one hand, categories of motivations: hedonistic – the need to obtain pleasure from life – self-giving – purchase impulses deriving from the desire to do good or to give something to the rest, which are above all family-related – and of self-expression – associated with self-fulfilment. And, on the other, different 'restraints': what he called 'inhibitions' associated with frivolous or ignoble motivations or those that cause embarrassment; and what he termed 'concerns', associated with people's different fears.

Evidently, the French advertising theoretician was a staunch advocate of psychology, even going so far as to claim, 'all men who sell are condemned to use psychology' (Joannis 1969: 8). Nonetheless, rather than referring to any old school of psychology, Joannis was openly committed to the psychology of motivation. He vindicated this reality throughout his oeuvre – particularly in his first book:

Motivation studies analyse the needs of men and the way in which these manifest themselves [...] It would seem that these studies of man as a consumer directly provide the industrialist with the necessary data to create products in accordance with the needs of the market and to conceive advertising and sales methods that are better adapted to the psychological traits of the consumer. Thus, for the last ten years or so, psycho-sociologists have started to apply their techniques in the commercial field.

(Joannis 1969: 7)

4.2. Joannis's proposals as addendums to Reeves's theories

All things considered and despite his acknowledged motivational leanings, Joannis maintained an ambivalent stance on such a rationalist strategic mechanism as the unique selling proposition (USP). For even though he denied that the rational attributes were the proposal around which a 'strategic axis' revolved, and doubted that one sole reason was behind a purchase decision, for defining his 'psychological axis' he used a methodology very similar to that of Reeves's persuasive mechanism. For example, in his view, owing to the fact that there is little time available in advertising communication, the reasons for purchasing a product should be few and resort to repetition as a technique to drive them home to the target audience. This idea fully coincides with the premises of the USP. However, in the opinion of the French advertising man, if we resort to only one idea, we will be placed in a position of weakness: 'there is no room for mistakes in the choice of the driving element employed' (Joannis 1969: 148). For this reason this is an obvious bone of contention between both postures.

Nevertheless, as remarked earlier, these two proposals have quite a few elements in common. We might almost say that Joannis's notion of 'axis' supplements the thought of Reeves. The introduction of motivational research into communication and the fact of putting the accent on 'psychological' motives to the detriment of the product have led us to believe that the 'axis' is an evolution in the philosophy of the USP. Namely, the Frenchman's 'psychological axis' is basically an improved version of the USP. As Rom and Sabaté note, '[h]ere, we can observe some coincidences with Rosser Reeves' USP, which just goes to show that the succession of advertising philosophies is more an evolution of each one of them than the total substitution of some advertising practices by others' (2007: 146). In point of fact, positioning, another strategic mechanism indebted to the USP, was also envisaged by Joannis in his oeuvre. For this reason it is possible to claim that he anticipated the concept of 'shortlist' when referring to the 'proximity of the image'. He understood that the 'shortlist of brands' was the extent to which that 'image' was present in the mind of the consumer. And he illustrated this in the same way as Ries and Trout did in their famous work, when asking consumers to name brands, who then identified four or five (Joannis 1969: 55).

Basically, the novelty of Joannis's approach lay in really applying motivational research to communication from within, as part and parcel of advertising practice – we have previously observed that there are several outstanding approaches, but from fields other than advertising, including psychology, sociology and marketing. We say 'really' because the works on the subject published to date, although they observe the utility of motivational psychology for communication or vindicate 'brand image' as the soundest strategic advertising mechanism, at no time do they delve into the matter as Joannis did. On the whole, most advertising creatives who refer to advertising and motivational research in these terms limit themselves to brief personal reflections of a more informative and, above all, commercial, than academic or conceptual character. Indeed, this work of the French advertising man, indebted to a great extent to Freudian psychoanalytic theories and the motivational approaches of authors such as Dichter and Martineau – as he himself admitted (Joannis 1969: 9) – renovated the conception of advertising. As Checa (2007: 160) has rightly remarked,

> Joannis' principal work is *De l'étude de motivation à la création publicitaire et à la promotion des ventes*, published in 1964, which had a notable impact and which was followed by other books like *Le Processus de création publicitaire*, in 1978.

In this sense, we could conclude by claiming that Joannis was the first advertising theoretician to understand the field from an eminently motivational perspective, as shown in his oeuvre, although he did not reject contributions made from other standpoints, as we have noted as regards Reeves's postulates.

4.3. A mechanism for creating ads

To conclude, we believe that it is necessary to clarify that, in our opinion, Joannis's strategic mechanism does not refer to the brand, as do those that will be analysed further on, but is a mechanism of a strictly advertising nature. In effect, the star strategy and the Lovemarks marketing concept, albeit clearly advertising mechanisms, have a broader conception, and whose objectives transcend mere communication, also bearing in mind the brand. On the contrary, Joannis's mechanism is aimed solely at advertising communication. The theory in which it is grounded, the methodology that it employs and its subsequent application are aimed at conceiving ads, but under no circumstances at building brands.[4] In point of fact, Joannis insisted at all times on the creation of campaigns; his methods – very useful and before their time – belong exclusively to the advertising realm. In his first contribution, *De l'étude de motivation à la création publicitaire et à la promotion des ventes*, whose aim was to demonstrate the utility of psychology of motivation in advertising, the concept of brand is hardly mentioned at all. Notwithstanding the fact that other theoreticians – Martineau, Gardner, Levy and Ogilvy himself – had already emphasized the importance of brand building, long-term objectives and consistency in 'brand image', Joannis did not pay much attention to the brand phenomenon. Similarly, the purpose of his second book, *Le Processus de création publicitaire*, was to establish a working methodology for conceiving ad campaigns, the 'creative Z' that he proposed evincing what we have just said. Years later, his third book, *De la stratégie marketing à la création publicitaire* (1994), underscores this yet again. In fact, its subtitle, *Magazine, Affiches, TV/Radio, Internet*, and its content offering a detailed description of the process of ad creation by medium (TV, radio, press, etc.) both bear this out.

All considered, the theoretical influence that Joannis has had, and still has, on the literature on advertising, beyond the creation of one of the longest-standing and most rigorous strategic advertising mechanisms in recent years, is beyond doubt. The incorporation of strategy, the concept of 'axis' and the functional assimilation of the precepts of motivational research all bear his stamp. Likewise, his contribution to making communication processes more meticulous and systematic in advertising practice is also unquestionable. In our view, Joannis's influence still casts a long shadow, something that has a lot to do with the way in which advertising agencies work nowadays.

5

Jacques Séguéla's 'Star Strategy': Selling the Hollywood Star System to Sell Brands

According to Eguizábal, 'the Frenchman Jacques Séguéla described a second conception of advertising emerging in the 1980s in his book, *Hollywood lave plus blanc*, in which he offered advertising creatives a new "system of thought"' (Eguizábal 2007: 61). Indeed, the French advertising man Jacques Séguéla's 'star strategy' is another contribution in the field of communication to the 'brand personality' model, in our case the third emotion-related strategic advertising mechanism, following Ogilvy's 'brand image' and Joannis's 'psychological axis'. Likewise, it is the most analogous to the philosophy of personality branding, in the strict sense of the word, primarily for the fact that in the field of communication Séguéla was the first to posit the possibility of 'humanizing' brands – for in other fields such as psychology this had already been proposed. As a matter of fact, the star strategy is sometimes called the 'philosophy of personality', owing to the aforementioned characteristic of 'personifying' brands. Rom and Sabaté (2007: 148) explain this new persuasive mechanism in the following terms:

> The most comprehensive and serious interpretation that has been made of this advertising philosophy, devised by the French advertising man Jacques Séguéla, is called the 'star strategy', which understands brands as if they belonged to the star system of the worlds of cinema, music, television, celebrity magazines, etc. For this French advertising man, one of the founders of the advertising agency RSCG, advertising strategies had become outdated at the beginning of the 1980s. And, in order to update them, he created a strategic platform for his agency. If before brands had a good or bad image for consumers, with the star strategy they engaged consumers more closely and conveyed to them a more complex, less Manichaean, more elaborate personality [...] Namely, with Séguéla the brand-person was born.

5.1. The 'star strategy': A brand image evolution

Séguéla proposes a strategic mechanism that, to our mind, is somewhat akin to Ogilvy's brand image. Indeed, they share the same methodological approach based on pragmatism – it is not for nothing that, as with his English colleague, his conception is associated more with professional practice than with theory – disclosure and self-congratulation.[1] Checa (2007: 161) dutifully notes this when referring to the Frenchman in the following terms: 'More practical than theoretical, but who has made a substantial literary contribution,[2] Jacques Séguéla (1934) is one of the most controversial European advertising men.' In effect, there are important coincidences between the Englishman and the Frenchman. The most evident is the success that both achieved in their respective fields in the advertising industry. Just as Ogilvy, as already noted, had triumphed in the United States in the 1960s, so too did Séguéla in Europe in the 1980s, demonstrating a daring, courage and creativity beyond doubt. The editor-in-chief of *Paris Match* and *France Soir*, since the 1970s he had pursued an advertising career at RSCG, an agency that he founded and where he held positions of great responsibility. As in the case of Ogilvy, he is a fundamental figure in advertising for understanding the history of communication. Accordingly, Checa (2007: 161) describes him as an 'imaginative, audacious, spectacular advertising man who seeks to construct differentiated images for the companies and products with which he works; he never rejects any proposal'. However, the conspicuously professional roots shared by both is only the first of many links. In our opinion, beyond their professional activity, their theories also have the same roots.

To start with, both dispense with those product-centric strategic mechanisms based on the behaviourism inherent to more classical communication. As with Ogilvy, Séguéla is also no friend of rationalist advertising. But while the Englishman challenged the postulates of his colleague and mentor Rosser Reeves and his unique selling proposition (USP), Séguéla does the same with the copy strategy of the hygiene giant P&G. He himself acknowledges this when referring to his creation, the 'star strategy':

> We have baptised it as the 'star-stratégie', in opposition to its forerunner, the copy strategy, and in tribute to its inspiration, the star system. The former is a manual for demonstrating the efficiency of an object, the other, the star system, is a way of appropriating the supremacy of dreams. In our case, the choice has been made: all brands have to be stars, whatever their stature, no matter the magnitude that they may attain.
>
> (Séguéla 1991: 98)

According to Séguéla (1991: 99), while the

> copy strategy was a weapon that divided, the star-stratégie is a collaborative tool. It has an ecumenical will. Marketing dominates the physical, the creation of style. But character stems from common, or community, one should say, dialogue, from the reconciliation between marketing and creation.

Likewise, Ogilvy and Séguéla are also closely united by a primordial conception of brand creation versus the product sales perspective. In the words of the latter (Séguéla 1991: 48), 'the brand of tomorrow will not now be a yearning to have but a need to be, the marital union between the product and magnetism'. In this sense, he is of the mind that advertising does not attempt to sell the attributes of a product, but what they represent – functioning in the same way as Ogilvy's 'brand image': 'The true talent of a product is its capacity to make people dream. Not its economic sense. The public do not buy a commodity, but its image. They do not consume its effect, but its desirability' (Séguéla 1991: 122). As Rom and Sabaté (2007: 149) rightly remark,

> This advertising philosophy represents an evolution of product language towards brand language, an essential differentiating factor at a time when productive processes tend to correspond to the rational benefits of products. Additionally, brands tolerate an emotional advertising language much better.

However, one of the most important coincidences between the two advertising men is to be found in the symbolic conception of both creative-strategic philosophies. Just as Ogilvy is committed to the emotional, psychological and suggestive aspects, so too does Séguéla call for the need to sell dreams, rather than products.

> The new consumer is also a lover of dreams. He naturally buys a product to use it, but even more so for the magic that it offers him as value added. The successes of today are the product of the union between utility and imagination.
>
> (Séguéla 1991: 50)

According to the Frenchman, 'the act of consumption will become a cultural act. Advertising shall win the right to citizenship that the publiphobes deny it. It will be our model of daydreaming, our way of escape, our daily Hollywood' (Séguéla 1991: 19). It is precisely this coincidence between the two advertising geniuses that forms the very core of the mechanism proposed by Séguéla.

5.2. 'Star strategy' characteristics: The cinema world as an advertising metaphor

Indeed, Séguéla suggests a cinema metaphor to define what, to his mind, should be the advertising universe. More specifically, it refers to the popular star systems of classical Hollywood as a strategy that should be adopted by the advertising industry.

> For Séguéla, advertising should follow the star-system strategy, give products and characters style, enhance them, which is the eternal essence of advertising. Brands should be committed to imagination, to helping consumers to feel good about themselves, to recuperate the initiative buried under reports and data banks.
>
> (Checa 2007: 161)

This is one of the reasons why he continually refers to the cinema world and draws parallels between this and advertising throughout his book, apparent in its title, *Hollywood lave plus blanc*, and in remarks such as 'advertising is the permanent overproduction of consumption. The advertiser is its producer. The advertising man its manager, its stage director' (Séguéla 1991: 188). As he sees it, advertising is identical to cinema: 'the dream factory'.[3] Eguizábal aptly describes this idea by dividing it into two differentiated points:

> (1) Man is nourished by bread and dreams. Throughout the twentieth century, those dreams were supplied by cinema. The role of the 'dream factory', which until now has been played by Hollywood, should be assumed by advertising.
>
> Advertising should do more than sell products, it should sell dreams. 'Who could decently be interested', Séguéla remarks in relation to the classic slogan, 'Omo adds brightness to whiteness', 'in a detergent that does nothing else but wash?' A detergent (fancy that!) now has to contribute to liberate women, to their psychological welfare, to their personal fulfilment. Similarly, a soft drink cannot now merely refresh, but should be a tool for the emancipation of the young, their freedom from domestic ties and the development of their individualism.
>
> (2) The advent of marketing, after the Second World War, produced a wave of data, both rigorous but also lacking in imagination. 'And reason', Séguéla says, 'took the place of spontaneity, information took over from talent.'
>
> (Eguizábal 2007: 62)

Nevertheless, what is perhaps Séguéla's greatest merit does not usually appear in current advertising manuals; in the literature reviewed, very few works mention it.

One book that does is *Procesos y técnicas creativas publicitarias: ideas básicas*, by Ricarte (2000: 75), in which he lists what he calls the 'attributes of the brand-person':

- The brand's physique: the benefit, what it offers, its differentiation, what it does, its contribution, its objective qualities.
- The brand's character: security, the reliability of the environment that cultivates confidence, that with which the consumer identifies, what it is, its psychology, that for which it is desired and which fosters loyalty.
- The brand's style: the spectacle that the public needs, the symbols for creating the message, for which it is seen, for which it stands out among the rest, its performance.

(Ricarte 2000: 75)

Ricarte (2000: 75) states that 'it has been proven that a brand without a physique does not sell, without a character it does not last and without a style it is invisible'. In the same vein, Rom and Sabaté (2007: 149) note in *Llenguatge publicitari*:

> In the star strategy, Séguéla treats brands as if they were people and gives them attributes: physique, character and style. According to Ricarte (2000, p. 73–77), a brand is identified, becomes established and is desirable when it communicates correctly its physique (the physique is the product, its originality), its character (its psychological universe, the invisible part of the brand, which advertising reveals) and its style (that by which it is recognised, its performance that makes it immediately recognisable). A campaign without style goes unnoticed, without physique it is invisible, without character it does not last. A person who is noticed, who is visible and who lasts, is a star. This is the star strategy.

This brand conception, tiered in three markedly emotional stages, which Rom and Sabaté describe drawing from Ricarte, is, to our mind, the French advertising man's greatest contribution. Indeed, beyond the aforementioned considerations inherited from Ogilvy and the Hollywood metaphor that he proposes – which is certainly very interesting, but, on the one hand, seems to be excessively indebted to motivational psychology and, on the other, has a clear commercial interest – his consideration that a brand should first have a 'physique', then a 'character' and, lastly, a 'style', is for us one of the most brilliant reflections that have been made on branding for many years. Not only because of its significance as a working methodology for agencies – plainly indisputable, if only for setting forth in a practical way the principle of brand 'customization' – but also because of the theoretical track record of this reflection in the world of brand management and, by extension, strategic advertising mechanisms. Effectively, many researchers have assumed this perspective as a departure point for later studies: from the insistence on looking for human values in brands, to some brand identity theories. In fact, a number of theoreticians have embraced Séguéla's original idea in apparently new approaches, which actually only offer an embellished version of it – presenting it with a few slight changes, but without revealing the source, is practically a tradition in the literature on advertising.

Séguéla introduces this revealing theory with an apparently simple question: 'What is a person? The amalgamation of three criteria, each being necessary but never sufficient' (Séguéla 1991: 55). He then goes on to answer this question clearly and concisely: 'Physique, character, style: this is our daily trilogy. A brand is but a mysterious fusion of these three components' (Séguéla 1991: 56). The French advertising man understands that brands should possess these human attributes to achieve success. Thus, he begins by explaining the more tangible and immediate features that people possess – and which brands should seek to achieve by associating with the product[4] – namely, 'physique': 'a person is, above all, physique [...] In public, our physique is our calling card, what makes us be' (Séguéla 1991: 56). Immediately afterwards, however, he vindicates the relevance of the emotional aspects that go beyond the functional attributes making up the 'physique': it 'is our deep inner self, the character that makes us exist [...] Character determines our destiny' (Séguéla 1991: 56). Similarly, in his review of the Frenchman's theories, Ricarte contends that 'a brand that does not state its character is like an empty person. And a brand that unceasingly changes its character permanently runs the risk of not being understood or, in other words, of ceasing to exist' (Ricarte 2000: 75). In this regard, and given the importance of the concept that he coined, the French advertising man theorizes subtly on 'brand personality' – only that he employs the term 'character'[5], instead of 'personality', a more precise one in our view:

> A brand possesses character, like you or I. And it is that character that seduces us, it and it alone that makes us fall in love. Products are always treated like things; it is now up to us to invent an identity, a heart, for them.
>
> (Séguéla 1991: 56)

Likewise, as a staunch advocate of this strategic mechanism based on personality, for him advertising is the main vehicle for creating brand universes: 'In advertising, there are times when it is better to exhibit the character of the product itself' (Séguéla 1991: 123). When analysing this element of the Frenchman's theory, Ricarte (2000: 75) expresses himself in similar terms, claiming that 'only advertising is capable of revealing and giving centre stage to the character of a brand. To this end, an imaginary universe is created.'

Séguéla completes his 'brand personality' proposal by introducing the last piece of this strategic advertising mechanism: 'The third element of the alchemy of our being, style' (1991: 56). In a similar way to his colleague, the Frenchman Henri Joannis, he describes a creative process that ends in the 'style' – Joannis, for his part, speaks of the 'axis', 'concept' and 'manifesto', as already seen. 'In the lexicon of our star-stratégie, we have called creativity "style." Its inseparability from the physique and the character helps us to appreciate better its importance. The style is the expression of the character' (Séguéla 1991: 126). In other words, the 'style' corresponds to the forms of the brand, the packaging, for which reason it is associated with the stage of creative ingenuity. Ricarte (2000: 75) defines it as the 'language': 'A privileged realm of the copywriter, the style, namely, the language, the *mise en scène*, is more important than first meets the eye. The public needs something more to believe in the message.'

That said, with his mechanism what Séguéla achieves is bringing most of the theoretical premises that were in the air closer to the advertising field in a comprehensive but simple and functional way or, what is the same, bringing them down to earth. On the basis of the symbolic principles that he puts forward and his cinematographic metaphors, he manages to apply the controversial self-concept:

> Every single individual creates in his own image. Therefore, a manufacturer can only devise products that are mirrors of himself. At the other end of the chain of consumption, no consumer will feel attracted by a product in which he does not see himself portrayed. That is to say, the consumer does not acquire a product, but a producer.
>
> (Séguéla 1991: 197)

For Séguéla, as for many other advertising creatives nowadays, the success of a brand lies in loyalty. According to his theory, it is only possible to reach the brand by accomplishing the proposed stages: 'The brand-star is sincere. It is by force, if not by choice. Sincerity is to triumph what loyalty is to love, the guarantee of its longevity. Who can deceive the entire world permanently?' (Séguéla 1991: 119). All considered, Séguéla's theories can be understood as an evolution of – never a break with – previous strategic advertising mechanisms. It certainly derives from brand image, but he formulates it in an aspirational way. The difference lies in the fact that his self-concept is more what we would like to be than what we can actually become. This same evolutionary principle can be found in the strategic advertising mechanism that we shall now discuss below.

5.3. The Chevron model in 'give your brand in marriage': The 'star strategy' revisited

Nowadays, branding experts tend to compare the phenomenon of falling in love with the loyalty that people feel for brands. Jacques R. Chevron[6] laid the foundations of this theory some years ago in his paper entitled 'Give your brand in marriage' (Chevron 1985). The author compares the emotional relationship that is established between brands and consumers with getting married. In his opinion, to sell a brand in an efficient and lasting way, what is needed is a communication that emotionally engages consumers with it. Consumers thus become deeply involved and, in a way, 'marry' their brands and reject the proposals of competitors so as not to commit 'adultery'. When someone orders a Coca-Cola but turns down the Pepsi that he is offered, he is demanding a brand, not a generic product (a cola drink). These 'brand' individuals are what Kevin Roberts calls 'inspiring consumers' – a topic that will be discussed in further detail in the following chapter – and embody the mechanism touted by Chevron.

In Chevron's opinion, as can be observed, it is a game of conquest and falling in love. But how can a brand occupy that privileged place in the heart of a consumer? To the branding expert's mind, by providing the same type of information that people offer about themselves when attempting to woo someone. This is the basis of his theory. Accordingly, the first step involves seduction. Chevron understands that when individuals feel attracted to others, the first thing that they focus on is the 'packaging', on the most physical and bodily aspects. So, given that the initial attraction is physical, Chevron aims to enhance the physical attributes, to wit, the physical qualities – which Anglophones call 'appeal'. By the way, in other languages, it is called 'physical attraction' or even 'chemical attraction'. It is not about adjusting to a specific aesthetic canon – for example, Greek, Rubenesque or Picassian – which is a secondary issue. The idea is to attract attention with what can be seen at first glance and, in this way, to be pleasing to the eye. In Chevron's view, those physical attributes can be found in the packaging: symbols, colours, fonts, logos and the like – the case of Campbell's is paradigmatic in this respect. However, for the adman, to sell brands based exclusively on their physique means brands have the eternal obligation to justify themselves. They have to constantly vindicate their 'attraction', because consumers will only remain loyal until they find a more attractive brand. Indeed, according to this model, if a brand only possesses a tangible attribute like its physique, it runs the risk of losing consumers at the moment when they take note of another competing brand that they find more appealing. For this reason Chevron understands that physical attraction is a compelling reason for a 'sporadic relationship', but not enough to justify a lasting one, namely, a 'marriage'. And a brand should always do its utmost to retain its customers.

This is when the second stage of the process comes into play: the style – or what has been subsequently called the 'look' in the Anglo-Saxon literature. In this stage, consumers recognize that their brand is 'attractive' (it has appeal), but want something more from it. The style involves gestures, manners and tokens; the way one dresses, expresses oneself, wears one's hair or acts. Chevron claims that the style establishes a style, and this is difficult to copy because it is the sum of personal traits. He understands that, while aesthetic convenience sustains the vitality of relationships forged on the basis of physical attributes, the 'style' is the first step towards emotional involvement, an incentive for forging a lasting relationship with a brand. If consumers like the 'style' of a brand, they will establish a closer relationship with the product. According to Chevron, they may even (temporally) ignore a more 'attractive' brand and plump for one that has a more personal 'style' (consistent with their own). If having an alluring appearance was sufficient for a sporadic relationship, an attractive style can make that relationship stronger and more lasting. For instance, the brand Vespa (made by the Italian company Piaggio) managed to create an aesthetic, an attitude and practically a way of life. In this sense, those who used the company's scooters in the 1960s were associated with the 'mod' movement, something that, to a certain extent, is still going strong today: a common imaginary shared by an entire urban tribe. In view of the film *Quadrophenia* (1979) (original soundtrack by The Who, a paradigmatic mod band), it is possible grasp an idea of the aesthetic power – style – of this brand.

Lastly, according to Chevron (1985), the character is the most complex step in the branding process described here. The adman says that at the end of the process, it is necessary to show oneself as one really is, to disrobe before the other to reveal the character to which he is referring. For relationships that are based on an attractive physique or on a merely formal appeal have a shelf life, owing to the fact that, beyond outdated packaging and ephemeral styles, in the end what is left is the inner being, the character. Chevron considers that the inner being is what wins people's hearts – which, as we have seen throughout this chapter, is currently called 'brand personality' – and, according to him, is the culmination of the marriage process. 'It is the ultimate step towards love.' Insofar as they seek loyalty, instead of sporadic relationships, brands have to win people's hearts. He then states that they thus tend to show themselves as they really are in order that consumers should have the chance to like what they see inside. For example, many people have fallen in love with Coca-Cola. A commitment, which goes far beyond the generic, has been shaped. When people order a Coca-Cola, they are not drinking the product, but experiencing the brand.

However, Chevron believes that it is far too complicated to fashion a unique, exclusive and lasting personality through communication. He understands that 'personality' or 'character' is a concept that is not shown but felt. A person's character is determined on the basis of personal observations; it is complicated for us to define our own character. On the other hand, it takes time to forge – for humans, practically their entire lives – and even more so if what is involved is a specific personality. While physical qualities are perceived in a split second and style in a few minutes, much more time is needed to understand a personality fully.

So, as can be observed, what Chevron basically does to conceive his strategic mechanism of 'marriage' between people and brands is to base it on the three premises established by his colleague Séguéla, but changing the order and slightly modifying the presuppositions of each one of them. Thus, the first attribute proposed by the founder of RSCG and the first stage of Chevron's falling in love, namely, the 'physique', have an identical basis that in both philosophies corresponds to the product. By the same token, the 'character', the second attribute of the 'star strategy', is used by Chevron to refer to the third stage of his 'marriage', that is, the 'character'. Even the allusions in both cases to the importance of 'brand personality' coincide. Lastly, the third attribute to which Séguéla refers dovetails perfectly with the second stage of his colleague's 'falling in love', which we associate with the 'look'. As can been seen, the basis of Chevron's theory is a carbon copy of the model previously created by Séguéla.

Notwithstanding this, we believe, on the one hand, that the fact that Chevron employs the 'marriage' metaphor is striking, not only now because it is evidently indebted to motivational and personal branding theories, but above all because it seems to be a proposal more consistent with the reality of relationships between people and brands – in fact, many subsequent studies are based not on Séguéla's 'dream factory', but on that premise. And, on the other, we are of the opinion that the order proposed by Chevron represents the spirit of personality branding more faithfully, since it fits better with human logic – which is what this strategic advertising mechanism attempts to explain. At any rate, associating the brand-person with partner relationships is perhaps the most interesting aspect of Chevron's proposal. In conclusion, it is not at all novel from a conceptual point of view, but very creative as regards form. A formula that, as will be seen in the following chapter, has a considerable number of proponents.

6

Kevin Roberts's Lovemarks: The Return of Emotional Mechanisms in the New Century

In the middle of the first decade of the new millennium – and primarily during 2005 – there was a return to strategic advertising mechanisms, based on the personality branding paradigm, and a comprehensive review of the approaches to this previously proposed advertising philosophy. Indeed, there was a spate of publications dealing with branding recuperating ideas such as 'brand image', the humanization of brands – the so-called 'brand-persons' – the management of intangibles and the affective component of brands. Among the many publications, one stands out above the rest for several reasons – we are referring to Kevin Roberts's *Lovemarks: The Future Beyond Brands* (2004). The first reason has to do with the author, who is none other than the former worldwide CEO of one of the historical and most important multinational communication groups in the advertising industry: Saatchi & Saatchi. This communication guru has made quite a few shocking and controversial value judgements about different political, cultural, economic and, obviously, advertising issues.[1] His views, which have given rise to much debate in professional circles, have occasionally crossed the boundaries of the industry to affect public opinion in general.[2]

The second reason, which is directly associated with the former – and on which we will continue to insist because, as will be seen, it is intrinsic to the communication market – has to do with the advertising industry's need to reinvent itself on a daily basis in order not to lose market share (or, in other words, so as to manage to adapt to a dynamic, variable and uncertain environment in constant evolution). Or, as is the case more often than not, pretending that something perfectly familiar is new, for markedly commercial ends (instead of adaptation). As we have seen throughout these pages, many of the most important milestones in the history of advertising have been much more than merely indebted to previous theories, methods or tools – for example, Reeves's unique selling proposition

(USP), Ogilvy's brand image, Séguéla's star strategy and the like. In our opinion –
as we will explain when analysing the proposal in question – when popularizing
the Lovemarks effect,[3] Saatchi & Saatchi and, more specifically, its top executive
Roberts resorted to this same formula. Namely, the creation of a euphonic name
with commercial potential – in the case at hand, the outstanding feat of coming
up with the name 'Lovemarks'. It is not for nothing that it is the creation of one
of the most important and talented advertising agencies in the world – based on
a philosophy or theory with a long track record – as is the case with personality
branding – with the aim of marketing it as an innovative strategic mechanism for
managing brands – in other words, attempting to pass off as new a philosophy
that has been about for over 50 years now. Clear proof of this is the wide media
coverage given to Roberts in, for instance, the Spanish press just before and after
the publication of his book. And we are not referring to specialized publications
in the field of advertising – where his renown is relatively natural and justifiable –
but primarily to the popular press. There were Spanish newspapers that published
full-page interviews with the CEO because 'for several years now he has been
attempting to introduce a new concept into the advertising world, i.e. Lovemarks'
(Oppenheimer 2005: 17), in which he defines the concept – or 'movement', as he
also calls it throughout the interview – as 'a brand that has evolved from having a
mere functional attribution towards something for which you harbour passionate
feelings, a loyalty that goes beyond reason, something full of mystery, sensuality
and intimacy which you find irresistible' (Oppenheimer 2005: 17). His influence
was so great that, three years later, *El País* published another full-page interview
with him, in which practically the same was said (Carrizo Couto 2008: 12). With
the exception that, this time, the ulterior motive was crystal clear. Three years
after the publication of *Lovemarks*, this new interview was accompanied by sup-
plementary information that read as follows: 'Roberts' Lovemarks effect enabled
him to win the JCPenney account in 2006, with an estimated value of US$ 430 mil-
lion' (Carrizo Couto 2008: 12). All of this confirms the commercial intention
behind the concept. At any rate, the best way of understanding its real nature is to
analyse it.

6.1. What is the Lovemarks effect?

According to Roberts, the Lovemarks effect came about in response to the dwin-
dling efficiency of conventional brands. To his mind, '[b]rands are out of juice [...]
They can't stand out in the marketplace, and they are struggling to connect with
people' (Roberts 2004: 35), understanding that there were a number of reasons
behind this: 'As the brand manual grows heavier and more detailed, you know

you're in trouble' (Roberts 2004: 35). Second, he was of the opinion that they had lost their aura of mystery: 'There is a new anti-brand sensibility. There is much more consumer awareness, more consumers who understand how brands work and, more importantly, how brands are intended to work on them!' (Roberts 2004: 35). By his reckoning, the third cause had to do with the fact that current brands were incapable of understanding the new consumer, contending,

> The new consumer is better informed, more critical, less loyal, and harder to read. The white suburban housewife who for decades seemed to buy all the soap powder no longer exists. She has been joined by a new population of multi-generational, multi-ethnic, multinational consumers.
>
> (Roberts 2004: 35)

The fourth cause was competition – increasingly more intense, widespread and atomized. In his view, brands were still disputing the market with the same competitors as before, instead of coming to grips with the new market reality: 'The more brands we invent, the less we notice them as individuals' (Roberts 2004: 35). He believed that the fifth reason behind brand erosion had to do with the fact that brands had been enslaved by manuals, claiming that '[w]hen everybody tries to beat differentiation in the same way, nobody gets anywhere' (Roberts 2004: 35). And as to the sixth and last cause, he was of the opinion that brands had been domesticated by a flagrant conservatism: 'The story of brands has gone from daring and inspiration to caution and risk-aversion' (Roberts 2004: 35). In short, a context that led to the advent of this strategic advertising mechanism based on 'love', whose inner workings we shall now attempt to describe below.

6.2. The characteristics of the Lovemarks effect

So, according to the CEO of Saatchi & Saatchi, this complex marketing scenario favoured the success of the Lovemarks effect, for it contained the one and only element capable of countering all these factors: 'love'. In effect, the concept is a robust and insistent vindication of 'love': 'love' as the driving force behind consumption. In the words of Roberts (2004: 57), 'I knew it was Love that was missing. I knew that Love was the only way to ante up the emotional temperature and create the new kinds of relationships brands needed'. But what is the advertising man referring to exactly in his book when he speaks of 'love'? He himself specifies this by proposing a list of what he calls the 'Six truths about Love' (Roberts 2004: 52). First and foremost, he asserts that human beings need 'love' because '[w]ithout it they die. Solitary people without Love are three to five times more

likely to die early!' (Roberts 2004: 52). For Roberts, the second truth is of a qualitative nature, to wit, to love something is much more than liking something a lot,
which he then qualifies in the following terms: 'Love is about a profound sense of
attachment' (Roberts 2004: 52). The third truth refers to considering that '[l]ove
is about responding, about delicate, intuitive sensing' (Roberts 2004: 52), while
the fourth underscores its diversity. In this sense, he notes that it is important to
take into account who and what we love, explaining that there are very different
relationships and degrees of love. The fifth truth, in his view, is that love needs
time: 'Love takes an investment of years' (Roberts 2004: 52). He then concludes
with the sixth and final one: 'Love cannot be commanded or demanded. It can
only be given' (Roberts 2004: 52).

After clarifying the concept of 'love', Roberts associates it directly with what he
understands as the main factor of Lovemarks: 'respect'. 'Love needs Respect right
from the start. Without it, Love will not last [...] Respect is one of the founding
principles of Lovemarks' (Roberts 2004: 60). In his opinion, '[r]espect looks to
performance, reputation, and trust as its organizing principles. Within each of
these principles I believe there is an inspiring code of conduct to lead you forward'
(Roberts 2004: 60). He even indicates what shape the code of conduct based on
the respect that brands need would take (Roberts 2004: 62). In this regard, as a
brand 'psychologist', he offers a number of recommendations, from fulfilling the
promises made to consumers to having to gain the trust of the public, by not hiding.
As a matter of fact, he places so much trust in the relationship between 'love' and
'respect' that he proposes a positioning map in which the two axes precisely represent these two aspects (see Figure 6.1). He then justifies this conceptual intersec-
tion as follows: 'The axis format immediately showed Love as a goal above and
beyond Respect. Now we could clearly show the ongoing importance of Respect
and the urgency of moving into a relationship based on Love' (Roberts 2004: 146).

As can be seen from the foregoing, most of the premises of Lovemarks derive
from previous theories. The concept's very basis is more than repetitive: 'Lovemarks
are created by emotional connections with consumers in ways that go beyond
rational arguments and benefits' (Roberts 2004: 105). Obviously, the 'democ-
ratization of production' and the 'management of intangibles' are nothing new.
But they do indeed help to update the classical personality branding model and,
of course, 'to sell' the strategic advertising mechanism conceived at Saatchi &
Saatchi. That said, the commercial nature of Roberts's book does not prevent him
from putting forward some or other interesting theoretical proposals, such as the
way in which he develops the distinctive features of his Lovemarks effect. Thus,
he introduces what, to his knowledge, are its attributes. 'These didn't sound like
traditional brand attributes', he cautions. 'And they captured the new emotional
connections we were seeking' (Roberts 2004: 74). He then goes on to specify that

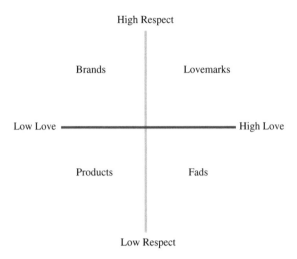

FIGURE 6.1: The Lovemarks love/respect axis. Source: Roberts (2004: 147).

the three pillars of the Lovemarks effect are 'mystery', 'sensuality' and 'intimacy'. Each one of these attributes is, in turn, generated by the following elements (Roberts 2004: 77): 'mystery' through 'great stories; past, present, and future; taps into dreams; myths and icons; inspiration'; 'sensuality' derives from the senses ('sound, sight, smell, touch, taste'); and 'intimacy' is achieved through 'commitment, empathy, passion'. In this way, Roberts develops each one of the attributes, all of which are of great interest to us here. To our mind, what he calls 'mystery' can be associated with current storytelling techniques that he had already envisaged. As to mystery, he remarks as follows: 'Mystery opens up emotion. Mystery adds to the complexity of relationships and experiences. It lies in the stories, metaphors, and iconic characters that give a relationship its texture. Mystery is a key part of creating Loyalty Beyond Reason' (Roberts 2004: 85). On the other hand, the concept of 'sensuality' acts as a nexus between classical motivational psychology and the new neuromarketing theories in the field of neuroscience. As he himself claims,

The senses speak to the mind in the language of emotions, not words. Emotions alert us to how important the findings of our senses are, not only to our well-being, but indeed to our very survival.

All of our knowledge comes to us through the senses, but they are far more than sophisticated gatherers of information. The senses interpret and prioritize. When we feel emotionally connected, we say, 'That makes sense.'

(Roberts 2004: 105)

Lastly, in our view, the third attribute that he proposes, namely, 'intimacy', is a critique of brand management models of the 'brand identity' kind, which, emerging in the 1980s, become firmly established only in the following decade. For Roberts, '[m]any of the big brands became standoffish over the 1990s. Removing themselves from the people who gave them their life – consumers – they fixed on another audience: shareholders' (Roberts 2004: 130). He understands that this results in a loss of trust and loyalty on the part of the public, for which reason he vindicates the traditional market:

> [T]here is a lot to learn from the intimate network of trust that the traditional market-place thrives on [while attacking the mass market]. As the mass market geared up, businesses lost their way. They became detached from personal relationships.
>
> (Roberts 2004: 132)

In this context, for Roberts it is a matter of understanding consumers again, of approaching people anew, which reveals once more its links to the brand management model of consumer branding:

> A crucial problem for brands in their battle against commodification is their growing apart from consumers. Distant, undifferentiated, unremarkable.
>
> Focused on growth and clamoring for attention, brands don't have a lot of time for nuance and sensitivity [...] Have the brands themselves changed? Or is it the other way around? Has what people want from brands changed?
>
> (Roberts 2004: 129)

All in all, it is obvious that the former CEO of Saatchi & Saatchi analysed, on the basis of the distinctive features described above, branding approaches transcending personality branding from which they derived. On the one hand, enriching their perspectives and, on the other – in our view, unintentionality – achieving a hybrid theoretical approach in which he conjugated 'brand personality' with 'consumer branding' – which we shall examine in the following chapter as the conceptual framework of the last strategic advertising mechanism addressed in these pages. Thus, Roberts considered 'relational' or 'cultural' approaches to the brand phenomenon that are not framed a priori in a strict 'brand personality' model. In this regard, for example, the term 'inspirational consumers' that he coined is grounded in complex consumer branding models of a relational nature. This provides us with additional information in way of a conclusion: the evolution of branding models without any marked discontinuities.

6.3. *Critiques of the Lovemarks effect*

Notwithstanding these theoretical achievements, which, as already noted, we do not believe to be among the work's main objectives, Roberts's Lovemarks strategic advertising mechanism is a more or less faithful rehash of previous ones. Its core, which can be summarized in the phrase 'brands are about emotion and personality' (Roberts 2004: 14), is indebted to the most basic motivational psychology and to the postulates of researchers like Dichter and Martineau. As Roberts would have us believe, the reasons why brands fall into decline and the solution that he provides with the Lovemarks effect – 'they need emotional pull to help them make decisions' (Roberts 2004: 36) – can be traced to Levy's (1959) first works and even to Ogilvy's brand image. Likewise, all the needs and emotions that he describes in his work are staples in the literature and advertising profession alike, and while doing so, he offers a number of different reflections that deserve comment.

First and foremost, we are of the opinion that some of the remarks that he makes on the different types of emotions – a key issue in his work – are excessively stereotyped: 'Primary emotions are brief, intense, and they cannot be controlled [...]: Joy, Sorrow, Anger, Fear, Surprise, Disgust' (Roberts 2004: 44). There is already plenty of literature on emotions that probes into this aspect and even questions it. Second, he creates a series of conceptualizations that lead to conclusions that are hardly new: 'To me what is really striking about the secondary emotions is how social they are' (Roberts 2004: 44). Appeals to the social character of human needs or emotions are already to be found in classics like, for instance, the works that Maslow wrote in the 1960s, while Joannis himself applied this concept to the advertising profession at the end of the following decade. And, lastly, the way in which he criticizes quantitative research produces a strong feeling of déjà vu at present: 'I'm looking for research that counts the beats of your heart rather than the fingers of your hand. Research that connects with the inner life of the consumer. Not as statistical constructs' (Roberts 2004: 157). Certainly, these ideas form the very basis of the motivation research model of the 1950s and were broadly disseminated by Ogilvy, among others, in the 1960s. In sum, as Roberts himself reveals halfway through his book, when echoing the words of Jim Stengel, the global marketing officer of P&G,

> Great brands have always been Lovemarks. What Lovemarks have done is give a structure in which to think about that. But I think as long as there have been brands with emotional attachments and connections and loyalty, there have been Lovemarks. One way to think about what a Lovemark might be is to consider how a consumer would feel if you took the brand away.
>
> (in Roberts 2004: 79)

That said, we should clarify that, by and large, the analysis performed by the former CEO of Saatchi & Saatchi in his book on the Lovemarks effect is superficial and vague. In this sense, it is more an informative and commercial work – as we have already cautioned – than an ostensibly conceptual or reflective one. With this in mind, it is relatively admissible for Roberts to define it as succinctly as he does in his book: 'The Lovemarks of this new century will be the brands and businesses that create genuine emotional connections with the communities and networks they live in' (Roberts 2004: 60). This work has a very different purpose. As already observed, regardless of its theoretical merits, what the Lovemarks effect does is to recuperate emotional strategic advertising mechanisms and apply them in the 2000s. However, other advertising theoreticians have also done this. Consequently, a multitude of strategic communication and marketing mechanisms, which on the whole are familiar and redundant, have been proposed. As analysing them one by one would have no bearing on our work, given their scant interest and input, we will exemplify all of these mechanisms in one paradigmatic case: Passionbrands.

6.4. Creating Passionbrands: An example of updating personality branding on the basis of the redundancy principle

Another strategic advertising mechanism based on the 'brand personality' branding paradigm known as Passionbrands also saw the light of day in 2005. Helen Edwards and Derek Day – two advertising experts with a long professional track record – published *Creating Passionbrands: How to Build Emotional Brand Connection with Customers* (2005), a book in which they describe the strategic tool referred to above. As with the Lovemarks effect, Passionbrands are a novel strategic advertising mechanism – apparently – linked to brand management. The basic difference lies in the fact that while Roberts talks about 'love', Edwards and Day speak of 'passion'. Another distinction, this time much more prosaic and far removed from the conceptual field, as will be seen, is the different reception that the Lovemarks effect and Passionbrands have had. Whereas *Lovemarks: The Future Beyond Brands* has been translated into more than twelve languages[4] by just as many national publishing houses, *Creating Passionbrands* is still only available in English – apart from a modest Spanish edition published by the Colombian publishing house Panamericana under the title of *Marcas Pasión*. That it has not been translated into any other language is responsible for the fact that the concept has not caught on at all outside the United Kingdom or, to a lesser extent, the United States – the publishing house Kogan Page publishes its books simultaneously in London and Philadelphia – and only then in Anglo-Saxon academic circles. This, in addition to the fact that Roberts's book was very favourably received, stresses the general lack of interest in *Creating Passionbrands* on the part of the press, academia and the public in general. For as much as it tries, it does not have the same commercial flair and drive as Roberts's work.[5] Even so, the book made a certain impression in academic circles, where it was received in the same way as with other similar works published at the time.

Nonetheless, and referring strictly to the book's content, it is only fair to remark that it is of greater theoretical value than is *Lovemarks*. In fact, it has more solid conceptual foundations and develops a more serious and accurate methodology than Roberts's book, written from an eminently informative and commercial perspective. *Creating Passionbrands* departs from the same point as *Lovemarks*, namely, explaining the reason why it is necessary to 'create a Passionbrand'. Thus, Edwards and Day are of the opinion that there are five symptoms, which they call 'symptoms of malaise of consumer-led brands'. Or, in other words, they perform an analysis on the environment to justify the application of the model that they are proposing. To wit: first, a growing similarity between brands; second, an inconsistency between 'brand image' and the product; third, a dearth of innovation and surprise; fourth, a distancing between the product and brand management capacity; and, fifth, the lack of a 'heart' in brands. For the authors, these causes warrant the claim that Passionbrands are the only answer to such a complex and competitive market: because those brands that 'unleash passion' rest on specific values, on defined beliefs, as with people:

> It is not hard to see why brands with a strong belief should be favoured in the hastening postmodern era. They give you more meaning for your money. They have more colour, more symbolic content, more utility as units in the project of self [...] These are brands that consumers don't just buy, but join. They are brands that become 'a part of me'.
>
> (Edwards and Day 2005: 54)

As can be observed in this passage, self-concept is presented as the driving force behind Passionbrands. To our mind, the strategic advertising mechanism, as with Ogilvy's 'brand image', Séguéla's 'star strategy' and Roberts' Lovemarks effect, is a vindication of self-concept.

> This is not a description of who your customers are, but of who they want to be. It is the self they imagine in moments of reflection, the self they aspire to, the self they believe, often against all evidence, that they could become. It is not to be confused with the fantasy self, which is the stuff of very pleasant daydreams and which, for most people, is no more than a diversion, a mini-movie to watch in the mind, of

which their alter egos are the star. The fantasy self is entertainment; the idealized
self is desire.

(Edwards and Day 2005: 193–94)

All in all, Edwards and Day describe what they understand as the defining characteristics of Passionbrands. First and foremost, they are brands with an active belief.
As their second trait, they highlight that the trust that they enjoy is thanks to their
internal capacity, what the authors call 'their roots'. And, lastly, Passionbrands
maintain their vibrancy in an ever-changing world (Edwards and Day 2005: 78).

Albeit more serious than Roberts's proposal, the methodology that they propose does not shed much new light on the matter. Broadly speaking – in the book
it is explained succinctly, for most of the space is dedicated to offering examples –
this is divided into two stages: an analytic stage and a creative stage. Obviously,
with the former their intention is to define the descriptive process of all of the factors shaping the reality of a brand. The latter, in contrast, refers to the executive
stage in which Passionbrands are creatively developed:

> The methodology comprises two distinct phases: an analytical phase, in which
> all aspects of the brand and its environment are studied; and a more creative
> phase, which uses that knowledge to crystallize brand belief and generate the
> Passionbrand identity. The process [...] is a four-corner diagram with a key word
> in each corner: ideology, capability, consumer, environment. The point where these
> four forces intersect is called the Passionpoint; this is where to focus efforts to create
> the brand's identity and total marketing offer.

(Edwards and Day 2005: 97)

In order to describe this process, they resort to a trampoline metaphor. Each one
of its legs represents one of the four listed forces that are the raison d'être of a
brand: 'ideology', 'capability', 'consumer' and 'environment'. If these four legs
rest on solid ground, they will be capable of successfully launching a brand. As
they caution, 'ideology' and 'capability' are internal and controllable factors,
whereas 'consumer' and 'environment' are external ones that are more difficult to
manage. Therefore, they should be handled coherently for the sake of the brand.
The authors express this idea in the following terms:

> The aim is ideological clarity: a short list of values that relate strongly to one another
> and exert a unifying influence on the identity as a whole. It is especially important
> that values and brand belief be mutually reinforcing. Brevity will help this cohe-
> sion. The list should be potent yet spare: three values, simply stated, strongly felt.
> Values you will hold forever. Values you will cherish, even when the world moves

93

on. Be particular; be pointed; don't be afraid to use words outside the accepted business lexicon.

(Edwards and Day 2005: 195)

At this point, it is unquestionable that the Passionbrand mechanism is, on the one hand, indebted to previous emotional strategic advertising mechanisms and, on the other, has a markedly commercial perspective. Some of the authors' allegations confirm this:

Passionbrands seek to achieve [...] to make the world a little better than it would be if the brand did not exist. There are two distinct aspects to this: first, to decide in what way the world could be made 'a little better'; second, to ensure that the brand plays an active part in achieving it.

(Edwards and Day 2005: 78)

Passionbrands tend to have a strong sense of their past but they live in the present and welcome the future. These are brands that have a seemingly instinctive feel for the zeitgeist, an eye for the subtle shifts in modern culture, an alertness to economic and environmental trends.

(Edwards and Day 2005: 80)

As can be observed, there is no theoretical reflection in this passage, but an evident desire to sell an advertising formula. And as already noted, these two features – plus the many fundamental aspects that they share – closely unite Passionbrands with the Lovemarks effect. As well as the level of analysis – much deeper and more rigorous in Edwards and Day's proposal – of the very few theoretical differences between both mechanisms that we have been able identify, including the individual loyalty that Passionbrands demand; there is an absolute loyalty that contrasts with the polygamy of Lovemarks. In this regard, Edwards and Day remark,

It is neither easy nor credible to apply real passion to half a dozen different things at once. Passion implies focus. This is reflected in the capability of Passionbrands, which tends towards the single and central rather than the varied and dispersed. Better to do one thing superbly well than many things tolerably well.

(Edwards and Day 2005: 194–95)

To conclude, it should be stressed that, beyond the evident legacy described in these pages, Passionbrands have some notable achievements, which although they have not been decisive for the history of advertising strategy or branding, are at least of some interest to business communication theory. In this sense, the passion brand thesis per se is, in our view, the book's most remarkable theoretical contribution. This is grounded in a critique of the classical consumer branding paradigm – which we will examine in the following chapters – namely, that brands place too much importance on the consumer and, as a result, lose their identity as such or, better said, their original values. Indeed, in our opinion, this initial hypothesis is one of the few valuable contributions of the book and, accordingly, of the Passionbrands strategic advertising mechanism. So, Edwards and Day recommend a new commitment to 'brand image' and emotional values, while dismissing the 'extreme measure' of placing the consumer at the centre of the process – as advocated by other strategic advertising mechanisms and brand management paradigms. As they themselves admit,

> At a brand level the objective is not to seek direction from consumers but to find better ways to serve them through the juxtaposition of enhanced understanding and the company's own distinct culture and capability. Implied in this approach, then, is the need for the company to have a *strong sense of itself*, not just the customers it serves.
>
> (Edwards and Day 2005: 17, original emphasis)

Edwards and Day understand that many strategic advertising mechanisms place the accent exclusively on consumers who know nothing about management, for which reason it is a blatant mistake to only do what *they* want: 'like all really strong brands it knows that, when it comes to the core, a brand must be consumer-leading not consumer-led' (Edwards and Day 2005: 81). It is precisely this theoretical contribution, intertwined with the strategic mechanism of positioning and, by extension, with the consumer branding paradigm – a mechanism that we will be examining in the next chapter – which underscore the discrepancies between this paradigm and the personality branding model discussed in Chapter 3. Otherwise, as has been explained, in the main Passionbrands are not a strategic mechanism involving an evolution, modification or break with previous ones. Quite to the contrary, the concept is predictable and continuist, more than likely due to its evident commercial spirit. As we have already remarked, it is paradigmatic of the many strategic advertising mechanisms that have emerged for the sole purpose of promoting a communication group, a working methodology or even a book.

7

Jack Trout and Al Ries's Positioning: The Appearance of Cognitive Psychology in Advertising

Positioning is perhaps the most widespread concept in the brief history of marketing. In lecture halls, it is an all-encompassing term employed to refer to any concept associated with strategy. Similarly, it is a constant in the literature where it is resorted to when addressing practically everything relating to the marketing reality of a brand or its communication. And in the corporate world it is certainly the most frequent term in business jargon for summarizing almost everything that has to do with brand management. Advertising agencies, business marketing departments, consultants, specialized journalists and even a substantial number of business professionals unrelated to marketing employ the term indistinctly to explain brand communication, to define brand positioning with respect to competitors, to gauge brand notoriety, to quantify brand value, to specify brand values or attributes, to implement a brand strategy and more besides.

With a clear cognitive legacy – Trout does hesitate to resort to Petty and Cacioppo, the fathers of the central and peripheral routes to persuasion, to vindicate its cognitive psychological basis[1] (Trout and Rivkin 2010: 148); according to Homs (cf. 2004: 78), this concept breaks with the old paradigms of the primacy of quality to give priority to the perception that consumers have of a product or service. Keller (2008: 98), one of the top international branding experts – closely linked to this psychological current through his Customer-Based Brand Equity (CBBE) model – holds that

> [b]rand positioning is at the heart of marketing strategy. It is the 'act of designing the company's offer and image so that it occupies a distinct and valued place in the target customer's minds'. As the name implies, positioning means finding the proper 'location' in the minds of a group of consumers or marketing segment.

Beyond its epistemological legacy, what is plain and clear is that it is the most popular concept to have emerged in the marketing world, proof of which is the revolution that it implied in every respect when it first appeared. This revolution was evinced in the academic literature,[2] in lecture halls,[3] in the advertising profession[4] and even in the battles over the concept's paternity. Indeed, as already noted, the term became so popular that different personalities from the marketing and advertising worlds would attempt to claim it as their own brainchild. And what is even more revealing, its original creators were obliged to embark on a public crusade in order to take credit for their own creation.

7.1. The origins of positioning

The first reference to the concept in question can be found in a brief paper entitled '"Positioning" is a game people play in today's me-too market place', by Jack Trout – an advertising executive working for Ries-Cappiello-Colwell, a communication and advertising consultancy firm based in New York – published in the American journal *Industrial Marketing*[5] in 1969. In his paper, the account supervisor uses a very simple example from the technology sector to predict the failure of those attempting to compete with IBM by offering the same product – the strategy known as 'me too', which was highly popular in the United States at the time. Two years later, in November 1971, and in the same vein as his previous work, Trout published another paper entitled, 'Positioning revised; why didn't GE and RCA listen?', in *Industrial Marketing*. Raúl Peralba (2003: 84), Trout's partner in Spain, has the following to say about it:

> In this case, the recently appointed vice-chairman of Ries-Cappiello-Colwell demonstrated that his prediction that both GE and RCA would fail to compete with IBM has come true. Neither of these two companies, the former a household appliance firm and the latter a record company, managed to change the perceptions that their clients had of them. Nor did they manage to weaken IBM's image as the leader in its speciality. On the contrary, they reinforced it.

The relative success of the two papers published by Trout prompted the well-known journal *Advertising Age* to ask the author to write a series of three papers with the aim of elaborating on his views on the concept of positioning. And the adman accepted, but this time they would be co-authored by Al Ries, his boss at Ries-Cappiello-Colwell. So, in issues dated 24 April, 1 May and 8 May 1972, *Advertising Age* published the papers under the title 'The positioning era'.[6] Nonetheless, as Trout's partner Peralba clarifies, 'in this case, signed by Jack Trout and

Al Ries, in that order' (2003: 84). Thenceforth, the concept became so popular that the consultancy firm began to see in positioning a very profitable business. Many clients were calling for brand strategies based on Trout's strategic advertising mechanism. To the point that, so as not to lose the succulent use rights of the concept devised by his former subordinate, Ries restructured the company, modifying not only its business philosophy – exclusively focusing on positioning consultancy – but also explicitly changing the roles of each one of its members. The new consultancy firm was called Trout & Ries Ltd. In the words of Peralba, Trout's vision carried a lot of weight:

> [T]he concept and the methodology invented by Jack Trout were transformed into the *star product* of the firm, which specialized in competitive strategy and which, recognizing the merits of Jack Trout, became to be known as Trout & Ries Ltd. That is, with the names in their original order.
>
> Thenceforth, they undertook many positioning projects for companies and institutions of different sizes and engaging in different activities. From a regional bank (Long Island Trust) to a multinational (Citibank) and from a country (New Zealand) to a religious institution (the Episcopal Conference of the Catholic Church, concerned about its dwindling flock).
>
> (2003: 84–86, original emphasis)

In this context, the only thing that was lacking is what has become one of the top bestsellers in the history of marketing – which to be sure also occupies a commendable place in the ranking of the most commercially successful non-fiction books.[7] We are referring to the enormously popular *Positioning: The Battle for Your Mind*. Published by McGraw-Hill in 1981, it went on to become a bestseller, translated into twenty languages and with millions of copies sold. As a matter of fact, a revised edition commemorating its twentieth anniversary was published in 2001, in which the authors comment on some of their theories and review points of view. This revised edition was also well-received.

In contrast with previous works, *Positioning* practically does not provide any new input. The theoretical framework that the authors created in their previous works remains basically unchanged and, as to the book's sole contribution, the consultancy firm's experience in applying the strategic mechanism of positioning is illustrated with a large number of practical examples. In this respect, Peralba, in reference to the book, claims 'that it had become a classic for many business schools and universities all over the world. It was a book with little theory and many real cases in which Trout and Ries had been involved over the years' (2003: 86). In short, if before the book's publication the concept of positioning was already in fashion, once it had seen the light of day, it became a marketing maxim. In this sense, it was the largest publicity campaign that positioning could ever have wished for.

Thenceforth, everything changed for the concept's creators, due to their overzealousness with the brand that positioning represented. First, for clearly commercial reasons they attacked all those professionals who used the concept, accusing them of misunderstanding its real inner workings. Second, for the same – albeit different – commercial purpose, they decried those management scholars or experts who included positioning in their books. Naturally, one of the main income sources of Trout & Ries Ltd. was the copyright of the bestseller, for which reason they had no intention of sharing the concept's literary profits with other authors. In this regard, the article published by Peralba, a partner of Trout & Partners Ltd., in *IPMARK* entitled '¿Quién inventó el positioning, Porter o Trout?'[8] is highly significant. In his article, the Spanish consultant lets fly, not without cynicism, against all those writers – from gurus producing a markedly informative business literature, such as Tom Peters, to eminent professors like Michael Porter of Harvard Business School, a very well-known author in the marketing world – who, in some way or another, had included the popular concept in their books. Accordingly, in this 'open letter' Peralba (2003: 84) explicitly condemned this state of affairs:

> There are many who think that it [positioning] is a relatively new idea and the invention of one of the gurus currently in fashion. People like Michael Porter, Regis Mackenna and Tom Peters intend to appropriate it and to present themselves as its creators.

And, of course, he makes it abundantly clear who is its real father: 'However, the real creator of positioning is Jack Trout, as can be verified by consulting any well-stocked library' (Peralba 2003: 84). Although his article is primarily a public vindication of the concept's paternity, he does not miss the opportunity to censor all those who use it. For instance, he is scathingly critical of Porter who, by his reckoning, is the personification of 'misappropriation'. According to Peralba, the Harvard scholar does not understand positioning: 'What is clear from Porter's words is that he has not grasped the concept's most important aspects' (2003: 84). And he justifies his accusation by resorting to the professor's academic provenance:

> What happens is that, occasionally, one's ego limits one's capacity. For a scholar like Porter it is certainly difficult to accept that, despite what he thinks or believes, it is potential prospects who have the power to decide from whom they should buy.
>
> (Peralba 2003: 84)

Trout himself followed suit in his bestseller *Differentiate or Die: Survival in Our Era of Killer Competition* (2000), in which he contends that '"positioning", [is] a subject we've been writing about since 1969. While many in business use this word, many still don't know the definition of positioning: how you differentiate your product in the mind of your prospect' (Trout and Rivkin 2000: 73). He would then say exactly the same thing in *Repositioning: Marketing in an Era of Competition, Change, and Crisis* (2010) ten years later:

> And yet to this day, while many people use the word positioning, not all of them truly understand what it is all about. And influential groups such as management consultants have little idea about perceptions or winning or losing in the mind.
>
> (Trout and Rivkin 2010: 207)

The zeal with which they protected their famous concept was such that it even led to petty squabbles between its two fathers. Peralba attempts to offer an aseptic account of how Ries and Trout parted company and even offers rational arguments to justify their separation:

> In 1994, Jack Trout and Al Ries decided to go their separate ways, since Ries moved because of family reasons and the United States is a very big country. In this *amicable divorce*, it was agreed that the concept of *positioning* should stay with its father, that is, Jack Trout.
>
> (2003: 86, original emphasis)

Be that as it may, Peralba (2003: 86) showed a certain degree of mistrust for the works that Ries would publish following their separation:

> Al Ries attempted to find something that allowed him to benefit from his association with Trout, publishing *Focus*. In reality, it was the same approach, but instead of talking about positioning a proposal in the mind of prospects, he proposed focusing on the activities of companies themselves aimed at achieving this, without mentioning the word 'positioning' at all. A complicated book that sold few copies.

In sum, the concept of positioning became an object of desire for all and sundry, for which reason Trout & Partners Ltd. continued to spare no effort to protect it:

> In recent years, other well-known gurus have wanted to jump on the bandwagon. From Tom Peters to Regis Mackenna who employ positioning and differentiation as keys to competitive capacity. Even Al Ries himself, who has not discovered his own line of thought, has realized that it is a powerful concept, and in the introduction to

his last book he recounts its advent and development in such a way that, for those who are neither familiar with the details nor know the story, he gives the impression that he is its 'father'.

(Peralba 2003: 86)

This evidently commercial vocation is undoubtedly one of its principal characteristics which, along with others, will be examined below. But, so as to gain a better understanding of them, we will first attempt to define the concept of positioning.

7.2. *What is positioning?*

As usually occurs with the most popular marketing concepts, although they are employed ad nauseam, it is difficult to find a more or less precise or minimally reasonable definition of them in the works of their creators. And 'positioning' is no exception. Effectively, despite having an outstanding curriculum of publications – at least quantitatively speaking – Trout and Ries have never made any concerted effort to offer a clear and precise definition of 'positioning'. By and large, in the book that they co-authored more than positing a definition, they make vague statements, such as: 'Positioning is not what you do to a product. Positioning is what you do to the mind of the prospect. That is, you position the product in the mind of the prospect' (Ries and Trout 2001: 2); '[p]ositioning is an organized system for finding a window in the mind. It is based on the concept that communication can only take place at the right time and under the right circumstances' (Ries and Trout 2001: 19); and '[t]o win the battle for the mind, you can't compete head-on against a company that has a strong, established position. You can go around, under or over, but never head to head' (Ries and Trout 2001b: 219). Independently, in their subsequent works – where there is always some or other passage in which they directly or indirectly allude to the mechanism – they say much the same: '*Positioning* is how you differentiate yourself in the mind of your prospect. It's also a body of work on how the mind works in the process of communication' (Trout and Rivkin 2010: 10, original emphasis); and '[r]epositioning is how you adjust perceptions, whether those perceptions are about you or about your competition' (Trout and Rivkin 2010: 10). Curiously enough, Trout provided the most orthodox definition in the first article that he devoted to the concept in 1969. In a rather ambiguous way, he says that it is important to find a simple idea/concept that differentiates the product and allows it to occupy a preferential position in the minds of prospects. But the idea/concept should be perceived by prospects as having a special benefit for them. It is not enough that the product be objectively different, for it should also be so in the minds of consumers. Otherwise, it will

101

not work (cf. Trout 1969: 51–52). It is perhaps due to the vagueness of the concept on the part of its creators that, in Sengupta's opinion, positioning is difficult to define: 'positioning, to this day, appears to be both a confusing and a confused concept, and there are almost as many definitions as there are writers on the subject' (2007: 14). By the same token, Ollé and Riu (2009: 100–01) claim that there is no firm or clear consensus – between the many existing definitions – on what the principle of positioning actually involves. For this reason, the two admen note thus:

> This is one of the so-called basic or fundamental concepts of the discipline, but curiously enough there is neither an academic consensus on its definition, nor a methodological one on its use by professionals.
>
> This is largely due to two problems. Firstly, the misuse of the term. It is clear that the same term has given rise to different definitions that, in many cases, lose sight of the original concept, since everyone positions themselves, but only a few do so clearly and efficiently, the rest limiting themselves to including grandiose statements or manifestos in their marketing plans, confusing rhetoric with strategy. At a conference, Ries himself said that it was one of the most used and least understood concepts in marketing [...] even Aaker accepts this vagueness as something normal [...]
>
> And, secondly, in our opinion this concept has changed a lot in the last fifteen years, so that some of the original ideas need to be reviewed and adapted owing to the fact that the concept of positioning is not only still current, but is also one of the most powerful marketing ideas.
>
> (Ollé and Riu 2009: 100–01)

Although Trout and Ries would complain bitterly, it is thus necessary to consult the works of other authors to find definitions in the strict sense of the word. The reality is very different in these works, for, in the main, the most outstanding brand management experts have aptly defined the popular concept. This is the case with the Frenchman Kapferer, who is of the following opinion: 'Positioning is the act of relating one facet of a brand to a set of consumer expectations, needs and desires' (1992: 96). In a subsequent work, he then qualifies this: 'Positioning a brand means emphasizing the distinctive characteristics that make it different from its competitors and appealing to the public' (2012: 152). As to the brand architecture guru Aaker, he understands that 'a brand position is the part of the brand identity and value proposition that is to be actively communicated to the target audience and that demonstrates an advantage over competing brands' (1996: 71). And in the fifth edition of his classic *Advertising Management* – co-authored on this occasion with Batra, in addition to Myers – he elaborates on his posture:

The key idea in positioning strategy is that the consumer must have a clear idea of what your brand stands for in the product category, and that a brand cannot be sharply and distinctly positioned if it tries to be everything to everyone. Such positioning is achieved mostly through a brand's marketing communications, although its distribution, pricing, packaging, and actual product features also can play major roles. It is often said that positioning is not what you do to the product, but what you do to the consumer's mind, through various communications [...] The strategic objective must be to have segmentation and positioning strategies that fit together: a brand must be positioned in a way that is maximally effective in attracting the desired target segment. A brand's position is the set of associations the consumer has with the brand.

(Batra et al. 1996: 190–91)

Or the case of Keller, another top branding expert, who defines the concept in the following terms:

The essence of brand positioning is that the brand has some sustainable competitive advantage or 'unique selling proposition' that gives consumers a compelling reason why they should buy that particular brand. Thus, one critical success factor for a brand is that it has some strongly held, favorably evaluated associations that function as *points of difference* and are unique to the brand and imply superiority over other competing brands. These potential differences should be judged on the basis of desirability (from a consumer perspective) and deliverability (from a firm perspective).

(1998: 77, original emphasis)

From that point onwards, many definitions can be found in the marketing literature. On the one hand, some of them show Trout and Ries's original concept great respect:

A position is a mental concept, a location of a brand relative to its competitors that exists in the mind of the consumer [...] 'Positioning is not something you do to a product, it's what you do in the mind of the prospects.' This is a much-quoted one-liner by Al Ries and Jack Trout, the inventors of the positioning concept. It is a one-sided or consumer-focused definition of the concept of positioning as a process that takes place only in the memory of consumers. The principle is that consumers classify a brand in a group or subgroup of other brands on the basis of the most salient category characteristics and distinguish the brand from other brands in the group or subgroup on the basis of its most differentiating characteristics.

(Franzen and Moriarty 2009: 165)

Similarly, Davis (2002: 32–33) defines brand positioning as follows:

> The place in consumers' minds that you want to own. Specifically, it is the benefit that you want them to think of when they think of your brand. It has to be externally driven and relevant. It has to be differentiated from competition and, most important, it has to be valued.
>
> A good positioning is a single idea to be communicated to your customers. A good positioning is a credible promise of value, delivered in ways that distinguish your brand from that of your competitors. A good positioning is a concise statement that summarizes your brand's promise to its customers.

Meanwhile, Heding et al. (2009: 14) come up with the following definition:

> The idea of brand positioning is based on the assumption that consumers have limited mind space for commercial messages and that the most successful brands hence are the ones able to position themselves in the minds of consumers by adapting the most congruent and consistent commercial message. The idea is linked to the information-processing theory of consumer choice.

On the other hand, there are definitions that have a pronounced marketing slant more in keeping with, for instance, Michael Porter,[9] than with the two admen who originally coined the term:

> Brand positioning refers to the specific, intended meaning for a brand in consumers' minds. More precisely, a brand's positioning articulates the goal that a consumer will achieve by using the brand and explains why it is superior to other means of accomplishing this goal.
>
> (Tybout and Sternthal 2005: 11)

This is also the case with another contribution made by Franzen and Moriarty, two authors who, as already observed, proposed a definition very much in line with that of the concept's creators. Their second – more Porterean – definition reads as follows:

> The concept of positioning refers to the strategy companies follow to reach a favorable, sustainable competitive position in a market. Positioning of a brand by companies refers to the choice of the customer groups to be served, the structure of the activities necessary to answer their needs and desires, and the competitive advantage a brand has over its competition.
>
> (Franzen and Moriarty 2009: 163)

Instead of defining the concept, some authors have attempted to explain how it works or have developed its objectives. Those who focus on the way positioning works in an attempt to understand it include Healey, who explains it by pointing out what it does not do: 'The basic approach of positioning is not to create something new and different, but to manipulate what's already in the mind, to retie the connections that already exist' (2008: 38). Tybout and Sternthal (2005: 25) follow suit, but divide it into three stages corresponding to the following three questions:

> Brand positioning plays a key role in the building and managing of a strong brand by specifying how the brand is related to consumers' goals. It can be thought of as answering three questions: (1) Who should be targeted for brand use? (2) What goal does the brand allow the target to achieve? (3) Why should the brand be chosen over brands that achieve the same goal?

For their part, Kelley and Jugenheimer (2004: 6–7) rely on the same premise when, extending it to the field of media planning, they claim,

> Brand positioning plays a critical role in the success or failure of your marketing program. Once the position has been determined, it must be translated into advertising; the positioning is meaningless if it is not supported in the advertising [...] Advertising media play an essential role in your brand's success and, ultimately, in your own success and progress.

On the contrary, Davis (2002: 109) grounds his definition of the concept in what he understands as its basic objective:

> A strong brand position means the brand has a unique, credible, sustainable, and valued place in customers' minds. It revolves around a benefit that helps your product or service stand apart from the competition. Good positioning gives you the direction required to focus the organization and focus your strategic efforts.

All considered, to assert that positioning is more focused on individuals, specifically on their capacity of reception, than on the abstract market, should come as no surprise to anyone with a cursory knowledge of marketing. As already observed, it is a marketing maxim. So, at this point, what should be understood by positioning? For its creators, it is a natural selection of brands that takes place inside the minds of prospects. It is a 'battle' waged inside their minds, to wit, the place occupied by a product or brand, according to their perceptions, in relation to other competitive products or brands or to an ideal product (cf. Santesmases 1996: 401). Thus 'the ultimate marketing battleground is the mind, and the better you understand how the mind works, the better you'll understand how positioning works' (Trout 1996: ix–x). As Al and Laura Ries note, '[t]he primary objective of a branding program is never the market for the product or service. The primary objective of a branding is always the mind of the prospect' (2004: 24). In plain English, so as to understand how positioning works, it is necessary to forget concepts such as the abstract market and the marketing of traditional products. For example, detergent brands are not vying with each other on supermarket shelves (or on the battle-ground of merchandising strategy) with a view to 'positioning themselves in the market'. Their battle begins when consumers reach supermarket shelves and have to decide on which detergent to buy. This is the synthesis of positioning: marketing is not a battle between products, but one of perceptions.

7.3. Theoretical bases of positioning

Throughout their prolific publishing careers – they are still churning it out – Trout and Ries have never developed a serious or rigorous epistemology of positioning from a theoretical perspective. Quite to the contrary, as is usually the case in all of their works, there is very little theoretical reflection or analysis. Although it is true that, in the main, they are replete with good intentions of a markedly func-tionalist nature, these are, to our mind, formulated with scant rigour and the-oretical consistency. Their approach in nearly all of their works is similar. They latch on to a specific idea to which they give a vibrant, euphonic and convin-cing name – 'positioning', repositioning', 'differentiate', 'divergence', 'obvious', 'focus', 'horse sense', 'marketing warfare' and the like – and then assemble an ad hoc theoretical construct, namely, adapting all sorts of psychological – 'posi-tioning', for instance, which is based on cognitive psychology – anthropological – 'differentiate', whose emotional basis rests on self-concept – economic – 'focus', which is developed as business targeting – and even biological principles – the principle of divergence draws from Darwin's hypothesis of natural selection – to the term in question. This method sometimes yields good results, as in the case of positioning in which recourse is made to the achievements of cognitive psychology, certain advertising techniques devised by Reeves, such as differen-tiated promise, and some product branding proposals, to justify the concept. However, it is often unsuccessful because it is impossible to find sufficient the-oretical consistency in these scientific resources to give it credence. This is the case with 'obvious', 'divergence' and 'focus', among others. Therefore, in their writings they resort over and again to positioning as an all-embracing justifi-cation. This does not detract from the fact that many of these works are pep-pered with ingenious and, on occasion, revolutionary ideas that, in some way or another, make it necessary to rethink brand reality. It is precisely here where the importance of their legacy lies, especially as regards positioning, their star proposal. Having said that, an additional problem is that not even positioning is sufficiently reasoned in the many works that they have devoted to this concept. As with its definition, we are of the mind that their oeuvre is sprinkled with the concept's more theoretical aspects. This theoretical anarchy has been resolved by scholars, who, appreciating the original idea's inestimable worth, have decided to delve deeper into the theoretical fundamentals of this strategic advertising mechanism.

As already observed, the notion of positioning rests on some very basic premises of cognitive psychology. Indeed, the concept of positioning is based on the limited memory capacity of human beings, to which should be added one of the innate principles of linguistic economy: the tendency to reduce all meanings to a summary or stereotype. Organizations are aware that it is unwise to overload their brands with connotations because consumers are not going retain everything that they are told, for which reason they should reduce their personality traits to a minimum. Nonetheless, positioning is also directly linked to the characteristics of the market system at the time when it emerged. It was a moment of business mergers and acquisitions like no other, which accentuated and atomized the concept of competition.[10] In other words, one of fierce rivalry, information saturation and the quest for differentiation that led to the need for oversimplifying messages. Positioning is grounded in the perceptive psychology of individuals. Owing to the fact that they are saturated with information and have a limited capacity to store it, it is essential to construct relevant messages that speak to them using their own codes and that are based on existing structures of meaning. On the one hand, messages should be tailored to target audiences, they should be spoken to in their own language, using their own jargon and common codes in search of stimuli that reveal the 'identity compact' between the emitter and the receiver. And, on the other, they should be constructed on a known basis, a pre-existing structure of meaning that does not hinder their reception. 'The basic approach of positioning is not to create something new and different, but to manipulate what's already up there in the mind, to retie the connections that already exist' (Ries and Trout 2001: 5). For, in theory, the receivers of those messages are not going to make any effort to memorize brands or their novel attributes and, obviously, commercial communication is not perceived as being strictly necessary. Thus, to construct brand messages it is necessary to leverage information that individuals already possess. Indeed, as most communication and marketing theoreticians hold, the minds of consumers are structured and there is no room for new information – and even less for the undesired kind – whereby it is necessary to look for already existing slots or positions. Having said that, there is no doubt whatsoever that positioning is more focused on individuals, specifically on their capacity of reception, than on the abstract market. As Trout and Rivkin (2010: 173) claim,

> You have to put your mind on the tactics of the battle you want to win. You have to focus on your competitors and their strengths and weaknesses in people's minds. You have to search out that one attribute or differentiating idea that will work in the mental battleground.
>
> Then you have to be willing to focus all your efforts to develop a coherent strategy to exploit that repositioning idea.

Thus, on the basis of the aforementioned premises, we will now assemble a theoretical construct with which to define the characteristics of the concept of positioning, which are as follows: (1) the problem of information saturation; (2) the problem of the mind's limited capacity; (3) the importance of being first; (4) the need to become generic in a category; (5) the importance of the reference brand; (6) the principle of differentiation; (7) the principle of difference beyond the product; (8) the principle of simplicity; and (9) the principle of permanence.

1. The problem of information saturation

The context of positioning coincides with what Semprini calls 'media pollution' (cf. 1995: 28), that is, an environment saturated with messages and information – the famous concept of 'noise' in communication theory. So, the concept is framed in a way very similar – albeit more complex due to the aforementioned economic trend of business mergers and acquisitions in the 1980s, which made competition stronger and information more relevant – to that of other consumer branding models. It is assumed that there is far too much information and that the human mind is incapable of retaining everything that it receives, an idea based on the second principle of positioning, which will be examined below. The idea of information saturation is a constant in the oeuvre of Trout and Ries. In fact, they even resort to authoritative citations to bolster their arguments, such as the interview that they perform with Dr Carol Moog:

> Consumer psychologists say that this sea of choices is driving us bonkers. Consider what Carol Moog, PH.D., has to say on the subject: 'Too many choices, all of which can be fulfilled instantly, indulged immediately, keeps children – and adults – infantile. From a marketing perspective, people stop caring, get as fat and fatigued as geese destined for foie gras, and lose their decision-making capabilities. They withdraw and protect against the overstimulation; they get "bored"'.
>
> (Trout and Rivkin 2010: 28–30)

Or the consumer expert Schwartz, who claims,

> People are so overwhelmed with choice that it tends to paralyze them. Too much choice makes people more likely to defer decisions. It raises expectations and makes people blame themselves for choosing poorly. You don't expect much if there are only two pairs of jeans to choose from. If there are hundreds, you expect one to be perfect.
>
> (in Trout and Rivkin 2010: 31)

This perspective is also shared by other brand management experts including Kapferer, Keller and Aaker.

This reality involves risks that Trout and Rivkin list in the aforementioned *Repositioning*, which takes up where the classic *Positioning* left off:

> Behavioral scientists say that there are five forms of perceived risk: (1) Monetary risk (There's a chance that I could lose money on this); (2) Functional risk (Maybe it won't work, or maybe it won't do what it's supposed to do); (3) Physical risk (It looks a little dangerous. I could get hurt); (4) Social risk (I wonder what my friends will think if I buy this); (5) Psychological risk (I might feel guilty or irresponsible if I buy this).
>
> (2010: 16–17)

For this reason advertising consultants also see the brand as a basic driving force of differentiation. This divergent quality of positioning can go a long way to putting an end to information saturation, provided that it is used correctly. The marketing literature is unanimous is this respect, as has been seen at the beginning of this chapter. For example, Homs (2004: 89) observes,

> In view of the confusion that an overabundance of options vis-à-vis similar products and services leads to, plus the uncertainty accompanying decision-making in these circumstances, brands become an element of reliability. Brands are depositories of positioning because of their attributes and values. When consumers feel incapable of making the right decision, they resort to the trust that publicly recognized brands foster.

For their part, De Chernatony et al. (2011: 105) also base their ideas on this information 'noise', but put forward a solution to the problem: the use of tools that connect with consumers.

> [T]o help the brand fight through the competing noise in the market, it is still essential to know what the brand means to the consumer, how the brand's values compare against competitive brands and how marketing resources are affecting brand values.

This brings us to the second principle of positioning, which is also based on presuppositions of cognitive psychology. Trout and Ries note that minds have a limited capacity and are incapable of retaining everything. Therefore, there is tendency to recall only that which, in some way or another, connects with individuals.

2. The problem of the mind's limited capacity

As advertising experts are perfectly aware, the 'mind/computer' metaphor is one of the maxims when applying theoretical cognitive presuppositions to marketing. As already observed, Trout and Ries borrow some notions from this current of psychological research to formulate their theory, something that they clearly admit in their work:

> Like the memory bank of a computer, the mind has a slot or position for each bit of information it has chosen to retain. In operation, the mind is a lot like a computer. But there is one important difference. A computer has to accept what you put into it. The mind does not. In fact, it's quite the opposite. The mind rejects new information that doesn't 'compute'. It accepts only that new information which matches its current state of mind. It filters out everything else.[11]

> (2001: 29)

Be that as it may, the two consultants are tremendously creative when inventing alternative metaphors to explain the hypothetical classificatory or selective functioning of the mind. On the one hand, those metaphors include the 'pigeonhole':

> The mind is like the sorting rack in a post office, which has a 'pigeonhole' for every name on a letter carrier's route […] So, too, with brands. The mind has a slot or pigeonhole for every category. If the pigeonhole is named 'safe cars', this is the hole for a brand called Volvo.[12]

> (Ries and Ries 2004: 250)

And, on the other, these include the association of 'nodes', as they are called in psychology, with 'holes in the mind': 'Marketing can be visualized as filling a hole in the mind' (Ries and Ries 2004: 228). They have even coined the less orthodox – and, we believe, regrettable – expression 'hole in the ground':

> A name in the mind is like a hole in the ground. You can deepen a hole, you can widen a hole, but the one thing you can't do with a hole is move it. Once a brand name becomes strongly identified with a category in the mind, the brand can't easily be moved.

> (Ries and Ries 2004: 152)

Nevertheless, Trout and Ries's maxim is none other than to stress that the marketing battle is not waged in the market, but in the minds of consumers, and they exploit some of the principles of cognitive psychology to this end. Sure enough, '[t]o find a unique position, you must ignore conventional logic. Conventional logic says you find your concept inside yourself or inside the product. Not true. What you must do is look inside the prospect's mind' (Ries and Trout 2001: 34). The two advertising consultants believe that this is the basic principle of any strategy: 'How do you find an open position in the prospect's mind? [...] The French have a marketing expression that sums up this strategy rather neatly. Cherchez le creneau. "Look for the hole"' (Ries and Trout 2001: 54). As a result,

[c]ritical to making correct branding decisions is the ability to differentiate between the market and the mind. The primary objective of a branding program is never the market for the product or service. The primary objective of a branding program is always the mind of the prospect. The mind comes first; the market follows where the mind leads [...] The mind doesn't think markets. The mind thinks categories. In this respect, the visual is only a means to an end. In Marlboro's case the end is a category the mind identifies as 'masculine' cigarette.

(Ries and Ries 2004: 24–25)

The 'mind/computer' metaphor and the functioning of branding on the basis of memory and recollections are very firmly established theories in marketing literature. For instance, Crainer takes a leaf out of David Hennessey's book when remarking that '[a] brand owns a little piece of memory in the mind of the consumer with a distinctive meaning' (1995: 85). Similarly, Cheverton states, '[t]he process of brand positioning is intended to identify and target those spaces in the customer's mind' (2006: 75). Indeed, there are many studies that have confirmed that the recognition or recollection of a brand has an influence on its purchase:

Although it seems intuitive that consumers would choose a brand based on an objective evaluation of the information they receive about a product, this is not always the case. People may purchase a brand because it comes to mind most readily, or because it is the brand their mother always bought, or because the brand is the easiest to justify to others.

(Sternthal and Lee 2005: 130)

All considered, the need to penetrate the mind of individuals became an obsession as of the 1980s. An obsession that, as has been seen, still exists judging by the words of Cheverton: 'Rather than share of sales, they will measure "share of voice" – the proportion of the total communication in the sector that their brand accounts for, or "share of mind" – the level of recognition their brand achieves in the customer's mind' (2006: 137).

3. The importance of being first

Inasmuch as it is a basically perceptive concept, another of the ideas underlying positioning is the need for brands to elaborate information in such a way that it penetrates the minds of consumers by assimilation. In other words, the message should be sufficiently relevant, appealing and simple to arouse the interest of individuals who should not be required to make too much of an effort to memorize it. As Homs notes, '[p]ositioning bases its structure on the phenomenon of perception and is therefore a strategy underpinned by the assimilation of regional cultural variables for the definition and instrumentation of commercial strategies' (2004: 29).

To ensure that this process of assimilation and significance in the mind is always effective, Trout and Ries propose being first. They understand that, in this way, the capacity of penetration is much greater and, as if it were a blank canvas, for them the hypothetical state of an unblemished mind is ideal. 'The first thing you need to "fix your message indelibly in the mind" is not a message at all. It's a mind. An innocent mind. A mind that has not been burnished by someone else's brand' (Ries and Trout 2001: 20). And they continue to insist on this point: 'The easy way to get into a person's mind is to be first' (Ries and Trout 2001: 19). And in the revised edition of their book commemorating its twentieth anniversary, they are even more categorical if possible: 'Better to be first than it is to be better' (Ries and Trout 2001b: 22). In this vein, they emphasize that the most effective type of 'differentiation' consists of being a leader, a leadership that can only be achieved by being the first brand in a specific product category. 'Leadership is your best "differentiator". It's the collateral for your brand's success' (Ries and Trout 2001b: 53). Under this principle of differentiation based on being first in the market, the authors contend that it is very difficult to lose strength as a brand. In their own words,

> brands are powerful brands not because they are better than competitive brands (although they might be), but because they are widely perceived to be the leader brands in their categories. Firstness creates leadership. If your brand is the only brand in the category, your brand must be the leader. And when competition arrives, leadership creates the perception of betterness for your brand. The first brand in the mind can survive a long time and still maintain its leadership […] Two things work in favor of the first brand into the mind. First is the perception that the leading

brand must be 'better'. It's axiomatic that the best product or service wins in the marketplace. Since the first brand into the mind is automatically the leader (there are no other brands), the first brand will tend to maintain its leadership. (It blocks the sunlight from competing brands.) Second is the perception that the first brand is the original. Every other brand is an imitation of the original.

(Ries and Ries 2004: 164–65)

They give such importance to being first that they even go far as to recommend thus: 'If you can't be first in a category, set up a new category you can be first in' (Ries and Trout 2001b: 25). In subsequent works, they qualify these forthright statements slightly:

Being first doesn't automatically mean your brand will become the leader in a new category. It only gives you a license to do so. If you're first, your brand starts off as the leader since no other brands are trying to occupy the same branch. Here's where evolution comes in. Your brand needs to evolve to maintain its leadership. In this respect, you need to be protective of your brand and be especially vigilant when competitors threaten your position. Sales, however, don't matter nearly as much as perception. To become successful, your brand needs to establish the perception of leadership in the minds of consumers.

(Ries and Ries 2004: 161–62)

In a more orthodox manner, Kapferer attempts to explain why it is so advantageous to be first in a specific category in a young market – despite the fact that such markets are currently few and far between. The branding expert understands that

[i]n young markets, where the product category is still finding its feet, the first brand to spread its message far and wide benefits from what we call the 'pioneer advantage'. Most brands which dominate a new market hold sway for decades afterwards [...] The psychological explanation is that when a market is first created, its customers have no system of preferences or set criteria of choice. The first brand which comes to be known in this market becomes the prototype – the market reference. Put another way, it characterizes the ideal brand – it bears the combination of attributes on which the purchaser will henceforth base his ideal of satisfaction. It is this brand which will define values, and for this reason subsequent entrants to the market are handicapped.

(Kapferer 1992: 90–91)

As will be seen, the Frenchman discovers the cause in cognitive psychology, which implies that, when being first in their category, brands act like 'pedagogical tools' for consumers, or we could even say that they educate them – they show them what they are, how they work, their usefulness, how they are used and so on. Ollé and Riu (2009: 116–17) endorse this point of view:

> [P]owerful brands 'paint the axes'. This means that they have been capable of teaching consumers their game rules, thus conditioning the strategy of the rest, which take the lead from a perceptual point of view [...] That is, they do not only communicate something about us, but also provide a point of view that makes us reshape the perceptions of all our rivals.

Judging by the literature, being first certainly helps a brand to gain a competitive edge. In his book entitled *Branding with Brains: The Science of Getting Customers to Choose Your Company*, Walvis reflects on cognitive psychology and neuromarketing, before concluding,

> The winning brand enters our awareness as the preferred option and will be adopted – unless our conscious mind deliberates or vetoes our choice. The preferred brand, the one that enters our mind *first*, is said to be the most 'accessible' brand. Accessibility is the end measure of the degree to which a brand has been built according to the three laws [relevance, coherence, participation] or, in other words, is favoured by the brain's algorithm.
>
> (2010: 45, original emphasis)

4. The need to become generic in a category

According to Trout and Ries (2004: 292),

> Having a brand name that is also used generically is an enormous marketing advantage. A generic brand like Kleenex is exceptionally strong and will almost certainly never lose its leadership as long as there's a market for pocket tissue [...] That's why brands that become generic don't generally lose their branding power.

The possibility of becoming the generic brand in a category is, in addition to being a marketing maxim, one of the most sought-after objectives of any brand. There seems to be a complete consensus on this point in the literature. For instance, Davis states that 'getting the customer to think only about your brand in your category. This is the position of power' (2002: 155). By the same token, Crainer asserts, '[t]he ultimate for any brand is to become the name people use automatically to describe a particular product or service' (1995: 45). For his part, Bassat (2006: 97) speaks in terms of achieving a mental monopoly over a category:

> Brands like Aspirin, Kleenex, Chupa Chups and Nocilla have lent their names to product categories. They are lexicalized categories. To lexicalize a product is to achieve a 'mental monopoly over that category', which leads to the name of a product being substituted by the brand [...] Lexicalized brands inhabit the highest spheres of our mind. This signifies that they will be the first to spring to mind when thinking about a category.

Davis (2002: 233) expresses himself in similar terms when referring to the 'short list' of brands:

> When a customer thinks about making a purchase in a category (whether it is long-distance service or toothpaste), usually a few brands come to mind as part of that customer's purchase set. In the future, companies who focus on getting a customer to think about their brand first, once the decision has been made to make a purchase in that category, will be successful. Recognizing that a brand, rather than the product or service, drives sales should motivate companies to organize around the brand.

However, to become the generic brand in a category also involves risks. It is essential to know how to maintain the lead and that the brand name continues to function as such. The problem is that when a brand name is assimilated by consumers, it can become solely generic, in other words, a commodity. According to Healey (2008: 54),

> English is littered with words that used to be trademarks [...] When a name is judged to have become generic, its former owners lose the protection of trademark, since language belongs to everybody and no one can lay claim to a particular word.

In this sense, there are brands associated with generic ones that maintain their philosophy and values. Nevertheless, the line between the generic product that a brand represents and its very status as a brand can be more blurred. If a customer orders a Coca-Cola and is served a generic cola drink, he or she will certainly insist on being served the brand that he or she has requested. On the contrary, if that same customer asked for Kleenex and he or she were sold any other tissue brand, would he or she react in the same way? Cheverton has the following to say in this respect:

> Becoming the generic is good, provided that you really *do* own the word, and continue to retain that ownership. That takes massive and continuous investment,

continued vigilance, continuing evolution, and a refusal to rest on your laurels. A great and glorious heritage is not enough.

(2006: 114, original emphasis)

And as Healey (2008: 55) notes,

The challenge for brands that risk becoming verbs is not to occupy the number one position in customers' minds – they have achieved that – but to keep customers mindful of why the brand means more than the product. They must achieve a higher insight that transcends product and stands for something more universally appealing.

5. The importance of the reference brand

According to LePla and Parker, '[p]ositioning is a method for showing how your company and/or products relate to others in the marketplace. One definition of positioning is *what currently distinguishes you in your customers', prospects', and other audiences' mind from your competition*' (1999: 77, original emphasis). Thus, positioning only makes sense if there is a previous reference brand involving other environmental, market and competitive factors.

A brand is never enough on its own to make a context grow, insofar as it always depends on other variables like its competitors or the cultural reality to make that context expand and become a mass idea that allows it to grow.

(Ollé and Riu 2009: 112)

In effect, it is a strategic mechanism based on comparison, whereby it is impossible for a brand to position itself if it is not in relation to another. For Kapferer, it is an analytical task: 'It has become common to analyze brands according to their positioning. The term applies to a process of emphasizing the brand's distinctive and motivating attributes in the light of competition' (1992: 39). Chevalier and Mazzalovo also understand it in this way when remarking thus: 'A positioning or an argument is only valid inasmuch as it has an advantage over its competitors […] beyond the operational levels of brand management, its identity implies differentiation and relativization in relation to competition' (2005: 117). And, for his part, Moliné (1996a: 60) expresses himself in identical terms:

[B]rands should adopt a relative position in relation to other brands and in terms of the characteristics, image, target audience, the use or occasion to which the product is specifically destined, etc. This signifies that the mind accepts things in relation to others more easily and resolutely. It classifies, compares and places the brand according to the category in question, in relation to other stimuli or competing brands.

Trout and Ries had already noted this reality: 'Yet too many companies embark on marketing and advertising programs as if the competitor's position did not exist. They advertise their products in a vacuum and are disappointed when their messages fail to get through' (2001: 32). However, it is other admen who have gone to the greatest lengths to explain what the reference brand of a positioning involves. Ollé and Riu (2009: 116) call this operation 'painting the axes of a positioning', remarking,

> [i]n our opinion, the advantage of entering into a debate on positioning is to analyse competitive positions in search of relevance, creating different scenarios and introducing new ideas for reflection or different messages that imply completely changing the layout of a perceptual map of brands.

The authors explain that the current 'game' of positioning consists in how to change the perception that prospects have of us by focusing on their environment. To their mind, 'everything is relative', for which reason absolute judgements can only be made if a reference brand exists. This is decided on by the brand, and is thus the first step towards positioning. They call this process 'contextualization' (cf. Ollé and Riu 2009: 103). The methodology rests on the following principles:

> The exercise is always the same: to think about the reference brand that benefits us most and to contextualize ourselves there. The real challenge of a strategy is not to 'play better' than one's competitors, but to establish the rules of the game so that the rest can follow [...] at a distance. This is what leading brands do: to educate consumers in order that they should buy according to those attributes that benefit them most [...] Contextualizing so as to find the correct core idea is 50 per cent of a good positioning strategy, the other 50 per cent depending on communicating it simply and efficiently. This is when the second step comes into play: to find the concept that best communicates our new context. It is what we call 'conceptualization'. Conceptualization is the correct communication of contextualization. It is the simplest and most popular expression that we are capable of coming up with to define our offering. It is a word, a value proposition, a verbalized idea that allows us to situate ourselves in the appropriate competitive context.
>
> (Ollé and Riu 2009: 104)

6. The principle of differentiation

Since Theodore Levitt published his article entitled 'Marketing success through differentiation of anything' – nowadays a classic – in *Harvard Business Review* in 1980, which begins with the following famous statement: 'There is no such thing as a commodity. All goods and services are differentiable' (1980: 83), the term 'differentiation' has become one of the pillars of marketing, as well as one of the most hackneyed concepts in the business literature. Indeed, as Franzen and Moriarty (2009: 176) note,

> David Aaker (1996b) states that differentiation is the bottom-line characteristic of a brand. Everything can be differentiated, even parity products like sand, concrete, copper, grains [...] Harvard professor Ted Levitt (1991), another pioneer of marketing theory, also emphasizes the need to differentiate as one of the most important strategic and tactical activities that companies can pursue. Levitt claims that there is no such thing as standard products: there are only people who see them as a commodity. He insists that everything can be differentiated – no company has to stay put in a commodity or parity position.

Differentiation forms the backbone of this process: 'Positioning allows marketing communications to focus on differentiating brand messages that relate to the immediate competitive environment. Differentiation is central to the branding process' (LePla and Parker 1999: 78). As already noted, some years after writing *Positioning*, Trout himself published *Differentiate or Die*, which is entirely based on the principles of the concept of 'differentiation'. In it, he claims, '[t]here are books and books on branding but very few books talk much about differentiation. And if it does get mentioned, rarely do authors go much beyond talking about the fact that branding is important to do' (Trout and Rivkin 2000: 13). Its central idea is that advertising professionals forget about the product and its differentiating functional attributes: 'Unfortunately, the fact is that many advertising people don't appreciate the need to offer the prospect a unique selling proposition' (Trout and Rivkin 2000: 14). For which reason, Trout concludes,

> [m]ost of these people feel that selling isn't cool and that people only respond to companies that don't try to sell them. Besides, many will argue, there often isn't enough 'difference' to talk about in the products. What they ignore is the fact that, whether or not people like to be sold, in a sea of choice a prospect still has the problem of figuring out what to buy or not to buy. In other words, alternatives are but the raw material of decision making. And decisions must be made.
>
> (Trout and Rivkin 2000: 14)

So, back in 1981 they saw 'differentiation' as one of the basic characteristics of positioning. As in previous cases, however, in their book they only mention the concept in passing, without taking the time to delve deeper into anything. In this context, the most lucid reflection on the concept is to be found in the work of other authors. This is the case of Homs (2004: 85) who observes that

> differentiation is the essence of commercial identity. A brand or a product that is not identifiable cannot generate competitive edges, because it is lost in anonymity. The first step towards possessing an identity is to distinguish oneself from the rest.

He then qualifies this:

> Differentiation is the key to identity. When two or more products or services resemble each other, their own attributes cease to be appealing and consumers opt for the cheapest [...] Differentiation is the essence of positioning, and without a correct positioning, it will be impossible to become a leader. The essence of a brand is identity, and this is nurtured by differentiation.
>
> (Homs 2004: 222)

In a similar manner, Nilson (1998: 132) warns of the risks that differentiation poses when establishing a positioning:

> There are two effects of positioning which sometimes are forgotten. The first one is that a distinct positioning does mean that some aspects and targets are excluded [...] The second is that by clearly positioning your own brand, you can also reposition competition.

For his part, Davis (cf. 2001) understands that differentiation fosters loyalty and that a company can benefit from having a strong brand because loyalty leads, in turn, to repeat business. In his view, strong brands give credibility to newly launched products; they offer a clear, valued and sustainable point of differentiation in relation to competitors; and the most loyal customers will also be the most understanding if the company makes a mistake.

7. The principle of difference beyond the product

In the words of Riezebos (2003: 37),

> [a] branded article can be composed of different attributes [...] On the basis of the attributes that consumers can perceive, they must form a picture of the branded

119

article. In this process of evaluation, consumers will often not use all the attributes available to them. Consumers will also often find one attribute more important than another – consciously or not. In other words, consumers will attach more value to some attributes than to other attributes. This normally leads to consumers (unconsciously) making an order of ranking between attributes relating to a certain branded article.

Positioning tends to look for a sales proposition in the attributes, advantages or solutions offered by a product. Although this additional trait of positioning, directly associated with the previous one, is never mentioned in the original texts – it would be necessary to wait for the identity approach theories to appear before it was elaborated on – some advertising creatives include it as a trait inherent to Trout and Ries's famous concept, extrapolating it to the present. We are referring to 'differentiation' based on psychological attributes (as has been seen in the strategic advertising mechanisms covered in Chapters 3, 4, 5 and 6). This is the case of Ollé and Riu (2009: 102) who, under the title of 'the current problem with positioning', state that,

> basically, nowadays products cannot be positioned. Formerly, an offering was launched in the market and, with time, experience and recognition (and a bit of advertising), it became a brand. At the time, positioning strategies tended to become a sort of brainstorming in search of concepts that fitted in with whatever perception of that offering was intended to be highlighted.
>
> Currently, to triumph in the market not only the tangible, but also the intangible, aspects of the offering have to be considered. And if a brand is a portfolio of meanings, the product or service of course provides the basis, but the consumer or the moment of use can be aspects that differentiate it. We therefore believe that the classical process of positioning based on attributes comparable to those of competitors has become more sophisticated and needs to be reconsidered. The idea is not to offer a new definition of positioning, but to deal with how it should be done today.

As already observed, in their works Trout and Ries resort exclusively to the properties of the product, refusing to bear in mind its emotional or psychological attributes. Likewise, the many examples contained in their oeuvre evince a type of strategy based on attributes, uses, solutions or advantages linked to the product. And, despite the passing of time, they have not changed their mind. Quite the opposite, judging by the views that Trout expresses in *Differentiate or Die*, an authentic plea in favour of communicating the objective advantages of a product, and a vindication of the unique selling proposition (USP) and the figure of Reeves as a mechanism and a thinker that are both still valid. The fact of alluding to the virtues of the product – in the same way as the strategic mechanisms framed in the context of the product branding paradigm (described in Chapters 1 and 2) operate – is a step back in the evolution of strategic advertising mechanisms, in particular, and in brand management, in general. Their proposal systematically overlooks the emotional strategic mechanisms addressed in the previous chapters. We concur with Rom and Sabaté when blaming this 'regression' on the abuse of models based on the 'brand personality' paradigm. Effectively, 'a certain exaggeration of the brand personality philosophy leads us to the following advertising philosophy' (Rom and Sabaté 2007: 150).

8. The principle of simplicity

The Power of Simplicity: A Management Guide to Cutting Through the Nonsense and Doing Things Right (1999) is the title of another book by Trout, which, as occurred with the principle of differentiation – the seed of the aforementioned *Differentiate or Die* – also emerged from an idea borrowed from his bestseller *Positioning*: the principle of simplicity. In fact, in this work Trout mostly repeats himself, focusing on many problems that he had already addressed in his 1981 book, while broadening the scope to include business management and even anthropology – that is, the chapters devoted to personal aspects – instead of advertising strategy or brand management. Both books have the same starting point: things should be done simply. As already mentioned, in *The Power of Simplicity* this idea is applied to management in general, and in *Positioning*, to advertising strategy and brand management. Similarly, Ries also takes up the cudgels for simplicity in most of his works, claiming, '[w]hat matters most is not describing exactly what the benefits of the new category are, but expressing the essence of the new category in as simple a way as possible' (Ries and Ries 2004: 229). However, it is yet again Trout who inquires more deeply into the concept of 'simplicity' as regards positioning, specifically in another fairly recent book entitled *Repositioning: Marketing in an Era of Competition, Change, and Crisis* (2010). The arguments that he deploys are based on a key idea: 'All this means that your differentiating idea must be as simple and as visible as possible and must be delivered over and over again on all media' (Trout and Rivkin 2010: 12–13). He then recommends how this should be done:

> If they are to work, positioning and repositioning ideas must be obvious ideas. That's because they are evident ideas. And if they are evident to you, they will also be evident to your customers, which is why they will work.
>
> (Trout and Rivkin 2010: 197)

Before warning against the pitfalls:

Meanwhile, the so-called experts in the field have worked hard at trying to keep things complicated and confusing. My final advice is, try not to overresearch or overthink your positioning or repositioning strategy. Simple and obvious will do the trick.

(Trout and Rivkin 2010: 205)

Most scholars summarize 'positioning' in this idea, which the authors called 'over-simplified' in their first book. Ellwood[13] explains it in the following terms: 'a simple message for all audiences that summarizes and reinforces the brand. This statement should include a maximum of two or three words and be accompanied by a longer sentence that explains each element' (2010: 97). In the words of Ollé and Riu, '[a]t present, we cannot communicate effectively if we do not do so with simplicity […] This is the essence of any exercise of brand positioning […] a tremendously simple and powerful idea' (2009: 105).

9. The principle of permanence

According to Trout and Ries, '[p]ositioning is like the game of life. A long-term proposition. Name decisions made today may not bear fruit until many, many years in the future' (2001: 89). This phrase summarizes the last principle on which positioning rests. Indeed, in the authors' opinion, the position of a brand should not change more than is absolutely necessary over time, because that would make it difficult to recognize for consumers. For them, positioning is a long-distance race in which, even though coming in first provides a substantial competitive edge, it is essential to know how to maintain that position, something that only the most robust and best managed brands are capable of achieving: 'Positioning is a concept that is accumulative […] You have to hang in there, year after year. Most successful companies rarely change a winning formula' (Ries and Trout 2001: 197). In a previous work, it would be Ries himself who would yet again refer to the need for perseverance: 'Perception is a long-lasting phenomenon. You can lose your sales leadership and still maintain your brand leadership in the mind […] Perception is an immensely valuable attribute […] Perception is sticky' (Ries and Ries 2004: 191). In this connection, persevering with the chosen brand concept is a fundamental attitude in advertising, since it implies the permanence of the message.

7.4. *Positioning seen from afar*

Positioning rests, on the one hand, on some very simple notions of cognitive psychology – practically intuitions in their first expressions – which have already been

122

covered and, on the other, on several of Reeves's product branding proposals and rationalist theories, which will be dealt with below. Regarding the fact that an attempt has been made to make the concept extremely complicated – suffice it to recall the many definitions and theoretical bases discussed above – we are of the mind that, rather than a coincidence, this has been intentional for two basic reasons. The first has to do with the urgent need for some eminent scholars and theoreticians to give the concept an academic sheen – conspicuous by its absence in its original conception – in order to make it researchable. It is important not to forget that this concept very swiftly became a scientific methodology or analytical tool in fields such as marketing and communication, being exploited above all in the 1980s and 1990s. Thus, it is relatively understandable that authors like the prestigious professor of Harvard Business School Michael Porter[14] – one of the researchers who has insisted most on this markedly academic approach to positioning, as if it were a complex issue with a long conceptual track record – have given positioning a new theoretical dimension which directly frames it in an academic context.[15]

The second reason has less to do with science and more with business. In our view, since it was originally such a simple, clear and understandable strategic advertising mechanism, at first sight it might seem excessively easy for anyone to apply it professionally. In this sense, the creators of positioning Ries and Trout, the director and account supervisor, respectively, of the then small communication and advertising consultancy firm in New York, called Ries-Cappiello-Colwell, were not convinced by this point for evidently commercial reasons. Given its formal simplicity, if their clients had access to the tool – they had now been publishing articles and books on the subject since 1969 – they could easily put it to use, which was not economically viable. Thus, so as to profit on their investment, they were obliged to complicate ostensibly the strategic mechanism's inner workings – without hardly any theorization in this respect – and to make it known that only the consultancy firm that had conceived it possessed the methodological key. As seen above, the company changed its name to Trout & Ries Ltd. – in this case, the order of the names had a notable effect on the product – in tribute to Jack Trout, the original creator of 'positioning'. As can be observed, with this strategy the authors intended to board up the application of the concept. In the hypothetical case of not engaging Trout & Ries Ltd. to implement the strategic mechanism, it would not work, in consonance with the following advertising maxim: everyone is talking about positioning but very few really know how to apply it (cf. Trout and Rivkin 2000, 2010) – a sales strategy very much in the style of Reeves who had previously done the same with the USP. In fact, as has been seen, Trout & Partners Ltd., the company that Trout opened back in 1994, devotes itself to pursuing and decrying anyone who uses the concept without its permission. After parting company with Trout in 1994, even Al Ries, the concept's adoptive father, had to renounce its use expressly. Nevertheless, this has not stopped him from insisting on the very basis of 'positioning' in everything that he has written since, while making slight conceptual modifications to the concept and resorting continually to his achievements with Trout.[16] Although with one small difference: in each new work, he coins very different terms as substitutes for 'positioning'. These range from the initial 'focus' appearing in the eponymous book *Focus* (1996)[17] to 'divergence', the most sophisticated aesthetically speaking, created in collaboration with his daughter Laura Ries and included in the relatively more well-known *The Origin of Brands* (2004).

By our reckoning, this is reason enough for why something as simple and practical as 'positioning' has undergone such far-reaching modifications. Indeed, it is significant that an allegedly simple concept has given rise to so much debate. Because we are of the mind that, as already explained, the idea behind the famous term is just as candid, a carbon copy of previous theories. In a paper entitled 'Positioning revisited', published in the *Journal of Marketing* in 1976, John P. Maggard wondered if positioning was new, old or just a loan (cf. 1976: 63). The author's theory was that it was a formula that had already been assumed by marketing experts: 'For the most part, positioning strategy is used in such general terms as to be essentially the same thing as the target selection and consequent promotional aspects of marketing strategy' (1976: 63). Four years after Trout and Ries had proclaimed the arrival of the era of positioning, he wrote, '[t]he use of positioning strategy by marketers is as old as the ideas of market segmentation and product differentiation' (Maggard 1976: 66). Sengupta expresses himself in the same terms when remarking, '[a] few, indeed, believe that it is no more than old wine in new bottles; a mere rehash of the ideas of market segmentation and product differentiation' (2007: 16). And he resorts precisely to Maggard, according to whom, '[t]he author does not agree with those who would proclaim positioning like something new and revolutionary in marketing strategy' (1976: 66). Certainly, positioning has very clearly been influenced by previous theories, which means that it is not very novel conceptually speaking. At any rate, its worth would lie in the application of cognitive sciences in its formulation, although it is not clear that Trout and Ries were the first to do so (moreover, nor has it been demonstrated that they were fully aware that they were using such psychological mechanisms, because until subsequent works like *Repositioning* recourse was not strictly had to theories applying cognitive psychology to communication). This suggests that what is valuable is not the concept per se, but its very name, 'positioning'. It is therefore a 'word' that has sparked the marketing revolution, rather than a theoretical reflection and its subsequent application, as would be expected. What makes matters worse is that some researchers see Reeves as the promoter of the term in question (Keller 1998: 116–17; Sengupta 2007: 16–17). We will now examine this issue.

7.5. *The USP as the forerunner of positioning*

To associate 'positioning' with 'promise' is not at all uncommon in marketing literature. Quite to the contrary, it is fairly normal: 'A good positioning is a credible promise of value delivered in ways that distinguish your brand from others. It is a concise statement that summarizes your brand's commitment, or promise, to customers' (Davis 2002: 110). Well then, it should be recalled that for Reeves the USP is that basic promise that any advertisement should make. As can be seen, the concept of positioning is essentially indebted to this premise of his: to highlight only differentiating attributes. However, this conceptual coincidence is but the first of a series of more profound and closer links, if possible, between both concepts.

First, the influential 'mind/computer' cognitive metaphor that Trout and Ries popularized to such a great extent is addressed in a suspiciously similar manner in Reeves's *Reality in Advertising*. It is true that the Madison Avenue adman, deeply influenced by current fads, was a firm believer in conduction psychology and everything associating a 'stimulus' – the USP – with a 'response' – the purchase. Nonetheless, this very well-known stance of Reeves's appears to be closer to the commercial arguments that he deployed with his clients than to judicious readings of the theories of Watson or Pavlov. Proof of this is that, in his book, Reeves makes – intuitively, we assume – many references to cognitive psychology. These range from rather timid statements – 'we are discussing penetration – which may be defined as "what it is possible for the consumer to carry in his head". For most people do not rush right out and buy' (1961: 36); 'our competitors' penetration is moving down – as we seize a larger and larger share the consumer's brain box' (1961: 42). 'You will discover the reason for the short life expectancy of advertising, which we discussed a little while back. You will begin to see the tremendous difficulty of owning a bit of space in the box' (1961: 39) – to others akin to advertising maxims – '[t]he U.S.P. almost lifts itself out of the ruck and wings its way to some corner of the mind' (1961: 52). As with Trout and Ries years later, Reeves (1961: 27) theorizes about information saturation:

> We must keep in mind that $43,000,000,000 a year is being spent for penetration. This is the rather staggering sum of $117,000,000 a day, spent in a desperate attempt to buy brands a bit of space in the memory box of the consumer. He is a

beleaguered consumer, a confused consumer, battered by television, assailed by print, assaulted by radio, bewildered by posters. It is very difficult to get him to remember, and he is very prone, indeed, to forget.

And, as in the last sentence of the aforementioned passage, he stresses the limited capacity of the public's memory: 'The public has an appallingly ephemeral memory; penetration, bought and paid for with millions and millions of dollars, can drift away like morning fog' (Reeves 1961: 25). As can be observed, the theoretical basis and backbone of 'positioning' coincides exactly with the theories put forward by Reeves, who also talked about information saturation, the 'mind/computer' metaphor and the limited capacity of an individual's memory. Meyers (1984: 29) is an author who expresses this reality in a curious fashion:

> He [Reeves] believed that every person's mind was divided into a series of purchasing receptacles marked 'soap', 'headache remedies', 'toothpaste', 'cigarettes', and so on. There is only so much room in each container, he said, so the advertiser must be certain that his sales message is crammed into the right space.

However, it would be Reeves (1961: 38–39) himself who most clearly expressed his point of view in this respect:

> For students of advertising are likely to assume that penetration is an expanding universe, and that, as more and more advertisers come splashing into the market, people put more and more into their heads. This is not true. There is a finite limit to what a consumer can remember about 30,000 advertised brands. He cannot remember all the advertising he reads, any more than he can memorize the *Encyclopaedia Britannica* [...] It is as though he carries a small box in his head for a given product category. This box is limited either by his inability to remember or his lack of interest. It is filled with miscellaneous data, and, when a new campaign forces in more, some data are forced out, and the box spills over [...] You will discover that the limits of his knowledge, or interest, are very finite indeed.

Second, there is another important point of convergence between the USP and positioning, which is rooted in the purported longevity of both philosophies. As cited above, Trout and Ries assert that 'positioning is a concept that is cumulative and of a long-range nature, and thus the most successful companies rarely change their positioning' (cf. Ries and Trout 2001: 197). While, years before, Reeves (1961: 42) held,

Being aware that there is 'no more room in the box', we have begun to sharpen our copy, to gather its energies together into that tight coil, for higher penetration. Aware, too, of the volatile nature of penetration – its almost vapor-like quality – we have stopped changing campaigns. Having discovered that a long-range campaign is worth a whole cluster of short-range ones, we are striving now for a campaign that can run for years, for we know that a good campaign will not wear itself out.

Third, notwithstanding the fact that Trout and Ries have experienced the many advertising models and mechanisms deriving from personality branding, as with Reeves they are committed to product branding, namely, proclaiming the attributes, uses, solutions or advantages of a specific product and converting them into the pivotal element of positioning. But this maxim is clearly none other than the persuasive functioning of the USP. Despite the relevance of the image when positioning first saw the light of day, like Reeves twenty years before them – albeit at a time when the technical control of the image was very limited – Trout and Ries became resolutely committed to the verbal at the expense of the visual. In their view, the mind works by hearing, not by sight. Every successful positioning program studied has been oriented towards the verbal, not the visual (cf. Ries and Trout 2001b: 113). We do not believe that it is necessary to cite Reeves to demonstrate this. As a matter of fact, as has been seen in Chapter 2 of this book, *Reality in Advertising* is an argument against image theory and brand image, or as the guru of Madison Avenue called them disdainfully, 'the window dressers'.

At this stage, there should be no doubt that Reeves's oeuvre had a powerful influence on the postulates of Trout and Ries. They did not only resort to the USP, even going so far as to cite Reeves himself to define what they called 'the product era' in one of their seminal articles in the 'The positioning era cometh' (1972a) series. It is more than significant that in his *Differentiate or Die* the former, the self-confessed father of the concept, continually resorts to Reeves's USP – devoting more than two chapters to the famous adman, in which he cites his theories and acknowledges the original source – fully endorsing everything he says – if some of the precepts were already controversial in the 1950s, they are frankly moot in the twenty-first century.[18] However, besides this more or less solid evidence of a conceptual nature, the ultimate confirmation of the loan can be found in the theories of some researchers who are of the opinion that Trout and Ries plagiarized Reeves. This critical movement is partly based on the following statement that Joe Sacco attributed to Reeves: 'Positioning is the art of selecting out of a number of unique selling propositions the one which will get you maximum sales' (1986: 13). Apparently, this statement appears in an alleged lost chapter of *Reality in Advertising*, which has not been included in its many reeditions. This is the reason why

127

it has not become so well-established in the advertising industry as other ideas devised by Reeves. According to Sengupta (2007: 15),

> These words are taken from what is described as the 'lost chapter' of *Reality in Advertising*, the famous book written by Reeves, which was reissued but without the 'lost chapter'. 'Positioning, because it is imprecise (he went on to write), can be a dangerous buzzword. Too often, it is pseudo-marketing, seeking to seize a segment of the market which exists only in the eye of the beholder.'

Beyond these conjectures and wrangling over paternity, the sole difference between both formulas, in our opinion, is that positioning is a broader and slightly more complex concept for a basic reason. For, unlike the USP, it does not refer to a specific type of advertisement but to the brand. The idea of positioning brands, instead of selling products, via advertisements is one of Trout and Ries's valuable contributions. As already noted, it is simplistic and its cognitive theoretical basis is more the product of intuition than of empirical research or the theoretical reflections of the human mind. Nonetheless, the fact remains that it is one of the few strategic advertising mechanisms with a cognitive basis that has had professional and academic repercussions. In fact, it is one of the last great contributions to advertising strategy and, therefore, worthy of being included in this book.

8

Douglas Holt's Iconic Brands: When Cognitive Psychology and Motivation Research Converge

8.1. Theoretical bases of iconic brands: The birth of cultural branding

Of the different approaches that have been taken to brand management since the advent of cultural branding[1] the one proposed by Douglas B. Holt has had the greatest impact on the literature. He has described his approach in numerous academic papers – 'Conceptualizing the social patterning of consumption in postmodernity', 'Does cultural capital structure American consumption?', and 'Why do brands cause trouble?' published in the *Journal of Consumer Research* in 1997, 1998 and 2002 respectively, and 'Toward a sociology of branding' appearing in the *Journal of Consumer Culture* in 2006 – professional articles – 'What becomes an icon most?' and 'How global brands compete', both published in *Harvard Business Review* in 2003 and 2004, respectively – and books – *The Consumer Society Reader* (2000) and *Cultural Strategy: Using Innovative Ideologies to Build Breakthrough Brands* (2010). But the work that catapulted the Oxford professor of marketing to fame was *How Brands Become Icons: The Principles of Cultural Branding*, published by Harvard Business School Press in 2004. Holt comprehensively develops his cultural branding theory in this book, a now seminal work that has served as a guide for other researchers in the field of cultural branding, in particular, and has influenced many other experts in brand management, in general.

Notwithstanding the fact that it was first published at the beginning of new millennium, encyclopaedic books on brand management resort to his theory to exemplify the basic mechanisms of cultural branding. This is the case of Heding et al., who borrow Holt's methodology to develop 'the cultural brand management process' (cf. Heding et al. 2009: 216). Likewise, scholarly works like Torelli et al.'s 'Cultural symbolism of brands', and O'Guinn and Muniz's 'Toward a sociological model of brands', exploit the professor's research to refer to the inner workings of cultural branding. Torelli et al. (2010: 116) adopt his definition of iconic brand:

Holt (2004) defines an iconic brand as a consumer brand that carries consensus expressions of particular values held dear by some members of a society. Iconic brands carry a heavy symbolic load for consumers, who frequently rely on them to communicate to others who they are or aspire to be. For these brands to become culturally influential their symbolic meanings should be widely and durably distributed in the culture.

They also assume his conception of self-concept: 'As stated by Holt (2004), "consumers flock to brands that embody the ideals they admire, brands that help them express who they want to be"' (Torelli et al. 2010: 123). For their part, O'Guinn and Muniz – also the creators of brand community, namely, the more implicative and participatory theory of the user in the framework of brand management – also resort to Holt to introduce their theoretical frame (cf. O'Guinn and Muniz 2010: 134).

All considered, the main reason why we have chosen iconic brands to conclude this book has to do with their professional application, as with the rest of the strategic advertising mechanisms that have been discussed in these pages. By our reckoning, iconic brands – as an optimum cultural branding methodology – have made their way into the industry, consolidating their position as a relatively established method of creation in the advertising world. They have proliferated to such an extent that some advertising agencies have adopted culture-based approaches to develop their working methodologies. To offer a good example, according to the 'transformation sessions' of VCCP Partnership (London), the agency's working methodology includes the concept of 'populate culture' to refer to the exploitation of culture or to its population with brand content; a methodology guiding many of the projects that the multinational group has developed to date. VCCP Spain, the agency's delegation in Madrid, applied cultural approaches to conceive 'Caja de ahorros mi colchón',[2] one of the campaigns picking up the largest number of awards at the 2013 Cannes Lions International Festival of Creativity. This ad, created for the small mattress brand DeS'S, leveraged the cultural tension generated by the economic crisis to launch the first mattress to incorporate a safe. This distinctly cultural campaign, which received news coverage in 74 countries, resulted in 8 million earned media impressions and greatly boosted the company's sales.

As already noted, it is very commonplace for advertising agencies to assume cultural principles, and, more specifically, those bequeathed by Holt, as a strategic or technical philosophy for generating ideas. Paradoxically, despite the proliferation of the iconic brand mechanism in the advertising industry, its creator Holt is not a top marketing executive of a corporate advertiser investing huge sums in advertising. Nor does he work for a multinational advertising agency that needs to reinvent its methodology to engage new clients. Quite to the contrary, Holt hails from academia. He is a scholar who has managed to consolidate a theoretical construct as the seed – when not the basis – of professional work in such a pragmatic discipline as advertising. And his conception of iconic brands has had a notable impact on the advertising market. Unlike what tends to occur most of the time, as can observed in the different strategic advertising mechanisms described in this book – mechanisms from different periods and places – in which academia is always one step behind the profession, in this case theoretical research has permeated the industry to develop or perfect a specific working methodology: all of which underscores the fact that what is known as 'knowledge transfer' in academic circles is sometimes viable in the social sciences. All in all, the success of his conception has allowed the university professor to pursue a career as a brand consultant.

Holt's transition from academia to consultancy is not surprising when his proposal is assessed objectively – the purpose of this chapter. Iconic brands unquestionably represent a very advanced model of brand management with a huge potential for generating brand content and, therefore, a very succulent proposal for advertisers. However, it also retains most of the arsenal of traditional brand management, such as its evident commitment to advertising, which makes it even more appealing, if possible, as a methodology – owing to its constrained newness. When compared with other contemporary approaches, such as its rational or community counterparts, much more participatory and consumer-centric – and less controlled by brand managers – Holt's cultural perspective appears to be quite a bit more conservative – communication content, albeit collective, is under the firm control of companies. As a matter of fact, the most developed models of the consumer branding paradigm in which cultural branding is framed (Fernández Gómez 2013) normally transcend a strictly advertising reality, involving hybrid approaches in which co-creation is commonplace. In light of the much more complex new markets in which advertising plays a different – and sometimes marginal – role with respect to previous conceptions and stages, being occasionally dependent on other communication tools, the iconic brand model maintains the advertising status quo in something as complicated and controversial as investment in communication and the generation of brand content. Also, there is the pull that if a culture-based campaign is a success, it will lead to a good dose of publicity in the shape of the so-called 'earned media impressions'.

For this reason, we could say that this is the most recent strategic mechanism of a purely advertising kind – the new consumer branding approaches make hybrid interpretations of communication tools, which in rare cases are strictly of the advertising kind, as already observed. Holt borrows an idea that has been amply elaborated on in motivation research – which was developed in parallel by symbolic interactionism, before being perfected in the field of consumption sociology (Fernández Gómez and Gordillo 2020) – to wit, self-concept. This is the concept that we all have of ourselves and which brands help to complete with the meanings that they convey. Accordingly, the Oxford professor turned consultant explains,

> Cultural branding applies particularly to categories in which people tend to value products as a means of self-expression, such as clothing, home, décor, beauty, leisure, entertainment, automotive, food, and beverage. Marketers usually refer to these categories as lifestyle, image, badge, or ego-expressive products.
>
> (Holt 2004: 5)

The fact that firms attempt to have a meaning for consumers is linked to the need for brand semantics comprising psychological values and the meanings associated with them; semantics that are largely developed by advertising through its storytelling nature. Consequently, Holt, as with the motivationalists, also considers advertising as the best storyteller: 'Most iconic brands have been built through the mass media, usually with television advertising' (Holt 2004: 7). Indeed, Holt's iconic brand theory involves the generation of a brand discourse in which advertising is capital when creating identity myths that respond to existing tensions.

8.2. The iconic brand concept

The basis of Holt's theory is what he calls the 'culture icon', a concept that he defines in the following way:

> [A] cultural icon as a person or thing regarded as a representative symbol, especially of a culture or a movement; a person or an institution considered worthy of admiration or respect [...] cultural icons are exemplary symbols that people accept as a shorthand to represent important ideas. The crux of iconicity is that the person or the thing is widely regarded as the most compelling symbol of a set of ideas or values that a society deems important.
>
> (Holt 2004: 1)

For Holt, an icon is an element that is regarded as a representative symbol in relation to something, particularly one of a culture or movement, as already seen. Accordingly, the first idea of his strategic conception that should be highlighted is that an iconic brand is a symbol representing ideas that are relevant for the target audience. In this context, the concept of cultural icon establishes conceptual relationships with dimensions that we have had the opportunity to examine in previous chapters, like deep psychology, for according to Testa et al. (2017: 1491), '[i]cons represent sets of meanings embedded in the collective unconscious of different groups and are shortcuts to feelings, myths, and values.'

From Holt's perspective, the concept of icon can be typologically varied. We have already explained in *Branding Cultural* (2019) that cultural icons can be real people (like, for instance, the ex-US president Ronald Reagan, who ended up symbolizing the quintessence of conservative ideas for the right in the United States) or fictional characters (e.g. Superman, who can be interpreted as an icon of truth, justice and the American way of life). There are also companies, organizations and institutions that iconically represent relevant ideas for the public (as is the case of the non-governmental organization Greenpeace, a global symbol of the ecologist movement). And the same also applies to certain places (the French capital Paris is doubtless a cultural icon representing the city of love) and even specific objects – Holt (2004: 1) employs, among others, the example of the iconic character of Coca-Cola during the Second World War. Icons can be surpassed and replaced by other very similar ones in the same field, as occurs with pop stars who are eclipsed by other more novel ones, but they can also prevail over time, as is the case with the Eiffel Tower (cf. Testa et al. 2017: 1492). To his mind, individuals strongly identify with cultural icons, and these frequently become symbols that form part of their daily lives. Thus, he contends that icons serve as fundamental guides for society in the shape of anchors of meanings, which continually refer to entertainment, leisure, journalism, the arts and the like (cf. Holt 2004: 1).

After defining the notion of 'icon' as Holt understands it, we will now dwell on how the concept is applied to commercial brands. It is evident that, in view of the definition of 'icon' established here, the idea of a cultural icon is as old as civilization itself; its connection with brand management lies in the fact that this concept currently forms part of the business of cultural industries and, in the main, consumer society: 'The market gravitates to produce what people value most. Today, the culture industries – such as films, music, television, journalism, magazines, sports, books, advertising, and public relations – are bent on cultivating and monetizing these icons' (Holt 2004: 2).

These icons are represented through stories. In Holt's opinion, until the story has not left a mark on consumers, it does not attain iconic status and become a basic symbol: 'What sticks are stories that affect how people think about themselves in the world' (Holt 2004: 35). In this connection, as in other cultural branding approaches – an idea recuperated from mechanisms pertaining to personality branding, that is, which operate in an emotional context – the brand story becomes yet again the fundamental element. In the words of Holt (2004: 3),

A brand emerges as various authors tell stories that involve the brand [...] Brand stories have plots and characters, and they rely heavily on metaphor to communicate and to spur our imagination. As these stories collide in everyday social life, conventions eventually form. Sometimes a single common story emerges as a consensus view. Most often, though, several different stories circulate widely in society. A brand emerges when these collective understandings become firmly established.

As in most of the European advertising tradition, Holt's approach analyses the brand as a semiotic device that moves through the story, to wit, a narrator with cultural meaning and an important factor in the intricate network of cultural meanings that are useful for the collective identity projects of consumers. Thus, brands are vehicles of meaning and creators of myths: narratives that will be successful in terms of the affinity of consumers. Askegaard holds that brands form new consumers, who are aware of the symbolic universe with which they provide them, and help to construct their identity (2006: 100). For Holt, this is a key notion. His approach understands that consumers are highly committed to the universe projected by brands – a universe of which they are fully aware and which they understand, and in which they even participate, according to relational branding theories. Thus, he talks about the 'merchant man' who is the result of the feedback between brands and consumers. In his view, both mechanisms derive from meanings. These meanings become part of an individual's self-esteem, as we have seen when analysing the strategic advertising mechanisms framed in the context of personality branding, a social distinction that generates similarities and differences between people. Indeed, from the anthropological perspective of these new approaches, self-concept evolves. In the words of Holt (2004: 4),

> Customers value some products as much for what they symbolize as for what they do [...] Consumers flock to brands that embody the ideas they admire, brands that help them express who they want to be. The most successful of these brands become iconic brands.

From the point of view of brand management, the value of an iconic brand is established when its associations become unquestionably social. Its value lies in the fact that it represents collective identities and allows consumers to express what they want to be (cf. 2004: 4–6). As Torelli et al. (cf. 2010: 115) interpret them, iconic brands contain consensual expressions of the values of certain members of society and '[i]t is precisely this shared understanding of the symbolic meaning of an iconic brand that facilitates the communication of ideals and aspirations to others through brand usage or consumptions' (2010: 115–16). Icons are, in effect, of a collective and participatory nature.

In this context, the interest of Holt's theory resides in the fact that it brings to light that many of the most valuable brands have been developed according to principles akin to those of cultural icons. In other words, iconic brands would act according to the same principles governing the symbolic character and cultural relevance of political leaders, fictional characters, social organizations and so on. Consequently, we could claim that this is the branding approach that, in the commercial field, mimics mechanisms that operate in other cultural spheres. So, it would seem natural to assert that Holt's cultural branding would be the set of principles that facilitate the transformation of a brand into a cultural icon, that is, an iconic brand. In this task, and coupled with other media discourses like journalism (cf. Holt 2006: 358), advertising occupies a preeminent place as a crucial tool for generating the type of value that converts a brand into an icon. As a matter of fact, Holt himself observes that brands usually resort to advertisements to create myths (cf. 2003). This is in keeping with the relevance that advertising has in marketing communication and for constructing brand stories with an iconic vocation (cf. Fernández Gómez 2013: 158). The principles underpinning the construction of an iconic brand will now be examined.

8.3. *Principles underpinning the construction of iconic brands*

Holt's theoretical proposal – comprehensively analysed in previous studies (Fernández Gómez 2013; Fernández Gómez et al. 2019) – can be summarized in the following way: on the basis of the aforementioned definition of cultural icons, an iconic brand is basically understood as 'an identity brand that approaches the identity value of a cultural icon' (Holt 2004: 11). Torelli et al. (2010: 116), who assume this conception, propose three characteristics of an iconic brand:

> (1) It symbolizes culturally relevant values, needs, and aspirations; (2) it is connected to diverse elements of cultural knowledge including values and other cultural icons; and (3) incidental exposure to an iconic brand can bring to mind its attendant cultural meanings.

We will now offer a detailed description of the principles underpinning the construction of an iconic brand.[3]

Identifying social tension. The first principle of cultural branding does not imply any communication or advertising action, but research. The conceptual key to Holt's approach – moreover, the why and wherefore of the functioning of an iconic brand – resides in the fact that a brand that has achieved iconic status is aimed at the collective anxieties and desires of a nation; social tensions that, in addition, are not ephemeral, but tend to last for years. Those social tensions are felt by the populace as a contradiction between their own lives, on the one hand,

and the ideas predominating in society, on the other. In plain English, it is a contradiction between ideology and individual experience, which gives rise to anxieties and desires – in this sense, those anxieties and desires are a result of national ideologies (cf. Holt 2003). Thus, the first step towards designing a strategy is to determine what Holt (cf. 2016: 46) calls 'cultural orthodoxy', namely, the predominant social conventions that cause tensions, anxieties and desires in culture. An idea that connects with Maslow's hierarchy of needs theory, one could say that an iconic brand also functions as a 'psychologically complex social benchmark', and that its appeal has nothing to do with the constituent elements of that theory, but with social needs.

In any case, what is important is that the design of an iconic brand should start with research on the society and culture in which it is to be introduced, with a view to discovering that social tension which is supposed to be the raison d'être of its construction. Studying the culture revolving around a brand from a sociological approach, paying attention to the prevailing ideology, becoming familiar with the cultural history of a nation, considering the main trends in the social psychology of a people, etc., form the knowledge base essential for identifying a social tension. Methodologically speaking, this knowledge is not attained employing techniques such as focus groups, ethnography or trend reports, but through the approaches taken by cultural historians, sociologists and literary critics to the phenomenon of ideology – how it develops and dissipates, the contradictions to which it gives rise and how it is culturally addressed.

On the other hand, the fact that the situation of nations, societies and cultures are studied as a whole has an important strategic implication: iconic brands are necessarily aimed at a mass audience (cf. Holt 2003); 'a large group of people – often a nation – ', according to Testa et al. (2017: 1492). On this point, it is interesting that Holt asserts that traditional segmentation models are insufficient for identifying the ideological response of a brand (cf. Holt 2016: 50), and that he draws parallels between social tension and collective desire, insofar as they are concepts that reveal the psychoanalytic (when not directly motivational) roots of cultural branding.

The identity myth. Once the culturally inspired strategy has identified a social tension and collective desires, it is necessary for the brand to generate a semiotic and narrative response to that tension. This response is the identity myth, a symbolic fiction that addresses, relaxes and even 'repairs' that social tension – it is no coincidence that, in this context, Holt recognizes that myths play a conservative political role, 'smoothing over contradictions and challenges to ideology' (2006: 360). The contradictions between the promises of the official ideology and individual life experiences generate intense anxieties, resulting in the demand for a myth that assuages them. In other words, social disruptions make cultural orthodoxy lose steam, thus encouraging consumers to look for alternatives (cf. Holt 2016: 47). Just as a cultural icon is a symbol that *represents* collective ideas, iconic brands should symbolically *represent* social anxieties – as Holt notes, 'the name of the game is symbolism: The strategic focus is on what the brand stands for, not how the brand performs' (2003). In other words, this representation can be understood as 'the matching process, i.e. the alignment of the brand with emerging sociocultural trends' (Testa et al. 2017: 1493). So, by constructing an identity myth, a brand aligns itself with emerging cultural trends, thus responding to social tensions.

It is the identity myth that converts a brand into an icon, its substance: 'Icons are encapsulated myths', Holt (2003) remarks. On the basis of the observations of Testa et al. (cf. 2017: 1493), one could say that the identity myth is actually one of the fields of semantic content with which brand managers should provide a brand: the former comprises the abstract characteristics that define the culture in which brands operate; and the latter (equivalent to the identity myth) would be the novel ideological response that intends to resonate with consumers.

The identity myth is essentially a story, a narrative – in keeping with the power of stories in the advertising discourse described above. In point of fact, for Holt it is a question of storytelling:

> [I]cons come to represent a particular kind of story – an *identity myth* – that their consumers use to address identity desires and anxieties. Icons have extraordinary value because they carry a heavy symbolic load for their most enthusiastic consumers. Icons perform the particular myth society especially needs at a given historical moment, and they perform it charismatically.
>
> (2004: 2, original emphasis)

It is perhaps not by chance that the ideological proposal of a politician like Reagan, regarded as a cultural icon of conservatism, was occasionally based on narratives, on storytelling: 'By telling real or invented, true or exaggerated stories, he managed to humanize abstract problems, personify political issues in the lives of "ordinary" citizens' (Martín Salgado 2002: 115). Those brands attaining the level of cultural icons do the same.

It is important to note that the identity myth generated by the market to relax or dissipate a social tension does not have to be unique, inasmuch as different brands can offer symbolic solutions to the same cultural contradiction. For instance, in the United States during the 1950s and 1960s, and owing to the suburban culture, the integration of the individual into a planned corporate life and the conformism prevailing at the time, the 'myth markets', in the words of Holt, 'soon sprang up – using the Western frontier, the Beats' bohemia, and the hillbilly backwater – to provide salves for these tensions' (2003).

Also in relation to the identity myth, it is worth stressing that this does not imply a pure conceptual abstraction. The myth of an iconic brand would not lie, following Greimas, in the axiological dimension, but in narrative and discourse. This property can be seen in the case of the Mexican beer brand Corona in the United States. In response to the ongoing changes in the US labour market, which was becoming increasingly more competitive and stressful, Corona proposed the idea of *doing absolutely nothing* and chilling out on the beach as a counterbalance to this situation: 'Unplugged. Find your beach', as one of the brand's graphic advertisements read – the beach scene would evidently form the core of Corona's identity myth. This core can be clearly appreciated in Corona's groundbreaking spot 'Pager', in which a couple are relaxing on a beach. When the man's pager sounds, he chucks it into the sea. The ad's tagline, 'Miles Away from the Ordinary' (cited in Holt 2004: 18), also evinces the type of narrative that Corona pursues with its identity myth and the reaction to a negative situation. This case indicates that it is necessary to avoid an excessive conceptual abstraction in the design of an identity myth, for the value of a brand is to be found in 'the particular cultural contents of the brand's myth and the particular expression of these contents in the communication. For Corona, the brand exists in the Mexican beach and its "nothing's happening" style of advertising' (Holt 2004: 36), instead of the abstract concept of 'relaxing'. In light of Holt's considerations, Corona's identity myth actually resides in the type of story that the brand tells (at a narrative level) and in empirical indicators (at a discursive level) such as the characters or the setting. In sum, he is of the opinion that brand semantics should essentially be sought in discourse.

The narrative format possessed by an identity myth leads to another concept relating to the construction of iconic brands. According to Holt, consumers appreciate the narratives of brands for their *identity value*: brand stories are valuable for constructing the identity of consumers, expressing what they want to be (cf. 2004: 3–4). This idea is important because it reveals that an identity myth should not only respond to a cultural tension, but should also offer something to mitigate its psychological effects. That 'something' is the *identity value* that the myth's narrative provides: a representation of what consumers want to be. This is where the idea that a brand that has achieved iconic status and which has known how to reflect the collective desires of a nation, that is, a collective's identity value, makes sense. In short, the most successful brands with identity value become iconic brands.

In view of the foregoing, the fundamental concepts explaining how an iconic brand operates are shown in Figure 8.1.

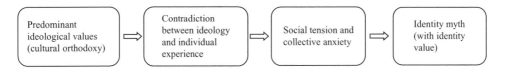

FIGURE 8.1: Operationalization of iconic brands. Source: Fernández Gómez et al. (2019).

It is worth noting that the concept of 'myth' employed by Holt does not correspond to the meaning of 'myth' associated with the pool of cultural symbols present in the Jungian or Campbellian monomyth, which is linked to other cultural branding models like the one developed by Mark and Pearson in *The Hero and the Outlaw: Building Extraordinary Brands Through the Power of Archetypes* (2001). As with the classical myths, Holt's idea of myth is akin to storytelling, the narrative format, but lacks their classical, timeless meaning. In iconic brand theory, the mythical is rather understood as a sort of story of (not necessarily fantastic) legitimization that acquires contextual meaning for a particular culture at a specific moment, acting like a guide; for instance, Nike's myth of personal achievement through perseverance (cf. Holt 2003), which would naturally dovetail with the values of contemporary American society. In the words of Holt: 'Simple stories with compelling characters and resonant plots, myths help us make sense of the world' (2003: n.pag.).

Ritual experience. Another principle underpinning the construction of iconic brands establishes that the use of a product permits consumers to experience *ritually* their identity myths. It should be noted that this reference to the ritual dimension yet again links Holt's theory to broader cultural branding issues; on this occasion, to the rite, a fundamental aspect of McCracken's (1988) Meaning-Transfer Model. At any rate, from this it can be inferred that the reception of an iconic brand should go beyond advertising and other marketing communication resources: consumers should become involved in actions that allow them to experience the meaning that an identity myth evokes. For example, the coffee brand Starbucks staged a corporate social responsibility action in New York, in which thousands of people exchanged their paper cups for reusable ones. If the concept of ethical consumption is understood as a symbolic response on the part of Starbucks to the anxiety generated by the possibility of an environmental disaster, the action of each individual citizen exchanging his or her paper cup can be understood as a way of experiencing the meaning of its identity myth, in this case the idea of contributing to environmental sustainability – as can be seen in a video of this action of Starbucks' on YouTube: 'One person switching can save trees [...] together, we can save forests' (cf. eccesignu 2010: n.pag.).

Creation of worlds. Or, more specifically, the creation of *populist worlds*, according to Holt. The term 'populist', in this context, has little to do with its current pejorative uses in politics, being conceptually related instead to the idea of movements of subaltern social sectors far removed from the political stage, which have emerged as a result of the legitimacy crisis of the traditional liberal order and which defend large-scale economic interventionism and a popular nationalist discourse (Gallego 2016: 262–63). In iconic brand theory, populist worlds are rather places where actions are guided by values. In other words, they are authentic worlds governed by moral principles and not by money or power. Furthermore, they are worlds of rebellious and marginal ideals. Holt has even gone so far as to say, '[t]he most successful icons rely on an intimate and credible relationship with a rebel world' (2003: n.pag.). So, given that populist worlds provide the cultural materials for constructing identity myths (cf. Holt 2004: 11), those that are generated by brands should draw inspiration from marginal ideological and cultural aspects, while rejecting mainstream ones: 'To assemble a credible populist challenge to the national ideology, iconic brands draw on people who actually live according to alternative ideals' (Holt 2003: n.pag.). Or, as the author would remark some years later, '[i]n cultural branding, inverting marginal ideologies is one of the tricks of the trade' (Holt 2016: 46).

It is therefore paradoxical that, albeit only in the discursive and communication dimensions, these brands reject the values of the capitalist world in which they exist and prosper (money and power), designing instead rebellious worlds where ambition, among other things, is not the rule. This perhaps explains the idea that identity myths relax social tension and anxieties in *imaginary* worlds (cf. Holt 2004: 8). The populist universe created by iconic brands is fictional, an idealized moral and ideological counterweight that acts as a sort of placebo in the face of the system's real contradictions.

An example of the authenticity of popular worlds can be found in Snapple, an iconic American tea and juice brand. At the beginning of the 1990s, Snapple created an amateur anti-corporatism identity myth. This myth was based on the rejection of conventional marketing in response to the fact that the neo-liberal revolution of President Reagan, which had got underway in the previous decade, was only benefitting the corporate elites. Thus, in response to the social tension resulting from the failure to keep the ideological promises of Reaganomics – namely, the orthodox ideas of popular capitalism and generalized enrichment, versus the real benefit of a few – Snapple created an identity myth in which the 'losers', who had remained on the sidelines of the dominant yuppie culture of the 1980s, lived in an original populist world that had nothing to do with the demands and professionalism of the standard corporate world, with some of its spots in the 1990s being characterized by a completely amateur aesthetic (cf. wtcvidman 2009; MrClassicAds1990s 2011).

Cultural avant-garde. Directly related to the idea that iconic brands should adopt a rebellious discourse (cf. Holt 2003), the principle of the cultural avant-garde blatantly contradicts the notion that advertising is a discourse essentially one step behind the predominant cultural trends surrounding it, ads thus tending to reflect mainstream elements with little innovation. Accordingly, Lomas (cf. 1996: 27) speaks in terms of *imitation* to refer to the way in which advertising borrows things from cinema, art and journalism, while, citing Baudrillard, decrying that simplifying perspective of the advertising discourse. It is precisely the French sociologist who, from this critical angle, insists most on advertising as 'a simplified form of operating', accusing it of being 'superficial [...] The lowest possible form of the power of signs [...] in which all singular content is annulled' (Baudrillard 1989: 5). Unlike homogenizing trends of this sort, the advertising of an iconic brand should be an avant-garde discourse of cultural change: 'Unlike conventional branding, icons don't mimic pop culture; they lead it' (Holt 2003). In line with the rebellious and marginal inspiration of populist worlds, Holt describes how brands and media outlets disseminate non-mainstream ideas as part of their avant-garde cultural role: 'Historically, cultural innovation flowed from the margins of society – from fringe groups, social movements, and artistic circles that challenged mainstream norms and conventions. Companies and the mass media acted as intermediaries, diffusing these new ideas into the mass market' (2016: 42–43). Yet, the fact that an iconic brand uses avant-garde ideas does not imply that it creates an identity myth:

> Iconic brands rarely rework significantly existing symbolism. Cultural products other than brands – including films, television programs, politicians, sport teams, and novels – do the ideological heavy lifting in modern culture, reconstructing myths to pioneer emerging ideals, creating what I term myth markets. Brand marketing laps up what these other media produce.
>
> (Holt 2006: 374)

The leading role of brands is therefore to offer a different worldview: 'Iconic brands function like cultural activists, encouraging people to think differently about themselves' (Holt 2004: 9). After all, it is only to be expected that an iconic brand should be obliged to communicate a world-view differing from that of orthodox culture: given that social tension is a result of the rifts and contradictions deriving from cultural orthodoxy, it would be absurd for an iconic brand to react to it by yet again reflecting elements from that same culture. On the contrary, iconic brands should offer a new world-view or, at least, a discourse differing from cultural orthodoxy. In this context, it is interesting that Holt (cf. 2003) has remarked that iconic brands obtain 'political authority' over their audiences, owing to the way in which their identity myths have tackled ideological contradictions; an authority that allows them, at a given moment, to reformulate their myths in different circumstances.

It is important to observe that, in light of Holt's writings, the cultural innovation or avant-garde role played by brands does not always have to revolve around the discovery of visions of new worlds; in fact, the cultural avant-garde role can paradoxically consist of recuperating an ideological stance from the past. This is the case with the 'rugged individualist' ideology typical of American Wild West culture. This individualism was recuperated by the bourbon brand Jack Daniel's in response to the crisis of masculinity in the United States and to the anxieties arising from the Cold War and the threat of nuclear war; anxieties that were countered by 'the gunslinging rugged individualist of the Old West, who, in the American mythos, had helped forge the country's success' (Holt 2016: 46). With the popularity of westerns as a frame pointing to the potential of this cultural change, Jack Daniel's bourbon was a suitable symbol for those Americans who wanted to relive the frontier myth through an imaginary all but copied from the nineteenth century, rapidly becoming an aspirational product among urban upper-middle-class men (cf. Holt 2016: 46).

Influential communication. The iconic character of certain brands derives from a number of advertising coups, instead of from an avalanche of ads – 'People forget the vast majority of ads within weeks after they are broadcast', Holt (2004: 10) remarks. The construction of an identity myth is therefore more a question of quality than quantity: to come up with an advertising action that brilliantly defines the identity myth of a brand. Indeed, that brand can create a myth on the basis of a sole ad that is sufficiently striking and influential. With 'Hilltop', one of the most important spots in the history of advertising, Coca-Cola created an identity myth of peace and symbolic reunification as a solution to the social situation in a country wracked by civil rights and Vietnam War protests (Project ReBrief 2012); a myth 'that many Americans found useful as a symbolic resource to patch up their identities as citizens' (Holt 2004: 24). This perspective giving priority to qualitative aspects and the value of impact contrasts with repetition-based mechanisms like the unique selling proposition (USP) or copy strategy – covered in the first chapters of this book – and those of a cognitive nature like positioning.

Effects. According to Holt, a high identity value has consequences for other aspects of brands, such as the perception of their quality or their association with certain benefits. In the words of the author, iconic brands 'enjoy intense customer loyalty and superior sales and profits, and garner loads of free media coverage'

(2016: 46). In reality, this idea is as much a principle underpinning the construction of an iconic brand as an assumption about its positive effects.

8.4. Critiques of iconic brands

Holt's theory and, by and large, cultural branding approaches, embrace theoretical influences and management models that distance them from previous consumer-centric approaches. It is precisely this melting pot of influences and theoretical bases that can be understood as both a positive and negative trait. It is obviously a very positive approach owing to its conceptual diversity and strength: the theoretical bedrock of cultural branding models provides important guarantees for brand analysis and management. However, that is where the problem actually lies: the fact that it has many aspects can be considered as negative because some brands and advertising agencies understand that, for them, it is difficult to implement or simply inapplicable. The approach's complexity and multifariousness would then be its main asset and, in turn, its Achilles' heel.

The description of the mechanism that has been offered here clearly points to this duality. On the one hand, the fundamental premises and resources that this brand management approach exploits convert it into a first-class theoretical and conceptual tool that undoubtedly enhances the intellectual level of branding work; and, on the other, cultural branding can become a demanding form of conceptual work for many advertising agencies and brand managers. For instance, for Heding et al., Holt is the inspirational driving force behind a branding model in which brand managers should have a multifaceted and multidisciplinary profile, so as to be able go back in time and understand the heritage of a brand. They should employ the working methods of genealogists, so as to able to turn back the clock and understand the heritage of a brand. They need to understand ideology as cultural historians do on the basis of economic, political and cultural changes. As with sociologists, they must also understand the social contradictions linked to the aforementioned changes, which will allow them to create powerful myths. And, lastly, they should have the ability to explore popular and literary culture and possess the sensitivity and empathy of writers, in order to be able to observe life more than participating it. Their 'sixth sense' will allow them to become acquainted with the deepest feelings of people (cf. Heding et al. 2009: 230). For all these reasons, the intellectual demands of cultural branding have prevented this strategic approach from becoming firmly established in advertising agencies, as already noted.

Beyond epistemological and applicability issues, the iconic brand mechanism has several weaknesses that should be taken into account. First, together with the potential diversity of things that can become icons, it is important to stress that not all cultural content is a cultural icon. To be a cultural icon, a person, organization, place and the like must have attained a privileged symbolic status and to have been converted into the summarized representation of a concept for a collective. In sum, culture pervades (practically) everything, but not all cultural elements become icons.

Emphasis should also be placed on the fact that, just as not all cultural elements attain an iconic status, obviously not all brands are icons – indeed, the term 'iconic brand' is only applied to a small number of commercial brands that have managed to incarnate relevant meanings for the public: Coca-Cola, Nike, Starbucks, Mountain Dew, Jack Daniel's, Lego, Nutella, Google, to name a few (cf. Holt 2006: 357; Testa et al. 2017: 1492). So as to attain that status, brands first have to identify a social tension that causes anxiety and to construct an adequate identity myth whose storytelling offers a pertinent response to that tension, and, most importantly, to possess a high identity value. In other words, it is possible that, even though a brand identifies a social tension, through its communication it is incapable of creating an imaginary world that assuages that anxiety and caters to collective desires. As has been examined above (Fernández Gómez et al. 2019), Holt's work focuses more on brand management than on highlighting its cultural dimension, in addition to resorting to McCracken's theory to understand the relationship between consumption and the cultural context (cf. Heding et al. 2009: 213). Holt (cf. 2004: 6) draws from the premise that culture takes the shape of a universe of meanings of which brands partake, admitting that products acquire meanings when they circulate among society, and that only when they are accepted collectively is it possible to speak of brand culture.

It is equally necessary to underscore that as brands have to identify tensions and anxieties at a specific moment, this implies a certain degree of short termism – after all, an identity myth should respond to what is currently happening in society. This is in opposition to theories such as that of positioning – which, as already seen, is an accumulative concept that should be maintained over time and, therefore, does not change – iconic brands are subject to change:

> Since these brands derive their value from how well their myth responds to tensions in the national culture, when there are tumultuous cultural shifts, the brand's myth loses steam. I call these shifts *cultural disruptions*. When disruptions hit, iconic brands must reinvent their myth.
>
> (Holt 2004: 23, original emphasis)

Thus, cultural disruptions deactivate identity myths, because they give rise to new social tensions that replace the collective desires that they have hitherto satisfied, for which reason they must necessarily be 'reinvented'. As a result, iconic brand theory is relatively contextual, for the validity of an identity myth depends on persistence and not on the ideological, sociological and other similar conditions in which it emerged.

Similarly, this need to use narrative and circumstantial values to generate brand communication also hinders the creation of axiological or core contents that persist over time and help to construct a solid brand image that empathizes with consumers. In effect, the iconic brand mechanism depending on the context and with limited objectives – due to the voluble nature of the semantic construction subordinated to that context – is not the best way of designing a robust and long-standing brand or to conceive brand values whose aim is to survive the passing of time.

It is true that a way of surpassing the contextualization imposed by iconic brands consists of renewing their identity myth from time to time with other different forms. Be that as it may, that possibility leads to another potential limitation of iconic brands, because they require a constant flow of brand discourses to keep their identity myths alive. On the contrary, they can lose their iconic dimension. For example, Snapple distanced itself from what was occurring in society and culture (cf. Testa et al. 2017: 1493); with its ad 'Handshake', to give just one example, Snapple has lost its myth of amateur anti-corporatism and its rejection of conventional marketing, substituting them with mere humour (cf. Tyree 2015). This leads to the phenomenon of 'de-iconization', which poses a threat to brands (cf. Testa et al. 2017: 1493) since they are deprived of their iconic qualities.

Beyond its more or less accepted application in the advertising industry, Holt's iconic brand concept has had a profound impact on marketing literature, becoming a source of inspiration for subsequent researchers. To our mind, its popularity does not lie so much in its conceptual novelty – in reality, there is hardly any difference between general cultural branding theory and the author's approach – as in its specific treatment and context. Jung's notion of 'collective imaginary', semiotics – Holt, for instance, recognizes that he is indebted to Roland Barthes (cf. 2006: 359) – and the Durandian archetype or mythocritique have been widely studied in Europe from different perspectives, for which reason his concept is not especially original at first sight. What Holt does is to employ it in an applied manner: as an exercise of management consultancy, he integrates humanistic baggage into the business discourse. Furthermore, just as it is true that European academic tradition has strived to inquire into these cultural realms for some time now – something that can be transposed to Latin American countries in recent years – so too is the fact that the American literature has not taken into account this cultural and humanistic perspective until recently. All considered, Holt's principal novel contribution is that his theory is one of the first cultural–humanistic approaches to American brand management.

Notes

Introduction

1. Thus, any decision that is adopted in the advertising planning process – creative decisions, for example, popularly called 'creative strategy' in the industry – any sort of tactical solution that is implemented – a media plan or a sponsorship package, called 'media strategy' and 'sponsorship strategy', respectively – or the use of a specific communication tool – the organization of an event or the launching of a social media campaign, 'PR strategy' and 'digital strategy' – is usually regarded as strategic. Even though all of these decisions inevitably participate in a strategy – and they can sometimes ostensibly modify or change its course as such – most of the time they are only adaptations of language, process stages or logical continuities of an instrumental nature. Namely, in theory strategy is central and unique. In our view, the reason behind this urge to call everything strategy is more commercial than theoretical. Specialized firms, subsidiary companies, purchasing networks and the media themselves talk about 'strategy' to embellish their offering, to give them intellectual force. Indeed, we could challenge anyone to find a company in the advertising industry that does not highlight its expertise in strategic planning (although in many cases the company in question does not even have experts on the subject or professionals who play that role with a minimum of proficiency).

2. Notwithstanding this, the General Law on Advertising (título II, artículo 3°, letra D) in Spain, to name just one country, continues to prohibit the use of these 'perverse' subliminal techniques.

3. In the chapter entitled 'The Freudian hoax' in *Reality in Advertising*, the advertising wizard Reeves casts doubt on the roots of motivational studies and quips about the 'hidden persuaders' theory:

> They believe that we are manipulating people, that we have sunk pipelines down to the pre-Oedipal wellsprings, that we are practicing some dark, mysterious necromancy [...] Well, if these men did not find hidden persuaders in their own countries [Reeves is alluding rather contemptuously to the 'hidden persuaders' and to the European psychologists who conceived these motivational theories], they will certainly not find them in this one [the United States]; for, as all top

advertising men know, such talk is the sheerest nonsense. It may serve to make a best seller of Vance Packard's book; and it may pick up, along the way, people who are prone to believe in the sensational; but there are no hidden persuaders.

(Reeves 1961: 70)

1. Procter & Gamble's Copy Strategy: When the Advertiser Made Products and Advertising

1. As will be seen further on, there is a lack of consensus on who was the first to devise a rationalist technique borrowing from Hopkins's reason-why copywriting concept.

2. There is some controversy over who invented the term; the critics agree that the notion is Stuart Mill's, but not its designation: 'While John Stuart Mill is generally identified as the creator of economic man, he never actually used this designation in his own writings. But the term did emerge in reaction to Mill's work' (Persky 1995: 222). There is a vast amount of economic–anthropological literature on the concept. For an interesting overview from an etymological point of view, see Persky (1995); Henrich et al. (2001), for an ambitious empirical analysis in 'In search of homo economicus: Behavioral experiments in 15 small-scale societies'; or Fox (2015), for a comparative and more informative perspective.

3. From Walter Dill Scott's *The Psychology of Advertising* (1908), a work that can be considered as the first to have rigorously combined psychology and advertising, to the oeuvre of J. B. Watson and, albeit from an opposing stance, W. McDougall – with his essential *Behaviorism* (1925) and *The Battle of Behaviorism* (1928) – through B. F. Skinner's prolific work, especially *About Behaviorism* (1974), most of the approaches that advertising has borrowed from psychology are of a behavioural nature. Based to a great extent on Pavlov's conditioned reflexes and trusting in a sort of effectiveness – to find the right stimuli to obtain a purchase response – this school has been widely adopted in the advertising industry and comprehensively theorized in academia.

4. The AIDA and DAGMAR models are perhaps the most popular among the many that have been proposed in the context of the so-called 'hierarchy-of-effects model'. Formulated in 1898 by Elmo Lewis, AIDA is the acronym for attention – sometimes awareness – interest, desire and action, that is, the four states that advertising messages should produce in consumers. For its part, DAGMAR is an acronym coinciding with the title of the book in which it appears, *Defining Advertising Goals for Measured Advertising Results* (1961), by Russell Colley. It is also important not to forget the three heavyweights of behaviourist-related advertising research: the psychologists Daniel Starch, the father of the recognition concept; George Gallup, the inventor of the recall concept and the creator of the first formal research department at the agency Young & Rubicam; and the physicist Alfred Politz, a staunch proponent of statistics – all of whom represent what could be called the adulthood of research.

5. The field of marketing and, by extension, marketing mix techniques, began to be developed thanks to the efforts of people like Butler (1911), Shaw (1916), Converse (1930) and Culliton (1948), who already pointed to the need to create a marketing tool box. But it was not until Borden (1958) invented the term 'marketing mix' that it was possible to talk authoritatively about this famous concept.

6. The original text was published in Borden (1965). Nevertheless, before publishing this article Borden had already set out the concept's basic principles in another work: 'Note on concept of the marketing mix' (1958: 272–75), an article appearing in the collective book entitled *Managerial Marketing: Perspectives and Viewpoints*, edited by Kelley and Lazer and published by Richard D. Irwin in Homewood, Illinois in 1958 – which in turn is a re-edition of a previous text owned by Harvard College. All in all, *Classics* (Volume II), published in the *Journal of Advertising Research* in September 1984, is easier to come by than the seminal 'The concept of the marketing mix'.

7. To gain further insights into what P&G meant for the business management world, see Dyer et al. (2004); Harry and Swasy (1993).

8. For further information on Lasker and his influence on advertising, see Lasker (1963); Gunther (1960); Cruikshank and Schultz (2010).

9. Specifically, Hopkins wrote a book, currently regarded as an authentic copywriting classic, entitled *Scientific Advertising* (1923), that is, the name of this novel advertising concept.

10. When devising its copy strategy, P&G directly included the reason-why copywriting technique as a fundamental tool in its basic operational scheme.

11. Paradoxically, the so-called 'white label' brands are currently the company's chief competitors in practically every product category.

12. Tellis (1998: 9) summarizes this versatile contribution as follows:

> Procter & Gamble never gave up its commitment to research. It kept innovating with products improvements, line extensions and new products, even if they cannibalized the old ones. And it kept promoting with novel ads and sales promotions through new media. Its strategy of high-quality, innovative products, each uniquely branded with carefully designed advertising, led it to become the giant consumer products company it is today.

13. The creative work plan was originally developed by Kenneth Longman for Young & Rubicam in 1970. This model served as a basis for Shirley Simkin to create her CWP (a refined version of the former).

2. Rosser Reeves's USP: The Reality in Advertising Is the Product

1. Ollé (2005: 120) explains the reason behind its swift dissemination among and adoption by advertising agencies:

> The USP had become one of theories most used by advertising men and, in its early days, it was a highly effective way of working for two reasons. Firstly, because in the 1960s marketing focused on products, their attributes, their constant technical improvements, and secondly because the main objective of advertising was to communicate those improvements on a massive scale. Thus, if someone improved normal shampoo by adding conditioner, the campaign's USP was precisely 'with conditioner'. If a toothpaste's formula was improved with an ingredient combating plaque and tartar development, the campaign centred on conveying, 'it reduces plaque and tartar build-up'.

2. Mayer, a journalist specializing in advertising, portrays the historical moment that Madison Avenue signified for the industry. This central street in New York became the nerve centre of modern American advertising. During the 1950s, most of the major multinational communication groups either started business or expanded on Madison Avenue, to the point that it is often used metonymically for advertising, as noted in the essential *Madison Avenue U.S.A.: The Inside Story of American Advertising* (1958).

3. Reeves attempts to explain this concept in Chapter 12, 'The window dressers', in which he draws an analogy with the shop windows on New York's Fifth Avenue to define a type of advertising that is both aesthetic and brilliant (as regards its execution) but 'devoid of persuasion'. When he refers to this type of advertising, he does so to criticize its value: 'But these campaigns merely display the merchandise. They merely present it to the consumer and ask that it sell itself' (Reeves 1961: 44).

4. For the most part, known simply as Dr Johnson, he was one of England's most prominent literary figures: a poet, essayist, biographer and lexicographer, he was considered by many to be the most outstanding literary critic in the English language.

5. We have made such a categorical assertion for two reasons that we believe are important. On the one hand, from an educational and professional point of view, Dr Johnson had very little or nothing to do with the advertising world. And, on the other – and maybe more importantly – it is an eighteenth-century quote, a period during which advertising was, scientifically speaking, still in its infancy.

6. It is impossible to determine the date when this book was published because it does not include one. Moreover, nor is Internet Archive much help in this regard, although, as already noted, it has been dated to the 1910s as follows: '[191?]'.

7. Meyers (1984: 22) describes this period as the 'dark ages' in the following terms:

> The object was simply to keep the advertiser's name in front of the public. Ads were pedestrian, like the ones you find in the high school yearbooks today; unimaginative copy such as 'Compliments of Prudential Insurance' or 'Cameras by Eastman Kodak' prevailed.

We believe that the promotion of brands – although not of products, which is a completely different kettle of fish – began between 1880 and 1900 with the initiatives of people like William Hesketh Lever, the so-called 'commercial genius' who founded Lever (see Costa 2004: 79). In this regard, that an advertising agency should have written a treatise on 'scientific advertising' is certainly praiseworthy.

8. According to Pedro Prat Gaballí, the father of Spanish advertising, this journal published some of the most inspiring reflections on advertising at the time. For instance, in 1895 *Printers' Ink* claimed thus: 'It is likely that when our culture has improved, advertising copywriters will study psychology. However odd this may now seem to many, the advertising copywriter and psychology will share a common goal' (in Prat Gaballí 1990: 15). For a more in-depth discussion in this regard, see Prat Gaballí (1990), published on the 75th anniversary of the publication of the first Spanish-language book on advertising.

9. Notwithstanding the fact that this topic has not been elaborated on here inasmuch as it is beyond the scope of this work, the following words of Sánchez Guzmán (1989: 138) clearly illustrate the reality at the time: 'The bombastic claim full of praise for the product that it was promoting, was highly popular as a copywriting technique from the end of the nineteenth through the first third of the twentieth century.'

10. In a previous work (Fernández Gómez 2013), we explained that these economic theories form the reference framework for the product branding paradigm. In this sense, it would an ideal context in which to implement this sort of plainly product-centric brand management. As regards economics, references are made to the so-called 'classic theories' such as 'the invisible hand' and the 'economic man'. In the field of psychology, it is rooted in behaviourism, despite the paradox. With respect to branding, the paradigm involves traditional marketing management, in other words, based on the product, in theories such as the marketing mix and in communication approaches of a rationalist nature.

11. However, these two marketing concepts do not only share the feature of perseverance. The close relationship between the USP and 'positioning' will be described in detail in Chapter 7 of this work.

12. Such as the emotional selling proposition, Burtenshaw et al. (2006: 89) hold that

> the concept of USP has been largely replaced by another principle, which John Bartle, Managing Director of Bartle Bogle Hegarty, has dubbed the emotional selling proposition (ESP) [...] in the absence of a specific unique benefit (a USP) inherent in the brand itself, the ESP is based on a uniqueness that is created by the advertising and marketing campaign. At the core of the ESP is a 'brand truth'.

These authors contend that, by means of an ESP, 'marketing communication triggers connotations that appeal to the audience on an emotional level, and in doing so the brand establishes a personal connection with them' (Burtenshaw et al. 2006: 89). Moliné (2000: 191) proposes another variant of the famous acronym which he calls the 'unique buying proposition'. And García Uceda (2001) notes that it was the Ted Bates Group that developed the unique buying proposition (UBP), which, as with Moliné, she translates into Spanish as *única proposición de compra*. For this authoress, the UBP 'allows for a warmer, more emotional, humorous and human advertising' (García Uceda 2001: 140). There has also been talk of the multiple selling proposition (MSP), but with scant scientific reflection on the matter to date. Lastly, Huete (2010: 128) has introduced a number of variants with which we are totally unfamiliar, specifically, the 'organizational selling proposition', the 'branding selling proposition' and the 'holistic selling proposition', which he describes in the following terms:

> [T]he holistic selling proposition, which recommends that companies build a strong brand identity and communicate this by all sensorial means possible; almost as if it were a religious experience [...] The holistic selling proposition would replace the brand-based one [brand selling proposition] in which the architecture and value of the brand were the priorities [...] the organizational selling proposition, the emotional selling proposition [...] or the most classic unique selling proposition in which the accent as regards differentiation was placed on the product.

13. A case that illustrates this well is that of Cunard Lines, a most valued client of Ogilvy's agency which, after many years, took its account to Ted Bates.

> Rosser Reeves sent proofs of the new Bates ads to his brother-in-law. The campaign introduced a new message – fly to the U.K. one way, return by Cunard – but otherwise was a dead ringer for Ogilvy's ads in the type and style. Ogilvy called Reeves's office and spoke with his secretary. 'I am so grateful to you for sending the new Cunard campaign. Please tell Rosser it arrived just in time. I'm editing my new book, and adding a chapter on plagiarism.'
>
> (Roman 2009: 139)

14. This restraint was obviously due to the relationship between both men, as explained above. But, at the same time, to our mind, it was also down, in part, to the pioneering currents of advertising thinking that Ogilvy studied during the first years of his professional career in the United States. It should not be forgotten that Reeves was Ogilvy's mentor and teacher and that the American's very solid ideas left a lasting mark on the Englishman. Indeed, it is a recognized fact that Ogilvy went through an initial 'pre-brand image' phase in which he staunchly defended the precepts of Hopkins and Reeves:

> Ogilvy always acknowledged his debt to Reeves, in one testimonial placing him in the 'direct line of Apostolic succession' from Claude Hopkins [...] He commented that he and Reeves had the same patron saint (Hopkins), the same bible (Hopkins's *Scientific Advertising*), and belonged to 'the same true church, even if his advertising manner leave [*sic*] something to be desired'.
>
> (Roman 2009: 118)

When Meyers analyses Ogilvy's initial philosophy, he actually places it in the fairly close orbit of Hopkins's and Reeves's and, therefore, very much in line with the tangible benefits of products and sales. According to Meyers (1984: 35), Ogilvy's pedagogy was an advertising style based on 'know-it-all'. 'Ogilvy, a fact fanatic, claimed that the more he told, the more he sold, and he always loaded up his copy with detail in order to persuade readers or viewers that his client had built a better mousetrap' (Meyers 1984: 34). Far removed, as can be observed, from the strategic mechanisms of image theory that he would champion years later.

15. For his part, Reeves defended himself against this criticism by attacking those advertising creatives who claimed that the USP was a mechanism as restrictive and inflexible as the Procrustean bed (according to myth, Procrustes stretched or cut off the limbs of his guests to adapt them to the bed). For Reeves (1961: 67–68), the USP concept was not at all rigid, and he defended this stance in the following terms:

> A U.S.P. is not a tight, closed structure. Creatively, there is no Procrustean bed. A U.S.P. is an end result. It is a totality projected by an advertisement. It is a fluid procedure rather than an arrangement of static elements. It is what comes through. It is what is played back. The creative man can let his imagination run riot, for a U.S.P. may be realized through a complex of visual and verbal elements.

16. These claims discrediting basic research are curious to say the least because they contrast sharply with his way of working. As Roman (2009: 208) writes in his biography of the English advertising man, 'Ogilvy's attempt to make the practice of advertising more professional began with research and the knowledge it unearthed.' Sure enough, research formed an integral part of Ogilvy's creative philosophy and was one of secrets that enabled him to build up his agency. In this respect, he devised the following formula: 'Look before you leap.' 'A line', as Roman (2009: 208–09) goes on to say, 'that embodies two thoughts – look deeply into the research, then take an adventurous creative leap'.

17. Naturally, we are referring to the term's positive use, for he does indeed use it on more occasions to question its effectiveness. However, apart from this, Reeves only employs the word 'feeling' without derogatory connotations once: 'It is admittedly difficult in advertising to achieve both these objectives, and you will often find that you have to choose

either one or the other. But the best theoretical objective is to *surround the claim with the feeling*' (1961: 82–83, original emphasis).

18. For Reeves (1961: 77), the 'most persuasive and able defender' of image theory was Pierre Martineau, about whom he ironically said that he had little faith in words, alluding to his reflections on the persuasive power of images. 'By far the best exposition of it which we have read is in his book, *Motivation in Advertising*, published by McGraw-Hill in 1957' (Reeves 1961). In his opinion,

> Mr. Martineau is wrong when he claims that people cannot cope with words [...] You can say four blunt words and a man will hit you in the face. You can tell a story, and the same man will burst into tears. You can tell a joke, and he will roar with laughter.
>
> (Reeves 1961: 80–81)

3. David Ogilvy's Brand Image: The Rise of Emotion in Advertising Communication

1. The rational strategic advertising mechanisms examined in the first two chapters, for instance, are rooted in economy, psychology and what was then an incipient marketing science.

2. Dichter, one of the fathers of motivational psychology, with an eminently psychoanalytical basis, emigrated from Europe to the United States.

3. In should be recalled that, as will be explained in greater depth further on, the brand image to which we are alluding here is a recently coined and underdeveloped concept. In this sense, it is a brand image that is much simpler and more elemental than the meaning that the term has since acquired and which has been popularized in the marketing field relating to the identity approach.

4. This is best demonstrated by Ogilvy's own words: 'Finally, we have developed a technique for selecting basic promises which is so valuable that my partners forbid me to reveal it' (Ogilvy 1987: 95). 'The manufacturer who dedicates his advertising to building the most sharply defined *personality* for his brand will get the largest share of the market at the highest profit' (Ogilvy 1987: 102, original emphasis).

5. This conception of Ogilvy's is odd because it seems to contradict the principles of 'brand image'. Each communication action is supposed to contribute to brand building in the broadest sense of the word. In this respect, recommending strategic reiterations, which are closely linked to strategic axes or basic promises (a reflection that was destined to be called the 'USP'), is more in keeping with Reeves's theories than with the 'new' Ogilvy.

4. Henri Joannis's Psychological Axis: The Advent of Motivational Research in European Advertising

1. According to Checa, Joannis was the head of communication for the perfume company Rochas, created his own advertising agency and, from 1975 to 1985, was the vice president of McCann Erickson (see Checa 2007: 160).

2. In this work, we have used the respective Spanish editions: Joannis (1969, 1990, 1996).

3. The question arising form that 'what' can be posed in countless ways. But, in turn, that axis is expressed with a 'how', and when selecting that 'how' it becomes part of the very process of creation. In other words, the same idea can be expressed in many ways. For instance, something as basic as the health risks of consuming alcohol can be explained by using humour or, quite the opposite, by resorting to drama. According to Joannis, the concept 'has the mission to represent concretely, specifically and credibly the satisfaction selected by the axis' (Joannis 1990: 23). It is what the theoretician called the stage of creative imagination.

4. This assertion might have been confusing owing to the belief, increasingly more widely held in the communication sector, that an ad always helps to build a brand. This belief, which of course we share, needs to be qualified. In our view, it is a great mistake to assume that an ad always helps in brand building, because this will largely depend on the intentionality of the sender. On the one hand, no-one with a grasp of marketing would be surprised to learn that specific ads do not collaborate per se in brand building. Indeed, there are campaigns – owing to the fact that they have specific, partial or short-term objectives, for instance, promotional campaigns; because they have a biased or badly defined target audience; or simply due to strategic or creative negligence – that instead of contributing to brand building, hinder it. And, on the other hand, there is a long tradition vindicating sales, information, persuasion or the mere conception of ads, campaigns or communication actions as the central objective of advertising techniques. In this context, before rushing to assert that advertising builds brands per se, it is necessary to analyse the advertising technique, goals, intention and strategic mechanism in each specific case. Even though it is true that particular ad modalities do indeed help to strengthen brands from their own theoretical conception, as is the case with corporate communication, corporate social responsibility (CSR) and the so-called 'image campaigns', the fact remains that in many cases of what is currently known as 'marketing communication' – or 'commercial communication', as it was called before – the advertising spirit, technique, strategy and conception themselves are very far-removed from the notion of brand. That is, in theory it does not imply a corporate spirit – which will depend on the good work of the manager in question – but has a sales, informative or persuasive essence. In any case, in our view, good communication, regardless of the type of goal, segmentation, strategy or strategic advertising mechanism implemented, should in theory always bear in mind the brand.

5. Jacques Séguéla's 'Star Strategy': Selling the Hollywood Star System to Sell Brands

1. Passages such as the following justify our claim: 'To kill a dream is to kill a star. By the same token, to kill the imaginary is to kill the brand. But, however, this leap towards the unreal always alarms the advertiser' (Séguéla 1991: 121).

2. His fondness for literature is unquestionable judging by the titles of some of his best-known books: *Ne dites pas à ma mère que je suis dans la publicité, elle me croit pianiste dans un bordel* is a clear example of unadulterated creativity, in addition to the aforementioned *Hollywood lave plus blanc*, which also corroborates the foregoing. However, his theoretical contributions are not so relevant.

3. This analogy is described by the advertising historian Eguizábal in the following terms:

> Séguéla's book focuses on his campaign for Mitterrand and on the conversion of a 'brand-person' into a 'brand-star'. Séguéla's strategy, i.e. that of the star system, consists exactly in that: wherever there was an object, a 'brand-product', there should now be a star, after the appropriate process of elaboration. The products of Hollywood were not actually films, but stars, who were the studios' main asset. By the same token, for Séguéla the role of the advertising industry is not to make ads, but to create brand-stars, surrounded by the same fascination, the same suggestive power, converted into objects of desire as if they were film stars, but with an advantage: their accessibility for a (more or less) affordable price. Design and advertising contributed to create these other stars.
>
> (Eguizábal 2007: 63)

4. 'The physique is the product. For a person and a brand, alike' (Ricarte 2000: 75).

5. This use of the term 'character' can also be found in Martineau (1957: 168):

> Symbols are a summary of significations and sentiments. The advertiser gives its character, its commercial brand, its packaging or its name a huge number of attractions and associations. He creates a conditioned reflex. So, when the consumer sees its symbol, the bells begin to ring and those associations are triggered.

6. Unlike in the rest of this work, neither have the quotes from Chevron been placed between quotation marks nor has the cf. system been used due to the fact that the page numbers are unavailable (the version consulted, whose pages are unnumbered, was obtained online). For the original paper, see the bibliographic reference at the end of this work.

6. Kevin Roberts's Lovemarks: The Return of Emotional Mechanisms in the New Century

1. The way in which a journalist of the Spanish daily *El País* described him over a decade ago speaks for itself: '[P]ossibly one of the most influential executives in the advertising world. This Englishman at the helm of the multinational Saatchi & Saatchi is regarded as a "visionary" and a "communication guru"' (Carrizo Couto 2008: 12).

2. His ideological leanings are common knowledge, declaring himself to be 'politically to the right, socially to the left', a declaration that has made tongues wag in certain political and economic circles. However, to offer just one example of this, in an interview that he gave to *El País* before there was any indication that the colossal economic crisis in which we are still immersed was in the offing, he declared that '[c]apitalism is the only vital force for development' (Oppenheimer 2005: 17).

3. Roberts also coordinated *The Lovemarks Effect: Winning in the Consumer Revolution* (2006), a book with an evident commercial ambition in which Saatchi & Saatchi (the owner of the copyright) highlights the popular methodology and its achievements. Indeed, the last part of the book is devoted to presenting the communication group's credentials (with details of the agency's staff and its creative endeavours). It also includes some original contributions made by the professionals working at Saatchi & Saatchi, like Richard Hytner, Derek Lockwood and Philippe Lentschener. These are supplemented with interviews with clients such as Jim Stengel, Procter & Gamble GMO, Renzo Rosso, the founder and owner of Diesel, and Toyota's Inoue Masao; staff members of the communication group to which the agency belongs, including Maurice Lévy, the chairman and CEO of Publicis Groupe; science communicators and marketing gurus like Malcolm Gladwell and Tom Peters; and a number of mavericks such as the Nobel Laureate Arno Penzias. However, notwithstanding this combination of, let us say, original ideas and concepts – although in actual fact mostly borrowed from the book *Lovemarks* – it is no more than a compilation of case studies directly or indirectly linked to the Lovemarks effect. Accordingly, it not only reviews classic examples such as Benetton, Ben & Jerry's and Camper, but also other satisfied clients, including Lexus and Payless. From a conceptual point of view, it is less interesting than the original book, with its anecdotal character being its one and only appeal.

4. Besides the original American, Canadian and British edition, the book is currently available in Maori, Portuguese, Bulgarian, Hungarian, Danish, French, German, Italian, Japanese, Russian and Spanish.

5. Following the publication of their book, the authors founded a branding consultancy firm in London. The commercial identification is so blatant that the URL of the website that they created mirrors the name of the branding model in question and, at the same time, the title of the book itself: 'passionbrand.com'.

7. Jack Trout and Al Ries's Positioning: The Appearance of Cognitive Psychology in Advertising

1. For a contextualization of the cognitive basis of the strategic advertising mechanism of positioning and its framing in the context of the paradigm of consumer branding, see *Principios de Estrategia Publicitaria y Gestión de Marcas: Nuevas Tendencias de Brand Management* (2013).

2. From the moment that the term started to gain popularity at the beginning of the 1980s, in academia there was a before and an after with respect to its treatment in the scientific literature. Suffice it run a search on the term 'positioning' in any journal metasearch engine, for example from 1975 to 1985, to obtain a staggering number of results. Likewise, it is relatively easy to observe this by collating marketing or advertising manuals pre-dating the advent of the concept with those published afterwards, in which it is practically impossible not to find an explanation of this concept or, at the very least, a reference to it (that its creator gets a look in is quite another matter).

3. At universities, the curricula of communication or business studies modules are also very revealing. As a matter of fact, it is difficult not to find 'positioning' as a basic subject in modules such as 'strategic marketing', 'an introduction to marketing', 'advertising strategy' and 'brand management'.

4. The trade press offers irrefutable evidence in this respect. As with the scientific literature, there was also a turning point in the professional world regarding the conception of positioning. Accordingly, in publications of this sort it is relatively commonplace to find communication and marketing professionals referring to campaigns, explaining brand strategies or simply using the concept of positioning very naturally. Suffice it to read any trade journal to realize this.

5. This journal was subsequently replaced with a new one called *B2B Marketing* by the group to which it belonged.

6. Subsequently republished, as Trout himself noted on the website of Trout & Partners, 'and these articles were compiled in print. As many as 120,000 copies were presented by the co-authors'. The edition to which he is referring is Trout and Ries's *The Positioning Era Cometh* (1972d).

7. On the website of Trout & Partners Ltd., in a look back on the firm's most relevant milestones the book's relevance is underscored: 'In 2009, this book ranked the 1st among "Best Marketing Classics in History" by *Ad Age*.' The website of Ries's consultancy firm also enthuses about it: 'It has become one of the most famous and best-selling marketing books of all time. It has sold more than two million copies around the world and has been translated into over 20 languages.'

8. In English: 'Who invented positioning: Porter or Trout?'

9. When referring to positioning, Porter speaks of a set of activities differing from those developed by competitors (cf. Porter 1996: 65). In his view, from a purely business marketing perspective, strategic positioning is rooted in variety-based positioning, need-based positioning

and access-based positioning (cf. Porter 1996: 65–68). For further information on this topic, see Porter (1996).

10. According to Kapferer (1992: 265),

> since 1986 there has been a frenzy of mergers and acquisitions in which brands have formed the real stakes – thus explaining the overbids and high multiples affecting takeover bids and raids. It is no longer rare to find offers at a multiple of more than 25 times company results – two or three times the share value.

11. The fact that useless information has to been 'erased' from a hard disk drive to save new information leads to another feature inherent to this metaphor, which is a true constant in the oeuvre of Trout and Ries. We are referring to the claim that they continually make that the mind is not limited and, therefore, the fundamental objective of any brand should be to find a slot in the minds of consumers.

12. By the authors' reckoning, this is why it is necessary to use already existing 'pigeonholes' or 'slots': 'So new brands want to avoid trying to get into somebody else's pigeonhole. New brands want to create their own slots or categories' (Ries and Ries 2004: 250).

13. The collective book *Brands and Branding* (2003), coordinated by Clifton and Simmons, has a Spanish adaptation entitled, *En clave de marcas* (2010), coordinated by Brujó and Clifton himself (in that order), which includes a number of changes. As well as featuring an ad hoc prologue by José Luis Bonet and discarding (Anne Bahr's chapter entitled, 'Brand positioning and brand creation', for example) or substituting (the chapter entitled 'The social value of brands' is now signed by Giles Gibbons, instead of Steve Hilton) some chapters appearing in *Brands and Branding*, it also incorporates contributions by Luis Huete, Max Raison, Andy Hobsbawn, Antonio Abril and the like. So, Iain Ellwood's chapter entitled 'Estrategia de Marca' is one of those new contributions.

14. This can be verified in their first two books – directly linked conceptually speaking – which are also their most acclaimed and popular works: *Competitive Strategy: Techniques for Analyzing Industries and Competitors* (1980) has been re-edited 53 times and translated into seventeen languages. Similarly, *Competitive Advantage: Creating and Sustaining Superior Performance* (1985) has been republished 32 times.

15. In the commemorative revised edition of their classic, Trout and Ries derisively claim that Porter has made the concept of positioning his competitive edge (cf. 2001b: 243).

16. Suffice it to consult the homepage of Ries's corporate website (https://www.ries.com/, accessed 14 January 2021), emblazoned with its slogan in large font letters: 'The Positioning Pioneers'.

17. By the way, this book, which was not as commercially successful as *Positioning: The Battle for Your Mind*, was re-edited in 2005, in all likelihood to exploit the synergies generated by the successful twentieth anniversary revised edition of the latter.

18. In this connection, Trout explicitly bases himself on the oeuvre of Reeves: 'Well, you might think that this was an argument of the past and that Mr. Reeves's ideas have long been accepted by today's advertising practitioner. Wrong' (Trout and Rivkin 2000: 12). And he states that the popular advertising man's theories are current when saying that 'the argument still rages':

> What's stunning is that the argument still rages on Madison Avenue. A front-page article in *Advertising Age* that was published thirty-seven years after Mr. Reeves's book proclaimed: 'Poets vs. killers': Perpetual ad debate – stress art or stick to hard sell? – is reaching fever pitch with fortunes hanging in the balance. This article, that went on for pages, laid out the battle of the creatives that see their work as artful and emotional and the marketers who want advertising that is factual and rational. One group wants to bond with the customer. The other group wants to sell the customer. It's time we stopped arguing and faced not reality in advertising but reality in the marketplace.
>
> (Trout and Rivkin 2000: 12)

Thus, the only perceptible difference with the USP, in view of Trout's words, is the current concept of competition:

> When Mr. Reeves was talking about being different, the world was an easy place. Global competition didn't exist. In fact, by today's standards, real competition barely existed. The concept of being unique or different is far more important in the year 2000 than it was in 1960.
>
> (Trout and Rivkin 2000: 13)

For which reason, he concludes by reaffirming his views: 'Rosser Reeves had the will to differentiate. But 40 years ago, the way to differentiate was usually based on a tangible difference between products. Usually it included a benefit that could be dramatized by a comparison with competitors' (Trout and Rivkin 2000: 19). All considered, in his book he offers several alternative differentiation formulas, but others were created by Reeves himself.

8. Douglas Holt's Iconic Brands: When Cognitive Psychology and Motivation Research Converge

1. 'Cultural branding is the strategic principle behind how to create and manage a brand and alter it into an icon. Cultural branding is all about what culture can do for brand value creation' (Heding et al. 2009: 216). It is important to stress that cultural branding has to do, above all, with issues relating to the meaning that commercial brands acquire and generate. As observed by Testa et al. (2017: 1492), '[t]he activity of endowing commercial brands with evocative meaning lies at the root of the approach known as cultural branding.'

2. In English: 'My savings-bank mattress'.

3. This section is based on the chapter entitled 'La construcción de la marca icónica como estrategia de branding cultural' appearing in the book *Branding Cultural: Una teoría aplicada a las marcas y a la publicidad* (2019), by Jorge David Fernández Gómez, María del Mar Rubio and Antonio Pineda.

References

Aaker, D. A. (1996), *Building Strong Brands*, New York: Free Press.

Aaker, D. A. and Myers, J. (1982), *Advertising Management*, 2nd ed., Englewood Cliffs, NJ: Prentice Hall.

Advertising Research Foundation (1953), *An Introductory Bibliography of Motivation Research*, New York: ARF.

Advertising Research Foundation (1954a), *Directory of Organizations Which Conduct Motivation Research*, New York: ARF.

Advertising Research Foundation (1954b), *Directory of Social Scientists Interested in Motivation Research*, New York: ARF.

Arens, W., Schaefer, D. and Weigold, M. (2009), *Essentials of Contemporary Advertising*, Boston: McGraw-Hill.

Askegaard, S. (2006), 'Brand as a global ideoscape', in J. Schroeder and M. Salcer-Morling (eds), *Brand Culture*, Abingdon: Routledge, pp. 81–92.

Audy, R. (1971), *Stratégie Publicitaire et Marketing*, Paris: Dunod.

Bassat, L. (2006), *El libro rojo de las marcas: Cómo construir marcas de éxito*, Barcelona: Random House Mondadori.

Batra, R., Myers, J. and Aaker, D. (1996), *Advertising Management*, Upper Saddle River, NJ: Prentice Hall.

Baudrillard, J. (1989), 'Publicidad absoluta, publicidad cero', *Revista de Occidente*, 92, pp. 5–16.

Bendelac, S. (1997), 'Foreword', in R. Reeves (ed.), *La realidad en la publicidad: Un acercamiento a la teoría de la USP*, Barcelona: Delvico Bates, pp. 7–10.

Berman, M. (2017), *The Blueprint for Strategic Advertising*, New York: Routledge.

Boches, Edward (2014), 'Bill Bernbach and the beginning', Medium, 26 May, https://medium.com/what-do-you-want-to-know/bill-bernbach-and-the-beginning-7e49c2242390. Accessed 4 March 2020.

Bogart, L. (1967), *Strategy in Advertising*, New York: Harcourt, Brace & World.

Borden, N. (1958), 'Note on concept of the marketing mix', in E. Kelley and W. Lazer (eds), *Managerial Marketing: Perspectives and Viewpoints*, Homewood, IL: Richard D. Irwin, pp. 272–75.

Borden, N. (1965), 'The concept of the marketing mix', in G. Schwartz (ed.), *Science in Marketing*, New York: John Wiley, pp. 386–97.

Borden, N. (1984), 'The concept of the marketing mix', *Journal of Advertising Research*, Special Issue: 'Classics', 2, pp. 7–12.

Burtenshaw, K., Mahon, N. and Barfoot, C. (2006), *The Fundamentals of Creative Advertising*, Lausanne: AVA.

Butler, R. S. (1911), 'Selling and buying', in R. S. Butler, G. H. Harmon and L. Galloway (eds), *Advertising, Selling and Credit*, New York: Alexander Hamilton Institute, pp. 275–484.

Caro, A. (2009), 'Una fase decisiva en la evolución de la publicidad: la transición del producto a la marca', *Pensar la Publicidad*, 3:2, pp. 109–32.

Carrizo Couto, R. (2008), 'Entrevista a Kevin Roberts', *El País*, 6 April, p. 12.

Checa Godoy, A. (2007), *Historia de la publicidad*, La Coruña: Netbiblo.

Cheskin, L. (1957), *How to Predict What People Will Buy*, New York: Liveright.

Chevalier, M. and Mazzalovo, G. (2005), *Pro logo: por qué las marcas son buenas para usted*, Barcelona: Belacqua.

Cheverton, P. (2006), *Understanding Brands*, London: Kogan Page.

Chevron, J. (1985), 'Give your brand in marriage', *Advertising Age*, 22, July, p. 14.

Clark, E. (1989), *The Want Makers*, New York: Viking Penguin.

Clifton, R. and Simmons, J. (eds), *Brands and Branding*, London: Profile Books.

Colley, R. H. (1961), *Defining Advertising Goals for Measured Advertising Results*, New York: Association of National Advertisers.

Converse, P. D. (1930), *The Elements of Marketing*, New York: Prentice Hall.

Cooper, A. (ed.) (1997), *How to Plan Advertising*, 2nd ed., London: Cassell.

Costa, J. (2004), *La imagen de marca*, Barcelona: Paidós.

Crainer, S. (1995), *The Real Power of Brands: Making Brands Work for Competitive Advantage*, London: Pitman Publishing.

Cruikshank, J. L. and Schultz, A. W. (2010), *The Man Who Sold America: The Amazing (but True!) Story of Albert D. Lasker and the Creation of the Advertising Century*, Boston: Harvard Business Review Press.

Culliton, J. W. (1948), *The Management of Marketing Costs*, Boston: Harvard University Press.

Davis, S. M. (2002), *Brand Asset Management: Driving Profitable Growth Through Your Brands*, San Francisco: John Wiley.

De Chernatony, L., McDonald, M. and Wallace, E. (2011), *Creating Powerful Brands*, Oxford: Burlington and Butterworth-Heinemann.

Dichter, E. (1960), *The Strategy of Desire*, London: T.V. Boardman.

Dichter, E. (1964), *Handbook of Consumer Motivations: The Psychology of the World of Objects*, New York: McGraw-Hill.

Dill Scott, W. (1908), *The Psychology of Advertising*, Boston: Small, Maynard & Co.

Dru, J. M. (1996), *Disruption: Overturning Conventions and Shaking Up the Marketplace*, New York: John Wiley.

Dyer, D., Dalzell, F. and Olegario, R. (2004), *Rising Tide: Lessons from 165 Years of Brand Building at Procter & Gamble*, Boston: Harvard Business School Press.

eccesignu (2010), 'Starbucks: Make a difference. Take the pledge', YouTube, 14 April, https://www.youtube.com/watch?v=KRFofwu-0o4. Accessed 9 October 2018.

Edwards, H. and Day, D. (2005), *Creating PassionBrands: How to Build Emotional Brand Connection with Customers*, London: Kogan Page.

Eguizábal, R. (1998), *Historia de la publicidad*, Madrid: Eresma & Celeste.

Eguizábal, R. (2007), *Teoría de la publicidad*, Madrid: Cátedra.

Ellwood, I. (2010), 'Estrategia de marca', in G. Brujó (ed.), *En clave de marcas*, Madrid: LID, pp. 91–111.

Feldwick, P. (ed.) (2000), *Pollitt on Planning*, Henley-on-Thames: Admap.

Feldwick, P. (2015), *The Anatomy of Humbug: How to Think Differently About Advertising*, Kibworth Beauchamp: Matador.

Ferber, R. and Wales, H. (ed.) (1958), *Motivation and Market Behavior*, Homewood, IL: Richard D. Irwin.

Fernández Gómez, J. D. (2013), *Principios de Estrategia Publicitaria y Gestión de Marcas: Nuevas Tendencias de Brand Management*, Madrid: McGraw-Hill.

Fernández Gómez, J. D. (2014), *Mecanismos estratégicos en publicidad: de la USP a las Lovemarks*, Sevilla: Advook.

Fernández Gómez, J. D. (2020), 'An approach to motivation research from advertising strategy: From Freud to the iconic brand', in V. Hernández and M. Barrientos (eds), *Handbook of Research on Transmedia Storytelling, Audience Engagement, and Business Strategies*, Hershey, PA: IGI Global, pp. 239–54.

Fernández Gómez, J. D. and Gordillo, T. (2020), *Branding de Comunidades*, Barcelona: UOC.

Fernández Gómez, J. D., Rubio, M. and Pineda, A. (2019), *Branding Cultural*, Barcelona: UOC.

Fog, K., Budtz, C. and Yakaboylu, B. (2005), *Storytelling: Branding in Practice*, Berlin: Springer.

Fox, J. (2015), 'From "economic man" to behavioral economics', *Behavioral Economics*, May, pp. 78–85.

Fox, S. (1997), *The Mirror Makers*, Urbana and Chicago, IL: University of Illinois Press.

Franzen, G. and Moriarty, S. (2009), *The Science and Art of Branding*, New York: M. E. Sharpe.

Freud, S. (1992), *Sigmund Freud. Obras completas. El yo y el ello y otras obras (1923–1925)*, Buenos Aires: Amorrortu Ediciones.

Gallego, F. (2016), 'Populismo', in J. Antón Mellón and X. Torrens (eds), *Ideologías y movimientos políticos contemporáneos*, Madrid: Tecnos, pp. 261–75.

García Uceda, M. (2001), *Las claves de la publicidad*, Madrid: ESIC.

Gardner, B. and Levy, S. (1955), 'The product and the brand', *Harvard Business Review*, 33:2, March–April, pp. 33–39.

Gardner, B. and Moore, D. (1955), *Human Relations in Industry*, Homewood, IL: Richard D. Irwin.

González Martín, J. A. (1996), *Teoría general de la publicidad*, Madrid: Fondo de Cultura Económica.

Govers, P. and Schoormans, J. (2005), 'Product personality and its influence on consumer preference', *Journal of Consumer Marketing*, 22:4, pp. 189–97.

Griffiths, J. and Follows, T. (2016), *98% Pure Potato: The Origins of Advertising Account Planning as Told to Us by Its Pioneers*, London: Unbound.

Grönroos, C. (1994), 'Quo vadis, marketing? Towards a relationship marketing paradigm', *Journal of Marketing Management*, 10:5, pp. 347–60.

Gunther, J. (1960), *Taken at the Flood: The Story of Albert D. Lasker*, New York: Harper.

Harrison, T. (1989), *A Handbook of Advertising Techniques*, London: Kogan Page.

Harry, A. and Swasy, A. (1993), *Soap Opera: The Inside Story of Procter & Gamble*, New York: Random House.

Healey, M. (2008), *What Is Branding?*, Mies: RotoVision.

Heding, T., Knudtzen, C. F. and Bjerre, M. (2009), *Brand Management: Research, Theory and Practice*, New York: Routledge.

Henrich, J., Boyd, R., Bowles, S., Camerer, C., Fehr, E., Gintis, H. and Mcelreath, R. (2001), 'In search of homo economicus: Behavioral experiments in 15 small-scale societies', *American Economic Review*, 91:2, pp. 73–78.

Henry, H. (1958), *Motivation Research*, London: Crosby Lockwood & Son.

Herreros Arconada, M. (2000), *La Publicitat: Fonaments de la comunicació publicitària*, Barcelona: Pòrtic Mèdia.

Higgins, D. (1987), *The Art of Writing Advertising: Conversations with Masters of the Craft*, Lincolnwood, IL: NTC.

Holt, D. B. (2002), 'Why do brands cause trouble? A dialectical theory of consumer culture and branding', *Journal of Consumer Research*, 29, June, pp. 70–90.

Holt, D. B. (2003), 'What becomes an icon most?', *Harvard Business Review*, March, pp. 43–49.

Holt, D. B. (2004), *How Brands Become Icons*, Boston: Harvard Business School.

Holt, D. B. (2006), 'Jack Daniel's America: Iconic brands as ideological parasites and proselytizers', *Journal of Consumer Culture*, 6:3, pp. 355–77.

Holt, D. B. (2016), 'Branding in the age of social media', *Harvard Business Review*, March, pp. 40–50.

Holt, D. B., Quelch, J. and Taylor, E. L. (2004), 'How global brands compete', *Harvard Business Review*, 82:9, September, pp. 68–75.

Homs, R. (2004), *La era de las marcas depredadoras*, Mexico City: McGraw-Hill.

Hopkins, C. (1966), *Scientific Advertising*, London: MacGibbon & Kee.

Huete, L. (2010), 'Los clientes han de sentir y vivir la marca', in G. Brujó (ed.), *En clave de marcas*, Madrid: LID, pp. 127–37.

Joannis, H. (1969), *Del estudio de motivación a la creación publicitaria y a la promoción de ventas*, Madrid: Paraninfo.

Joannis, H. ([1978] 1988a), *Le processus de création publicitaire*, Paris: Dunod.

Joannis, H. (1988b), *El proceso de creación publicitaria: Planteamiento, Concepción y realización de mensajes*, Madrid: Deusto.

Joannis, H. (1990), *La creación publicitaria desde la estrategia de márketing*, Bilbao: Deusto.

Joannis, H. (1996), *La creación publicitaria desde la estrategia de márketing*, Bilbao: Deusto.

Jones, R. (2017), *Branding: A Very Short Introduction*, Oxford: Oxford University Press.

Kapferer, J. N. (1992), *Strategic Brand Management: New Approaches to Creating and Evaluating Brand Equity*, London: Kogan Page.

Kapferer, J. N. (2012), *The New Strategic Brand Management: Advanced Insights & Strategic Thinking*, Philadelphia: Kogan Page.

Keller, K. L. (1998), *Strategic Brand Management*, Upper Saddle River, NJ: Prentice Hall.

Keller, K. L. (2008), *Strategic Brand Management*, 3rd ed., Upper Saddle River, NJ: Prentice Hall.

Kelley, L. D. and Jugenheimer, D. W. (2004), *Advertising Media Planning: A Brand Management Approach*, London: M. E. Sharpe.

Kelley, L. D. and Jugenheimer, D. W. (2015), *Advertising Account Planning*, New York: Routledge.

Lannon, J. and Baskin, M. (2008), *A Master Class in Brand Planning: The Timeless Works of Stephen King*, Chichester: John Wiley.

Lasker, A. D. (1963), *Lasker Story: As He Told It*, Chicago: Advertising Productions.

LePla, F. J. and Parker, L. M. (1999), *Integrated Branding: Becoming Brand-Driven. Through Companywide Action*, Westport, CT: Quorum Books.

Levitt, T. (1980), 'Marketing success through differentiation-of anything', *Harvard Business Review*, 58, January–February, pp. 83–91.

Levy, S. J. (1959), 'Symbols for sale', *Harvard Business Review*, 37, July–August, pp. 117–24.

Lomas, C. (1996), *El espectáculo del deseo: Usos y formas de la persuasión*, Barcelona: Octaedro.

Maggard, J. P. (1976), 'Positioning revisited: Is positioning something old, new, or borrowed?', *Journal of Marketing*, 40:1, January, pp. 63–66.

Mark, M. and Pearson, C. (2001), *The Hero and the Outlaw: Building Extraordinary Brands through the Power of Archetypes*, New York: McGraw-Hill.

Martineau, P. (1957), *Motivation in Advertising: Motives That Make People Buy*, New York: McGraw-Hill.

Martín Salgado, L. (2002), *Marketing político*, Barcelona: Paidós.

Maslow, A. (1970), *Motivation and Personality*, 2nd ed., New York: Harper & Row.

Mayer, M. (1958), *Madison Avenue U.S.A.: The Inside Story of American Advertising*, London: Bodley Head.

McCarthy, E. J. (1971), *Basic Marketing: A Managerial Approach*, 4th ed., Homewood, IL: Irwin.

McCracken, G. (1988), *Culture and Consumption: New Approaches to the Symbolic Character of Consumer Goods and Activities*, Bloomington: Indiana University Press.

McJunkin, W. and Finn, J. (191?), *Master Merchandising and the Dominant Idea*, Chicago: McJunkin Advertising.

Meyers, W. (1984), *The Image Makers*, London: Orbis.

Mitchell, A. (1983), *The Nine American Lifestyles*, New York: Macmillan.

Moliné, M. (1996a), *La comunicación activa: Publicidad sólida*, Bilbao: Deusto.

Moliné, M. (1996b), *Malicia para vender con marca*, Bilbao: Deusto.

Moliné, M. (2000), *La fuerza de la publicidad. Saber hacer buena publicidad. Saber administrar su fuerza*, Madrid: McGraw-Hill.

MrClassicAds1990s (2011), 'Snapple commercial 1994', YouTube, 12 May, https://youtu.be/eYYgKXJ2x2I. Accessed 7 October 2018.

Muniz, A. M. and O'Guinn, T. C. (2001), 'Brand community', *Journal of Consumer Research*, 27, March, pp. 412–31.

Newman, J. (1957), *Motivation Research and Marketing Management*, Cambridge: Harvard University.

Nilson, T. H. (1998), *Competitive Branding*, Chichester: John Wiley.

Ogilvy, D. (1966), 'Introduction', in C. Hopkins (ed.), *Scientific Advertising*, London: MacGibbon & Kee, pp. 7–10.

Ogilvy, D. (1983), *Ogilvy on Advertising*, London: Prion.

Ogilvy, D. (1987), *Confessions of an Advertising Man*, New York: Atheneum.

Ogilvy, D. (2006), *The Unpublished David Ogilvy*, London: Profile Books.

Olins, W. (2003), *On Brand*, London: Thames & Hudson.

Ollé, R. (2005), 'El *planner*. La voz del consumidor en la agencia', in J. D. Fernández Gómez (ed.), *Aproximación a la Estructura de la Publicidad: Desarrollo y Funciones de la Actividad Publicitaria*, Sevilla: Comunicación Social, pp. 115–31.

Ollé, R. and Riu, D. (2009), *El nuevo brand management: cómo plantar marcas para hacer crecer negocios*, Barcelona: Gestión 2000.

Oppenheimer, W. (2005), 'Entrevista a Kevin Roberts', *El País*, 6 March, p. 17.

Ortega, E. (1997), *La comunicación publicitaria*, Madrid: Piramide.

Packard, V. (1957), *The Hidden Persuaders*, New York: David McKay.

Peralba, R. (2003), '¿Quién inventó el Posicionamiento, Porter o Trout?', *IPMARK*, 606, 16–30 September, pp. 84–86.

Percy, L. and Rossiter, J. R. (1980), *Advertising Strategy: A Communication Theory Approach*, New York: Praeger.

Pérez, R. A. (2001), *Estrategias de comunicación*, Barcelona: Ariel.

Persky, J. (1995), 'The ethology of homo economicus', *Journal of Economic Perspectives*, 9:2, pp. 221–31.

Petty, R. E. and Cacioppo, J. T. (1986), *Communication and Persuasion: Central and Peripheral Routes to Attitude Change*, New York: Springer-Verlag.

Porter, M. E. (1980), *Competitive Strategy: Techniques for Analyzing Industries and Competitors*, New York: Free Press.

Porter, M. E. (1996), 'What is strategy', *Harvard Business Review*, 74:6, November/December, pp. 62–78.

Prat Gaballí, P. (1990), *Una nueva técnica: La publicidad científica*, 75º Aniversario de la edición del primer libro sobre publicidad en lengua española, Barcelona: Cambra de Comerç de Barcelona.

Project ReBrief (2012), 'Coca-Cola, 1971 – "Hilltop" | "I'd like to buy the world a Coke"', YouTube, 6 March, https://youtu.be/1VM2eLhvsSM. Accessed 9 October 2018.

Reeves, R. (1961), *Reality in Advertising*, New York: Alfred A. Knopf.

Ricarte, J. M. (2000), *Procesos y técnicas creativas publicitarias: Ideas básicas*, Barcelona: Universitat Autònoma de Barcelona.

Ries, A. and Ries, L. (2004), *The Origin of Brands*, New York: Harper Collins.

Ries, A. and Trout, J. (2001), *Positioning: The Battle for Your Mind*, 20th Anniversary ed., New York: McGraw-Hill.

Riezebos, R. (2003), *Brand Management: A Theoretical and Practical Approach*, Harlow: Pearson Education.

Roberts, K. (2004), *Lovemarks: The Future Beyond Brands*, New York: PowerHouse.

Roberts, K. (ed.) (2006), *The Lovemarks Effect: Winning in the Consumer Revolution*, New York: PowerHouse.

Roman, K. (2009), *The King of Madison Avenue: David Ogilvy and the Making of Modern Advertising*, New York: Palgrave Macmillan.

Roman, K. and Maas, J. (2003), *How to Advertise*, New York: Thomas Dunne.

Rom Rodríguez, J. and Sabaté López, J. (2007), *Llenguatge publicitari: Estratègia i creativitat publicitàries*, Barcelona: UOC.

Rosenbaum-Elliot, R., Percy, L. and Pervan, S. (2011), *Strategic Brand Management*, New York: Oxford University Press.

Russell, G. (2013), *Planning Advertisements*, Abingdon: Routledge.

Sabaté, J., Solanas, I. and Martorell, C. (2010), 'De "Jumbo" a Internet: ¿no será que no hay nada tan nuevo en creatividad y en publicidad?', *Marketing News*, 23 April, http://www.marketingnews.es/varios/opinion/1047675028705/jumbo-internet-no-no-tan-creatividad-publicidad.1.html. Accessed 26 May 2019.

Sacco, J. (1986), 'Rosser Reeves' lost chapter', *Advertising Age*, 17, October, p. 17.

Salmon, C. (2008), *Storytelling*, Barcelona: Península.

Samuel, R. S. (2010), *Freud on Madison Avenue*, Philadelphia: University of Pennsylvania Press.

Sánchez Guzmán, J. R. (1989), *Breve historia de la publicidad*, Madrid: Ciencia 3.

Santesmases, M. (1996), *Marketing: conceptos y estrategias*, Madrid: Pirámide.

Schultz, D. (1981), *Essentials of Advertising Strategy*, Chicago: Crain.

Schultz, D. (1991), *Strategic Advertising Campaigns*, Lincolnwood, IL: NTC.

Scott, W. D. (1908), *The Psychology of Advertising*, Boston: Small, Maynard & Co.

Séguéla, J. (1991), *Hollywood lava más blanco*, Barcelona: Business Books.

Semprini, A. (1995), *El marketing de la marca, Una aproximación semiótica*, Barcelona: Paidós.

Sengupta, S. (2007), *Brand Positioning: Strategies for Competitive Advantage*, New Delhi: Tata McGraw-Hill.

Shaw, A. W. (1916), *An Approach to Business Problems*, Cambridge, MA: Harvard University Press.

Sirgy, J. (1982), 'Self-concept in consumer behaviour: A critical review', *Journal of Consumer Research*, 9:3, pp. 287–300.

Skinner, B. F. (1974), *About Behaviorism*, New York: Alfred A. Knopf.

Smith, A. ([1759] 1976a), *The Theory of Moral Sentiments* (ed. D. D. Raphael and A. L. Macfie), Oxford: Clarendon Press.

Smith, A. ([1776] 1976b), *An Inquiry into the Nature and Causes of the Wealth of Nations* (ed. E. Cannan), Chicago: University of Chicago Press.

Smith, A. (2008), *The Invisible Hand*, London: Penguin Books.

Smith, G. H. (1954), *Motivation Research in Advertising and Marketing*, New York: McGraw-Hill.

Soler, P. (1991), *La investigación motivacional en marketing y publicidad*, Bilbao: Deusto.

Soler, P. (1997), *Estrategias de Comunicación en Publicidad y Relaciones Públicas*, Barcelona: Gestión 2000.

Starch, D. (1914), *Advertising: Its Principles, Practice, and Technique*, Chicago and New York: Scott, Foresman and Co.

Steel, J. (1998), *Truth, Lies & Advertising: The Art of Account Planning*, New York: John Wiley.

Sternthal, B. and Lee, A. Y. (2005), 'Building brand through effective advertising', in A. M. Tybout and T. Calkins (eds), *Kellogg on Branding*, Hoboken, NJ: John Wiley, pp. 129–49.

Tellis, G. (1998), *Advertising and Sales Promotion Strategy*, Reading, MA: Addison-Wesley.

Testa, P., Cova, B. and Cantone, L. (2017), 'The process of de-iconisation of an iconic brand: A genealogical approach', *Journal of Marketing Management*, 33:17–18, pp. 1490–521.

Tomasi di Lampedusa, Giuseppe ([1958] 2002), *Il gattopardo*, Milano: Feltrinelli.

Torelli, C., Keh, H. T. and Chiu, C.-Y. (2010), 'Cultural symbolism of brands', in B. Loken, R. Ahluwalia and M. J. Houston (eds), *Brands and Brand Management: Contemporary Research Perspectives*, New York: Routledge, pp. 113–32.

Trout, J. (1969), '"Positioning" is a game people play in today's me-too market place', *Industrial Marketing*, 54:6, June, pp. 51–55.

Trout, J. and Ries, A. (1972a), 'The positioning era cometh', *Advertising Age*, 24 April, pp. 35, 38.

Trout, J. and Ries, A. (1972b), 'The positioning era cometh', *Advertising Age*, 1 May, pp. 51, 52, 54.

Trout, J. and Ries, A. (1972c), 'The positioning era cometh', *Advertising Age*, 8 May, pp. 114, 116.

Trout, J. and Ries, A. (1972d), *The Positioning Era Cometh*, Chicago: Crain Publications.

Trout, J. and Rivkin, S. (1996), *The New Positioning*, New York: McGraw-Hill.

Trout, J. and Rivkin, S. (1999), *The Power of Simplicity: A Management Guide to Cutting Through the Nonsense and Doing Things Right*, New York: McGraw-Hill.

Trout, J. and Rivkin, S. (2000), *Differentiate or Die: Survival in Our Era of Killer Competition*, New York: John Wiley.

Trout, J. and Rivkin, S. (2010), *Repositioning: Marketing in an Era of Competition, Change, and Crisis*, New York: McGraw-Hill.

Tybout, A. M. and Calkins, T. (2005), *Kellogg on Branding: The Marketing Faculty of the Kellogg School of Management*, Hoboken, NJ: John Wiley.

Tybout, A. M. and Sternthal, B. (2005), 'Brand positioning', in A. M. Tybout and T. Calkins (eds), *Kellogg on Branding*, Hoboken, NJ: John Wiley, pp. 11–26.

Tyree, Adam (2015), 'Snapple "Handshake" commercial', YouTube, 28 May, https://youtu.be/fOql7QaBPL0. Accessed 7 October 2018.

Walvis, T. (2010), *Branding with Brains: The Science of Setting Customers to Choose Your Company*, Harlow: Pearson.

Watson, J. B. (1925), *Behaviorism*, New York: W.W. Norton.

Watson, J. B. and McDougall, W. (1928), *The Battle of Behaviorism*, London: Kegan Paul, Trench, Trubner & Co.

Woodruff, J. F. (1979), 'The allusions in Johnson's *Idler* no. 40', *Modern Philology*, 76:4, pp. 380–89.

Woods, W. (1959), 'Psychological dimensions of consumer decision', *Journal of Marketing*, 24, July–April, pp. 15–19.

wtcvidman (2009), '1993 Snapple commercial #1', YouTube, 29 December, https://youtu.be/knfpZvW6GOU. Accessed 7 October 2018.

Wulfeck, J. and Bennett, E. (1954), *The Language of Dynamic Psychology: As Related to Motivation Research*, New York: McGraw-Hill.

Index